Watchman...
Vol 1

Watchman ... Vol. 1

FROM MY CONGREGATION ON FACEBOOK

Rev. Steven Bailey

Deeann D. Mathews, Editor

ISBN: **978-1981377596**

Rev. Steven A. Bailey
Olivet Baptist Church
1667 Revere Avenue
San Francisco, CA 94124
bstephanos7@aol.com
https://www.facebook.com/steven.bailey.355?fref=nf

First published in the United States by Rev. Steven A. Bailey

Printed in the United States of America

Dedication and Acknowledgments

To the Lord Jesus Christ, my Savior; to my beloved wife Nina and our beloved children; to Mr. Adam Banks; to Rev. Milton Williams, Pastor Emeritus of Bayview Baptist Church of San Francisco, Rev. Edwin H. Watkins, pastor of Mt. Zion Baptist Church of San Francisco, and Rev. Bryant Wyatt, pastor of Mt. Calvary Baptist Church of Sacramento. I also thank all my Facebook friends who encouraged me to make this volume happen.

Foreword

Some time ago, I was warned concerning this new online computer thing that several young members of the Mt. Calvary Missionary Baptist Church were using to gossip, post pictures and tell people off. I was also alerted of information and pictures some of the young people of Mt Calvary Missionary Baptist Church were posting on this thing called Facebook. I would tell my young adult son to let me get on his Facebook account and check what the young people of our church were putting on this media.

It was then that my son suggested that I get a Facebook account. In doing so, I was able to find out some of the stuff my young people were posting on this Facebook thing. This Facebook thing is now a part of my daily routine; locating old school mates, checking messages, posts, the latest gossip and even some weird video clips.

A few years ago, while in conversation with a good preaching friend, we began discussing Facebook. He told me how he couldn't see himself on Facebook and what a waste of time he thought it was. I explained to him how I got on Facebook. I then suggested to my friend to get an account and make it anonymous. After some encouragement, he reluctantly got a Facebook account.

Since then, my friend's Facebook posts have become some of the most popular inspirational and Biblically practical meditations I have seen. People from different parts of the world are now audience to the many inspirational posts of my friend. His scholarly approach to biblical truths, his unusual stories and the practicality of the presented information is now becoming life changing and challenging information to people across the globe.

My good friend is Dr. Steven Bailey. I have seen Dr. Bailey confound Bible students and scholars alike with his working knowledge of the original Biblical languages; yet he has the ability to make it so simple that even those who do a shallow study of the Bible can grasp some knowledge.

And now, you can also be blessed by the wit, storytelling, as well as the scholarly approach to Biblical truths through the eyes and thought process of Dr. Steven Bailey. This collection of devotional messages has the potential of changing your very existence. It is also full of helps and stories that can add zest to sermons and Bible study lessons.

So, please experience the mind of a humble scholar who pens devotional messages that will cause you to think and at the same time gain a greater appreciation for the Word of God.

Dr. Bryant C. Wyatt
Pastor ~ Mt. Calvary Baptist Church, Sacramento, California

Preface

Toward the end of 2010, I was informed by some members of my church congregation that there might be a possible problem on the Internet with other members. After some urging, I checked into it and found essentially nothing.

I did, however, discover this media called Facebook. I realized that if used properly, Facebook could be used for ministry rather than misery. Here we are, 2,700 Facebook friends later, from all over the world. Only a Living God could do that. *Soli Deo Gloria*!!!

My wife Nina and I have had the privilege to travel to at least 5 countries with my mentor Dr. Joel C. Gregory and his Proclaimers Place Seminars, yet I have never set foot in many places where I have Facebook friends. That's further proof of what God can do.

Thanks to Dr. Joel Gregory for his guidance, instruction and mentorship at the seminars, and also the E.K Bailey Expository Preaching Conferences. It is an honor to know one of the greatest Biblical and theological minds "under the sun."

I started this ministry on Facebook, as I said in 2010. I set up my page so that you cannot post on it, but you can comment. That way the scripture, which is the main thing, will always be on the top. In seven and a half years, I have only had to delete 2 or 3 comments and 2 or 3 people. People are free to disagree, just not to disrespect the rest of you.

This book is a compilation of 365 posts, chosen from the last 7+ years as our "Facebook Congregation" grew. If you are looking for a profound theological treatise, this is the WRONG BOOK! This collection of posts is just the observations, gleanings, and illustrations from almost 40 years of preaching ministry.

Occasionally some sentences may sound incomplete, and you may notice the use of the ampersand sign and abbreviations quite often. This is because when I began posting on Facebook, there were word count restrictions that don't exist anymore! Also, occasionally, you may see a references to a previous post for which that day and year were not used in this publication.

The title is the inspiration from a "one word" response to many of our posts, "Watchman!" Whenever I posted something that caught his attention, my childhood friend Deacon Adam Banks would respond with that one word, "Watchman!" My use of the ellipsis symbol (...) on the cover, simply indicates that you are free to use your sanctified imagination as to what we who watch over God's Word do.

Deacon Banks reminds me of what I feel my ministry is to the Body of Christ. The term "Watchman" is used several times in the Bible. Suffice it to say, "Watchmen" in the Bible were charged with keeping watch in an agrarian society from a tower for protection of the fields and the animals.

Watchmen also kept day and night watch over cities from the top of the surrounding walls. Not only could they warn the people of the city from that vantage point of any approaching danger, but they could also observe the daily routines, habits, comings and goings of the people IN the city.

That's what I feel God has called me to do. It's also the purpose of this book: to observe everyday life on this earth, and to try and make simple sense out of what may be "darkness" to some of us (Isaiah 21:11-12). My #1 task as a "watchman"" is to report the Good News of our Lord and Savior, Jesus Christ.

Isaiah also said that those of us who deliver these Good Tidings (Good News), have beautiful feet (Isaiah 52:7-8)! Thanks, Isaiah. I've never had anyone compliment me on my FEET before!

Pastor Steven A. Bailey

Table of Contents

January

January 1
Plugging Our Meter!
Romans 8:34 ~ "Who is he that condemneth? It is Christ that died,
yea rather, that is risen again, who is even at the right hand of God,
who also maketh intercession for us."

Christ sits at the Father's right hand making intercession for us, not to CONDEMN US! I once worked graveyard shift in downtown San Francisco. Parking was free until 6am. After 6, cars were towed away if we didn't plug the meter. If we forgot, a co-worker would plug our meter. Thank God SOMEONE ELSE kept us from being towed away! That's what Jesus is doing at the Father's right hand, PLUGGING OUR METER!

January 2
FIRST THINGS FIRST!
Matthew 6:33 ~ "But seek ye first the kingdom of God,
and his righteousness;
and all these things shall be added unto you."

A boy's mother gave him TWO quarters one Sunday, one to put in church, & one to spend on himself. While walking to church & tossing the coins in the air, one of the quarters fell into the sewer. With tears in his eyes the boy looked down into the sewer and said, "What a shame: I LOST GOD'S QUARTER!"

Let's put the things of GOD FIRST! HE'LL take care of the REST! I prom ...no, HE PROMISED!

January 3
Tough Shoes
Deuteronomy 29:5 ~ "And I have led you forty years in the wilderness:
your clothes are not waxen old upon you,
and thy shoe is not waxen old upon thy foot."

Deuteronomy 33:25 ~ "Thy shoes shall be iron and brass;
and as thy days, so shall thy strength be."

There is a principle in God's Word that has BLESSED MY SOUL over the years. In 1989, I preached my mother's home-going service. If you had told me BEFORE her death that I would do that, I would have called you crazy. I learned something about God. He says to His people ...I'll give you TOUGH (Tuff) SHOES for a TOUGH TRIP. I'll also give you STRENGTH, based on how THAT PARTICULAR DAY IS GOING!

Comment ~ Don't borrow on TOMORROW'S TROUBLE. When you get there, He'll give you STRENGTH for that situation!!! (Isn't that what Jesus was saying in Matthew 6:34? :o)

January 4
Going to the "Service Bowl"
John 13:5 ~ "□Then He (Jesus) poured water into the basin (bowl),
and began to wash the disciples' feet,
and to wipe them with the towel wherewith He was girded..."

With all of the "Bowl" games going on this time of year, I have chosen to enter our church into the "Service Bowl"! Jesus was teaching His disciples to seek to be SERVANTS, and NOT simply to be SERVED. He took a BOWL of water and washed their dirty, stinky feet (I would emphasize dirty and stinky)!

Jesus told them in John 13:14, "If I as Lord and Master can wash YOUR FEET, then you ought to wash each other's feet! He said pretty much the same thing in Matthew 20:28.

Now go into 2012 and wash somebody's feet with a smile, a kind word, a pat on the back, a show of support, a hug, a handshake, a THANK YOU, etc. Can you think of a way you can be a better servant in the SERVICE BOWL this year?

January 5
Character Check!
2 Corinthians 4:2 ~ But have renounced the hidden things of dishonesty,
not walking in craftiness, nor handling the word of God deceitfully;
but by manifestation of the truth commending ourselves
to every man's conscience in the sight of God.

The verse speaks for itself. What we teach from the Word of God should line up with how we live!

I recently had a CHARACTER CHECK. I went to a store to get a refund on an item that didn't work. I had purchased 4 of them, and ONE was useless. When Jocelyn – yes, I try to remember the names of those that serve us – gave me the refund, she handed me almost DOUBLE what I had paid. She was going by the price it SHOULD have been that was on the wall behind her! The original salesperson charged me $4.99 per item when he should have charged me $7.99. I had not really looked at the receipt, I just knew I hadn't paid that much.

I immediately told Jocelyn that she gave me too much. She kept looking at the wall instead of the receipt. When she finally figured out what had happened, I went from giving her back some of what she had refunded me to also paying the difference on the OTHER THREE ITEMS!

Bottom line: my honesty cost me around $7 - $8 dollars. I also received a, "We need more HONEST men like you" from Jocelyn!

Now I can hear some of you saying, "Being a $7 or $8 dollar Christian is EASY. I wonder would he have been so honest if it had been SEVEN or EIGHT HUNDRED DOLLARS?" The answer is YES, and I HAVE!

Some 15 years ago when I went to Office Depot to purchase my first FAX machine, I saw one with ALL of the "bells and whistles" for $799.00. This was a beautiful piece of equipment. Those subtle curves, the beautiful big buttons, those sleek lines, her Ebony Blackness. Ah …I was IN LOVE! :o) I discussed the features at length with the salesperson, but decided to stay within MY budget and purchase a $200.00 model. (She wasn't as pretty! :o). While the salesperson went to the back storage room to get my cheaper model, I paid the $200 plus tax for the machine. The salesperson carried it to the car and put it in the trunk.

When I got home and unloaded the trunk, GUESS WHAT was in there?! You got it …the $800 Fax Machine!!! There I am AT HOME, with the most EXPENSIVE FAX MACHINE in the place and a RECEIPT that said I PAID for it! I was free & clear, RIGHT? On earth maybe, but NOT IN HEAVEN!

I got in my car, went back to the store and it took 15-20 minutes to CONVINCE them that I was returning an $800 machine (which was in my possession and untraceable) for a $200 one! Surely this man has lost his mind and is pulling our leg, is what they must have thought! No. I have learned something in this CHRISTIAN WALK. Your REPUTATION is who people say you are, based on what they have seen and heard about you. Your CHARACTER is who you ARE …when NOBODY (except God) IS LOOKING! How's your CHARACTER these days???

January 6
Pressure!

1 John 4:4 ~ "Ye are of God, little children, and have overcome them: because greater is he that is in you, than he that is in the world."

The world, the flesh and the devil put pressures on us, whether we are UP or DOWN. Success as well as failures bring PRESSURE!

Did you know that airplanes AND submarines are pressurized? The HIGHER you go in a plane, or the LOWER you go in a submarine, the GREATER the OUTSIDE PRESSURE!

The pressure inside airplanes and submarines is made to equal the OUTSIDE PRESSURE to keep the plane or the submarine (or persons) from being CRUSHED FLAT! God has placed His Holy Spirit INSIDE EACH of His children to keep us from COLLAPSING under the OUTSIDE PRESSURES of this world! That's what the verse says. :o)

January 7
Next of Kin

Ephesians 4:29 ~ "Let no corrupt communication
proceed out of your mouth,
but that which is good to the use of edifying,
that it may minister grace unto the hearers."

Colossians 4:6 ~ "Let your speech be always with grace, seasoned with salt, that ye may know how ye ought to answer every man."

Do our words reveal animosity in our hearts, or do they minister GRACE to the hearers?

A newly elected pastor who won the vote by a very NARROW margin, moved to the little town of his new pastorate. When his family arrived at the church parsonage (a home for the pastor, owned by the church), they found a DEAD DONKEY on the lawn of their new place.

The newly elected pastor reasoned that the donkey was put there by disgruntled members who DID NOT vote for him. He immediately made a call to the chairman of the church board and told him that there was a DEAD DONKEY on the parsonage lawn.

The chairman, who also DID NOT vote for the new pastor, said, "What do you want me to do? Isn't dealing with the dead YOUR JOB? Wouldn't that include a JACK-ASS?"

The pastor didn't miss a beat. He simply and calmly said to the chairman, "You're right. Dealing with the dead is my responsibility, including JACK-ASSES. I just thought I'd notify ...his NEXT OF KIN

FIRST!!! Now read those verses, if you haven't already. :o)

January 8
Don't Worry!
Matthew 6:25~ "Therefore I say unto you, Take no thought for your life,
what ye shall eat, or what ye shall drink;
nor yet for your body, what ye shall put on.
Is not the life more than meat, and the body than raiment?"

Matthew 6:25 says, "Don't Worry!" The Greek word "merizo [take no thought]" means to BE DISTRACTED or have DIVIDED ATTENTION. That's WORRY! If the devil can get your mind off of trusting Jesus, you will worry. Remember Peter walking on the water (Matthew 14:29-31)? When he SAW the storm, he lost FOCUS ON JESUS and began to sink. When storms come, keep a single-minded focus! When you start to worry, re-focus ...ON JESUS!

January 9
Godly Influence
Nahum 1:7—"The LORD is good, a strong hold in the day of trouble;
and he knoweth them that trust in him."

Harry Snyder and his wife Esther are with the Lord now. Harry died in 1976 and Esther in 2006, yet their INFLUENCE lives on in our lives to this very day. As Christians, they had their share of trials and tribulations like the rest of us. They had TWO sons, Harry "Guy" Snyder (born 1951), and Richard Snyder (born 1952).

Esther outlived both of their sons yet the legacy lives on. Guy Snyder died in 1999 of an overdose of painkillers. Richard Snyder, and four other people, were killed in a plane crash in 1993 when their small plane was caught in the "wake turbulence" of the larger plane they were behind, just before landing. That event led to changes in aviation laws.

While I'm here, let me say that we need to be CAREFUL of the path we set for those coming BEHIND US. Make sure it's a path that WON'T cause their destruction! Those "following" need to also be careful NOT to follow a destructive path. I'm sorry! That just hit me while I was typing!

The reason for this post is so that you will pay attention to the scriptures on several of the products from the BUSINESS the Snyder Family started in 1948, and remains a FAMILY business to this day. It has gone from ONE location to over TWO HUNDRED and THIRTY! Now the next time you eat at an IN-N-OUT Burger, slow down and check out the scriptures on the containers of the following products.

In-N-Out prints DISCREET references to Bible verses on their paper containers. These consist of the book, chapter and number of the verse, not the actual text of the passage, in small print on an INCONSPICUOUS area of the item. The practice began in the 1980s during Rich Snyder's presidency, a reflection of the Christian beliefs held by the Snyder family.

Burger and cheeseburger wrappers: Revelation 3:20—"Behold, I stand at the door and knock: if any man hear My voice, and open the door, I will come in to him, and will sup with him, and he with Me."

Beverage cups and replicas: John 3:16—"For God so loved the world that he gave his only begotten Son, that whosoever believeth in him should not perish, but have everlasting life."

Milkshake cups: Proverbs 3:5—"Trust in the LORD with all thine heart; and lean not unto thine own understanding."

Double-Double wrapper: Nahum 1:7—"The LORD is good, a strong hold in the day of trouble; and he knoweth them that trust in him."

Paper water cups (no longer in use for customers; they are now used by employees only): John 14:6—"Jesus saith unto him, I am the way, the truth, and the life: no man cometh unto the Father, but by Me.

License plate key-chains:1 Corinthians 13:13—"And now faith, hope, and love abide, these three; and the greatest of these is love."

P.S. ~ IN-N-OUT Burger is one of the FEW fast food restaurants where the FOOD actually looks like the PICTURE ...AFTER YOU GET IT! Praise God for CHRISTIAN entrepreneurs. Need MORE like them. :o)

January 10
Worship
John 4:24 ~ "God is Spirit, and those who WORSHIP Him
must WORSHIP in spirit and truth." (NKJV)

I have often used the word "WORSHIP," but never defined it. The Spirit told me NOT to assume that everyone knows what "worship" is.

Although my definition will by no means be exhaustive, I'm going to try to tackle this by giving you the English, Hebrew (Old Testament), and Greek (New Testament) definitions, and then my mentor's definition. The English word "worship" comes from two words, "worth" and "ship." That comes from the days when the value of a SHIP was determined by the value of the CARGO it was CARRYING at any given time.

The main Hebrew word for WORSHIP means to BOW DOWN. The lower, lighter, and lesser should always make himself or herself smaller... in

12

the presence of the HIGHER, HEAVIER, and HOLIER (John 3:30)!

The main Greek word for WORSHIP has an interesting root. Its root is the word "dog"! That New Testament word for WORSHIP means to "BOW DOWN and kiss the hand," as a dog would lick its master's hand!

Now I don't know about you, but I just want to bow down and kiss the hands (and feet) of JESUS when I think about my sins that He CARRIED away to yonder hill called Calvary (1 Peter 2:24)!

Dr. Rance Whiteside wrapped up WORSHIP in a neat package for those of us who sat under him. He said that WORSHIP is, "Perceiving the WORTH of GOD!" In other words, how you respond to (worship) God, will be determined by His WORTH to you! That's why Calvary is so important."

When I think about His goodness, and all He's done for me, when I think about His goodness, and how He set me free, I can..." Oh well, you get the picture! My question, "What is Jesus worth... TO YOU???" Go ahead... MOVE THE FURNITURE AGAIN! :)

January 11
The 49ers, or GOD?
Joshua 24:15 ~ "And if it seem evil unto you to serve the LORD,
choose you this day whom ye will serve;
whether the gods which your fathers served
that were on the other side of the flood,
or the gods of the Amorites, in whose land ye dwell:
but as for me and my house, we will serve the LORD (KJV)."

I know this won't be popular, but you all already know that's NOT why I'm here. Here is the S.A. Bailey version of Joshua 24:15 for today ~ "If you have a problem putting God first on this Championship Sunday, then you need to make a choice whom you're going to serve. Will it be the Ravens, 49ers, Giants, Patriots, or the GOD in whom you live, move and have your very being (Acts 17:28)!

Also remember that when you get in trouble, you CANNOT call Alex Smith, Eli Manning, Tom Brady, or Joe Flacco, but you can ALWAYS call on JESUS CHRIST! He knows all about your struggles, even how many HAIRS you have on your head ...or WEAVE! (Matthew 10:30 :o)

January 12
You Can't Handle the Truth!
Matthew 7:6 ~ "Give not that which is holy unto the dogs,
and don't cast your pearls before swine,

lest they trample them under their feet,
and turn again and attack you."

You know how some of us CAN'T HANDLE THE TRUTH? I feel that way about this post. I have a suspicion it won't be popular and it won't be up long, but it needs to be said. The verse simply says, that which is HOLY (or separated unto God) should not be treated LIGHTLY.

That would include YOURSELF! You are a Special Treasure (jewel) to God (Malachi 3:17). Giving yourself to someone unsaved and uncommitted would be like giving a Bible to a dog or a pearl necklace to a pig!

My friend and member, Deborah Lynn Davis-Payton, caused me to think about this verse when she said, "The Naked Truth: Having casual sex because you're horny is like eating garbage because you're hungry!" :o)

January 13
But GOD!!!!
Psalm 145:4 ~ "One generation shall praise thy works to another,
and shall declare thy mighty acts."

I heard it AGAIN! People my age and older saying, "Things I used to do, I don't do anymore ...and places I used to go, I don't go anymore." And some of us say that like it qualifies us for some special status with God.

LET'S BE REAL! The things we used to do, we CAN'T DO ANYMORE ...and places we use to go DON'T EXIST ANYMORE! Let's be truthful with these young people. Our generation should DECLARE God's GOODNESS, GRACE and MERCY to the next generation!

Let's tell our children the TRUTH about OUR YOUNG DAYS. Let them know that WE got abortions, used drugs, and had sex outside of marriage, ...BUT GOD!!!

Tell them how Auntie or Grandma raised our nieces and nephews that we THOUGHT were our COUSINS, and NOW we understand why SISTER (or some girl in the neighborhood), went missing for 9 months! Stop trying to make them believe that we lived up to standards that WE didn't keep ourselves. Then tell them how TRUSTING IN GOD will keep and/or deliver them from their mess! If they mess up, let them know that WE DID TOO ...BUT GOD!

January 14
A Story from Deacon Threat
Ephesians 5:16 ~ Redeeming the time, because the days are evil.

(The following story was sent to me a few years ago by my friend, Deacon James Threat).

Son: "Daddy, may I ask you a question?"
Dad: "Yeah sure, what is it?"
Son: "Daddy, how much do you make an hour?"
Dad: "That's none of your business! Why do you ask such a thing?" the man said angrily.
Son: "I just want to know. Please tell me, how much do you make an hour?"
Dad: "If you must know, I make $50.00 an hour."
Son: "Oh", the little boy replied, with his head down.
Son: "Daddy, may I please borrow $25.00?"
Dad: (furious) " If the only reason you asked that is so you can borrow some money to buy a silly toy or some other nonsense, then you march yourself straight to your room and go to bed! Think about why you are being so selfish. I don't work hard every day for such childish frivolities."

The little boy went quietly to his room and shut the door. The man sat down and started to get angrier about the little boy's questions. How dare he ask such questions only to get some money. After about an hour or so, the man calmed down and started to think. Maybe there was something his son really needed to buy with that $25.00. After all, he really didn't ask for money that often.

The man went to the door of the little boy's room and opened the door.

Dad: "Are you asleep, son?"
Son: "No daddy. I'm awake."
Dad: "I've been thinking, maybe I was too hard on you earlier. It's been a long day and I took out my aggravation on you. Here's the $25.00 you asked for."

The little boy sat straight up, smiling -- "Oh, thank you, daddy!"

Then the boy reached under his pillow and pulled out some crumpled up bills. The man saw that the boy already had money, and started to get angry all over again. The little boy slowly counted his money, and then looked up at his father.

Dad: "Why did you ask me for money if you already have some?"
Son: "Because I didn't have enough, but I do now! Daddy, I have $50.00 now. Can I buy an HOUR of your time? Please come home early tomorrow. I would like to have dinner with you."

The father was crushed. He put his arms around his little son and he begged for his forgiveness.

This is a reminder to ALL of us who work so hard in life. Don't let TIME slip through your fingers without having spent some TIME with those who really matter to us, those who are close to our hearts.

That's what the verse at the beginning says, "...making the most (redeeming) of TIME (*kairos*)." There are two main words for TIME in the New Testament, *chronos* and *kairos*.

Chronos is CHRONOLOGICAL time. Your watch or clock keeps track of that. Kairos (in the verse), is OPPORTUNITY, a specific time or season.

My dad, who is with the Lord now, use to tell us that there are TWO (2) things that God isn't making any more of ...land, and TIME!!! :o)

January 15
Bluing
Proverbs 20:30 ~ "The blueness of a wound cleanseth away evil:
so do stripes the inward parts of the belly."

When I met my wife Nina, she was washing clothes on a WASHBOARD in the tub. When we finally got a washing machine, she put what I thought was BLUE INK in the wash with my WHITE SHIRTS! I asked her if she had lost her mind? She assured me that she KNEW what she was doing and said, "BLUING cleans the DINGINESS out of white clothes."

BLUE is a color that represents "the heavens" in scripture. Now, Proverbs 20:30 makes sense! Do you have a WOUNDED body, heart, spirit, relationship, marriage, or friendship? I love Donny Hathaway and Roberta Flack's version of that old hymn, 'Come Ye Disconsolate' which says, "Earth has NO SORROW, that HEAVEN CANNOT HEAL!"

January 16
Get Out of the Kiddie Pool
Psalm 107:23-24 ~ "They that go down to the sea in ships,
that do business in great waters; these see the works of the Lord,
and his wonders in the deep."

Psalm 107:23-24 says launch out into deep water and see GOD AT HIS BEST! Have you ever caught BIG FISH in SHALLOW WATER? No, just GUPPIES! Launch out into DEEP WATER where you can see God do the MIRACULOUS. Deep water is trusting GOD TOTALLY. Pray and do your homework. Then start that business, make that career change, go back to school after all these years, get that degree, apply for that grant or scholarship, help someone else when you think you can't afford it! In other words, TRUST GOD and see HIS WONDERS IN THE DEEP! Now get your toes out of the KIDDIE pool!

January 17
Go with the Plan!
Jeremiah 29:11 ~ "For I know the PLANS (thoughts) that I planned
("have" is the same word) for you, says the LORD,
plans of peace, and not of evil, to give you a FUTURE HOPE!"

What contractor would try to build a decent house without checking the PLANS from the ARCHITECT?! Many of us do just that everyday. We go through an entire day of trying to build our lives, without ever having asked the ARCHITECT to show us HIS PLANS for our lives!

Joseph used the "root" of the same word when he told his brothers (who had planned to kill him), "You PLANNED evil against me, but GOD PLANNED IT for good. (Genesis 50:20)!" That means that no employer, employee, spouse, child, teacher, preacher, judge, lawyer, bill collector, politician, devil or demon in hell can stop what God has for you once you get in line with His plans for you.

GOD (The Architect) says HIS plans for us are SHALOM. That word means well-being, prosperity, safety, health and wholeness in body, soundness and tranquility in our relationships, peace and completeness! NO PLANS for evil whatsoever! The Bible word for HOPE is not a wish as it is in English, but an EXPECTED POSITIVE OUTCOME! I EXPECT things to go well for me, when I've checked the ARCHITECT'S PLANS FOR ME! And the DEVIL HIMSELF can't stop me! :o)

January 18
Truth and Tongues
1 Corinthians 13:1 ~ "If I speak in the tongues of men and of angels,
but have not love, I am a noisy gong or a clanging cymbal." (ESV)

I think I did say awhile back that I do what I do in a effort to impart truth as I understand it from the Word of God. The truth is NOT always comfortable. As a matter of fact, it will often make you down right mad, before you allow it to instruct you. The following subject is one of those truths. I pray I don't lose (as friends) too many of you, but the TRUTH will

FREE YOU ~ John 8:32.

I have been working toward making these posts shorter, then you all come up with a subject like this! This may take a minute. Feel free to copy and paste to a word processor for future reference. I have been in-boxed about the subject of "speaking in tongues." Yesterday I saw a post from my good friend, renowned Gospel singer and musician, Arvis Strickling-Jones. She posted that she heard a "Bishop" on television say that everyone who DID NOT speak in tongues, was going to hell! There is a day set aside for stuff like that. It's April 1!!!

Would you like to know what the BIBLE says about the subject, as opposed to some people? First of all, if that "Bishop" is correct in what he has said, you all might as well delete this page. That's because most of the folk on my friends list, including myself, would be on our way to hell. Can I appeal first to common sense? If speaking in tongues will get you into heaven, then the GOOD NEWS becomes a gospel of WORKS (something you do), and NOT of Grace. That would make Ephesians 2:8-9 a LIE!

Next, "other tongues" and "unknown tongues" are TWO DIFFERENT things! OTHER TONGUES (Acts 2:4), were KNOWN languages that the Holy Spirit imparted into those who preached at Pentecost. Those men AND women (Acts 1:13-15; 2:1-4), were all of a sudden able to speak to everyone there in the language of those listening to them (Acts 2.6-11)!

This was NOT some super spiritual language that was being spoken at Pentecost. In order to repeat what happened there, we who proclaim the Word would have to miraculously be able to speak Spanish, Mandarin, German, French, Italian, Japanese, etc. All the languages of any person of any country who would hear us preach!

UNKNOWN TONGUES are another matter. It is a special language (a gift from God) between an INDIVIDUAL person, and GOD! Look at 1 Corinthians 12:1. Paul said he did not want us to be IGNORANT about spiritual gifts. Now look at verse 4. The word "diversities" means VARIOUS gifts. Verses 8-11 teach that we all DO NOT have the same gifts.

My son, Adam Bailey, is a GIFTED keyboard player. NOT MY WIFE!!! If God gave everyone the same gifts, the organ bench at Olivet would not be able to hold the musicians who would be lined up to play. That's why God inspired Paul to write 1 Corinthians 12:12-31 on how DIFFERENT gifts should work... TOGETHER.

Now, have you noticed something about the LIST of gifts? Tongues is LAST on the list (12:10). Lists were often done in order of importance in Bible days, hence Paul and Silas... not Silas and Paul. Just an observation! 1 Corinthians Chapter 14 will open blind eyes to the truth of the gift of UNKNOWN TONGUES. Before I try to close this particular post in that chapter, let me say that by now, it should be apparent that I AM NOT one of those preachers who DO NOT believe in the gift of "tongues". I just KNOW that it is a gift... that I DON'T HAVE! I'm also convinced by what Paul says, that it is one that I don't need in order to help YOU.

I have good friends, as well as a Son in the ministry, who have this gift of a special prayer language. I have yet to meet someone with the gift of speaking multiple languages that they had never learned, as was done at Pentecost. Maybe you have. Can I wrap this up in 1 Corinthians 14? Paul says that when you exercise this special gift of unknown tongues, you are talking to GOD and NOT to me (verse 2)!!! That part of the gift makes it prayer (14:14)! Here is verse 5 in plain English: "I wish you all had the gift of speaking in tongues, but EVEN MORE I wish you were all able to prophesy (another post!). For prophecy is a greater and more useful gift than speaking in tongues, unless someone interprets what you are saying so that the whole church can get some good out of it (14:5)."

After a careful reading of the entire chapter 14, you can come to only ONE conclusion. Paul felt that speaking in an unknown tongue was more of a private, not public thing. He did, however, give instructions how it was to be done in public. Look at verse 27 and tell me if you have ever seen it done like this: Let TWO, no more than THREE of you speak. Speak ONE at a time (by course), and then someone tell those of us who DO NOT have the gift, or are unbelievers what in the world you are talking about. Otherwise, we might think you are crazy (14:23).

By the way, let me see if I will lose a few more (friends). This is free, no charge! Do you see chapter 14 verse 34, about women being "silent" in the church? Paul was STILL talking about speaking in tongues! He DID NOT change horses in mid-stream. It's on BOTH SIDES of the verse!

Haven't you ever asked yourself why he ONLY said this to the church at Corinth? Using it against women who preach or teach would be important enough to mention it more than just here, don't you think? Paul also would be contradicting himself, since he had just told the women how to dress when they prayed and prophesied... in chapter 11!

If you have studied the history of the church at Corinth, you would know that WIVES (14:35) in that particular church, were enjoying making their husbands (who didn't have the gift) look spiritually inferior by exercising the gift of tongues in public worship. Paul told those women, "STOP IT!!!"

If Paul meant what some of us have taught that 1 Corinthians 14:34 says, then EVERY CHURCH that I know of... IS OUT OF ORDER. No singing, welcomes, addresses, Amens, praises etc., would be allowed if Paul was saying to the women to SHUT UP IN CHURCH! He was talking to the women in THAT PARTICULAR CHURCH, about speaking in unknown tongues. Let's end this the way Paul did in chapter 14, verse 40.Verse 40 says, "Let all things be done decently and in order." Now for those of you who have the gift of tongues, exercise it in good faith and with love. Also do it decently and in order as Paul instructed. The rest of us who are idiots in this PARTICULAR area ("idiotes" is the Greek word for unlearned, ungifted, unskilled in verses 16,23, and 24), will wait for someone to tell us what you're saying.

Here's the bottom line. The verse at the top of the post says that if we don't do what we do, motivated BY LOVE... we'll probably end up where the good "Bishop" is trying to send us! Can I go soak my hands now? :)

January 19 (originally posted in 2011)
The Breath of Life
Genesis 2:7 ~ "And the LORD God formed man of the dust
of the ground, and breathed into his nostrils
the breath of life; and man became a living soul."

I remembered today... once in 2011, I came home from a three-service Sunday with a sore throat, and laid down. I had this sore throat for about three days. I woke later... GASPING FOR AIR! For two full minutes, I couldn't catch my breath (That's a LONG time when you can't breathe)!

I want to thank my son Marcus for grabbing me and praying for me, while I was stumbling around gasping for air. I do remember him saying, "Lord, don't take my daddy!!!" Thank You, Lord, for adult children who know and love you!!!

Do you all realize how precious AIR IS or how FRAGILE LIFE IS?! Every now and then, God reminds us of where it comes from! That's in the verse up top. God also reminds us that we can do NOTHING without Him (John 15:5; Acts 17:28). That's in the profile picture up top!

It's also a framed photo that I received from one of my Deacons, Al Carter. That picture was the first thing I noticed on the door of my home office when we returned from the hospital a short time ago. If you asked WHY the turtle is on the fence post, you asked the WRONG question! The question is, HOW did it get there? The answer? IT HAD HELP!

Interestingly, I mentioned Psalm 46:1 in my sermon yesterday, "God is our refuge and strength, a VERY PRESENT HELP in trouble." WOW!!! Just as I am typing this, there is a preacher on television who is talking about Psalm 46:1 !!! God is AMAZING! He is also a VERY PRESENT HELP when you need Him.

For those of you who teach that you have to WAIT on God for everything, let me ask you a question that Dr. Joel C. Gregory asked us in

Paris, France last year. "WHEN do you need help? ...WHEN YOU NEED IT!!!" Last night I needed breath... RIGHT THEN! There was no time to WAIT! SOLI DEO GLORIA, God ALONE gets the glory!!!

January 20
Caught in His Own Trap!
Psalm 7:15-16 ~ "He (the wicked person in verse 9) makes a pit, digging it out, and falls into the hole that he has made.
His mischief returns upon HIS OWN HEAD,
and on his own skull his violence descends." (ESV)

If you are a child of God, don't worry about those who mistreat or set traps for you. God has a unique way of causing a boomerang effect according to the verses. That's why Paul told the Galatians to be careful how they talked about others, because God can "flip the script" (Galatians 5:15)!

I saw a black and white episode of The Lone Ranger from 1950 today. At my age, one can appreciate the simple lessons in those old TV shows. In this episode, the Lone Ranger was on the trail of a man he had arrested years earlier. The outlaw had escaped from prison by taking the warden's son hostage. Tonto, the Lone Ranger's Native American friend, found the hideout first. What Tonto didn't know was that the outlaw had rigged the front and back doors of the hideout, with TRAPS! Over the front door was a heavy burlap sack, rigged to fall on whoever came through that door. The back door was tied to the trigger of a rifle, mounted to the side of a table in the middle of the small one room cabin. It was rigged to SHOOT anyone who came through the back door. Tonto came through the front door, and was knocked out when the heavy sack fell on his head.

Now the criminal has TWO hostages, tied up at the table in the middle of the room. The Lone Ranger finds the cabin. He cracks open the front door... SLOWLY. The trap had been reset, and Tonto had regained consciousness. Through the small crack in the door, Tonto warns the Lone Ranger with his eyes, that there is danger over his head! Let me pause here and say that a REAL FRIEND will warn you when others set traps for you!

The Lone Ranger kicked in the door, and got into a fight with the outlaw. As the Lone Ranger got the upper hand, the escaped convict broke loose and ran through... THE BACK DOOR! In case you didn't catch that, here are the words of The Lone Ranger as the outlaw went through the back door..."Caught in his OWN TRAP!!!"

January 21
On this Date in History...
2 Kings 6:1-7
"And the sons of the prophets said unto Elisha,
'Behold now, the place where we dwell with thee is too strait for us.
Let us go, we pray thee, unto Jordan, and take thence every man a beam,
and let us make us a place there, where we may dwell.'
And he answered, 'Go ye.'
And one said, 'Be content, I pray thee, and go with thy servants.'
And he answered, 'I will go.' So he went with them.
And when they came to Jordan, they cut down wood.
But as one was felling a beam, the axe head fell into the water:
and he cried, and said, 'Alas, master! for it was borrowed.'
And the man of God said, 'Where fell it?' And he shewed him the place.
And he cut down a stick, and cast it in thither; and the iron did swim.
Therefore said he, 'Take it up to thee.' And he put out his hand, and took it."

On this date in history, January 21, 1979 was a Sunday. At least three memorable things happened on that date. The Pittsburgh Steelers defeated the Dallas Cowboys in Super Bowl XIII, 35-31. Also on that day, TWO young men, twins by the name of Rufus and Julius Lucas were ordained as deacons at the Olivet Missionary Baptist Church where they serve to this day.

What was that third thing? Oh yes. Somebody by the name of Steven Bailey preached his first sermon at that same church, in that same service. He left the church in 1982 and returned in 1991, a little over 20 years ago, as pastor, where he remains to this day.

I thought the church would be empty because it was Super Bowl Sunday. Because of the three families, there were people standing around the walls that day. There was nowhere to sit. I remember making the statement that there were enough Black people in the church to make a Tarzan movie! (You have to be my age to know who Tarzan was. :o)

The crowd was not there because of the prowess of the preacher. Remember, I had never preached before! Many were there because of my "reputation." I had the same problem that the prophet Isaiah had in chapter 6 verse 5. I was a man of "unclean lips." I wrote the book on 'cussing'! People wanted to see if this person they knew was truly called to preach, and could string two CLEAN sentences together!

I've shared some details of that day because of the subject that I preached. It was taken from the scripture at the beginning of this post. Students of the prophet Elisha where cutting down trees to build a larger facility. One student was using a borrowed ax when the head came off and fell in the Jordan River.

Elisha cut down a tree (KJV says "stick", but the same word is translated "tree" 162 times), and tossed it into the Jordan. A MIRACLE took place! The iron ax-head (iron doesn't float), came to the surface of the water and was recovered!

Does all of this sound familiar? Our Lord and Savior Jesus Christ came all the way from heaven down into this sinful world and was nailed to a tree. I had been sinking deep in sin when He said, "And I, if I be lifted up from the earth, will draw all men unto me. (John 12:32)."

My subject on Sunday January 21, 1979 was ..."LOVE LIFTED ME"! It was a miracle, just like that ax head ...I was RECOVERED! :o)

January 22
Amazing Grace!
Ephesians 2:8-9 ~ "For by GRACE you have been saved □ □through faith,
and that not of yourselves; □it is the gift of God, not of □works,
lest anyone should □boast." (NKJV)

There is a song that you can sing in ANY prison in the world, and inmates will know it. It's the song "AMAZING GRACE"! Have you ever asked yourself why "Amazing Grace" is the most popular and well-known Christian song in the world?

Angels in heaven can't sing "Amazing Grace," because they've never been LOST. Sinners can't sing it, because they've never been FOUND. The only ones who can sing "Amazing Grace" are those of us who have been saved by GRACE through Faith!

By the way, some "politically correct" folk have tried to change the words of the song from, "...saved a WRETCH like me" to "...saved a SOUL like me!" I don't know about you, but I KNOW what I was when Jesus saved ME! I was a HOT MESS! In other words... He saved A WRETCH (Romans 7:24-25; 3:23) LIKE ME! ~ CUT annnnnnd ...PRAISE HIM!!! :o)

January 23
Moving Forward
Luke 9:62 ~ "□No one, having put his hand to the plow,
and looking back, is □fit for the kingdom of God." (NKJV)

Several comments on the last post have led to this post. Sis. Helen Gill-Smith said in a comment, "...sometimes it's good to remember where you have been delivered from..."

Paul Shotwell stated, "...Yep that WAS me both 1 and 2. An outcast and an exile."

Minister Robert J Kraft said, "Three days after my 14th birthday (referring to the death of M.L. King Jr.) ...I WAS very afraid of the world...the dawn's early light WAS beginning to dim."

Charlie Climp said, "YOU YOU AND YOU....PANIC! THE REST OF YA FOLLOW ME!"

Read all of the comments from the last post and tell me what they virtually ALL have in common. They all required a certain bit of "retrospection" (looking back), before one can look FORWARD! That would seem directly contradictory to the verse up there, wouldn't it? Not if you understand the verse. This verse has been taught to suggest that we should TOTALLY ignore the past.

First of all, that's IMPOSSIBLE. You may have a child with THE PAST, or some property with THE PAST! Secondly, some of you are sleeping with a TWIN of the person that "dogged" you, because you IGNORED lessons that THE PAST was trying to teach you! So what about the verse?

The word "looking" in the verse means to look "longingly, with a desire for". It even means to "orientate yourself in that direction!" Simply put, it's OK to look back and LEARN from the past. Some of us CAN'T MOVE FORWARD, because we haven't completely dealt with the past! It's dangerous to look back, with a desire to GO BACK!

In the verse up top, Jesus was choosing His disciples. He needed to be able to DEPEND on them. Jesus was headed for Jerusalem, and DID NOT have time for them to GO BACK to their old lives, even to say good-byes, or bury their dead (57-61).This was about PRIORITIES. What do you desire most? WHO do you desire most? Now the story of Lot's wife makes sense. She did not turn into a pillar of salt, simply for LOOKING BACK (Genesis 19:26; Luke 17:32). She looked back with a longing desire... TO GO BACK!

Do you REALLY want to return to a mess, or do you want to LEARN from it... so that you won't REPEAT IT? By the way, some of the past holds GREAT memories, like the day Jesus Christ came into your life!

January 24
Access
Ezekiel 16:49 ~ "Behold, this was the guilt of your sister Sodom:
she and her daughters had pride, excess of food,
and prosperous ease, but did not aid the poor and needy." (ESV)

Ephesians 2:18 ~ "For through Him [Christ Jesus in verse 13]
we both have ACCESS by one Spirit unto the Father."

As we approach Black History month, I pray for fair and equitable access to life, liberty, and the pursuit of happiness for ALL MANKIND with genuine needs.

Red, Yellow, Black and White men and women who desire to live in harmony with one another should have access to the basic needs of life. After all, JESUS gave us access to HIMSELF... and we DIDN'T DESERVE IT!

How often have you heard Sodom's (Sodom and Gomorrah) sexual sins, but not God's #1 problem with them? Sodom had so much wealth, but SHE DIDN'T HELP THE POOR! How many of you have heard this statement, "GIVE a man a fish, and he'll eat for a day. TEACH him to fish, and he'll eat for a lifetime"? My good friend John Hayes, taught me something that has stayed with me. He said, "Steve (He's Caucasian) :), all of that is good, but you have to give the person ACCESS TO THE LAKE!!!" Thank You Jesus for giving us ACCESS.. to YOURSELF! I never would have made it WITHOUT YOU! ♥

January 25
What God Desires
Amos 5:24 ~ "But let judgment run down as waters,
and righteousness as a mighty stream."

God desires JUSTICE & RIGHTEOUSNESS! So why are many of God's "sheep" silent about the injustice in society? I'm not talking about speaking against personal pet peeves, but about systemic evil inherent in the culture. Philosopher Edmund Burke said, "The only thing necessary for evil to triumph is for good men to do (say) nothing." My friend Dr. Larry Ellis calls this the "SILENCE OF THE LAMBS!!!"

January 26
It Floats!
Proverbs 10:19~ "In the multitude of words there wanteth not sin:
but he that refraineth his lips is wise."

TRUE!!! ~ First draft of an ad for a bar of Ivory soap: "The alkaline element & fats in this product are blended in such a way as to secure the highest quality of saponification, along with specific gravity that keeps it on top of water, relieving the bather of the trouble & annoyance of fishing around for it at the bottom of the tub during ablution." Final draft: "IT FLOATS!" Sometimes, less is MORE!

January 27
Name that Poem!
1 Corinthians 2:1-5~ "And I, brethren, when I came to you,
came not with excellency of speech or of wisdom,
declaring unto you the testimony of God.
For I determined not to know any thing among you,
save Jesus Christ, and him crucified.
And I was with you in weakness, and in fear, and in much trembling.
And my speech and my preaching was not
with enticing words of man's wisdom,
but in demonstration of the Spirit and of power:
That your faith should not stand in the wisdom of men,
but in the power of God."

"Scintillate scintillate globule vivific, fain that I fathom thy nature specific. Loftily poised in the ether capacious, strongly resembling a gem carbonaceous. Scintillate scintillate globule vivific, fain that I fathom thy nature specific." This is a version of an ENGLISH poem we learned in kindergarten! Paul teaches us to keep God's word ...plain & simple. What? Oh... Twinkle, twinkle, little star!... :o)

January 28
Give AS You Have Received
Matthew 10:8 ~ "Heal the sick, cleanse the lepers, raise the dead,
cast out devils: freely ye have received, freely give."

The Bible does NOT say "freely you give, freely you receive!" Read Matthew 10:8 again S-L-O-W-L-Y. Jesus was trying to teach his disciples that just as you have RECEIVED so much from me (context), GIVE the same way! Freely you HAVE RECEIVED, freely GIVE! Stop giving in order to GET. Give because of what you HAVE RECEIVED...like salvation, grace, mercy, protection, healing, etc. All from HIM! :o)

January 29

Propped Up Fronts
2 Corinthians 11:13-15 ~ "For such are false apostles, deceitful workers,
transforming themselves into the apostles of Christ.
And no marvel; for Satan himself is transformed into an angel of light.
Therefore it is no great thing if his ministers
also be transformed as the ministers of righteousness;
whose end shall be according to their works."

My favorite sitcom was Amos & Andy. (Say what you like & pretend that many of you didn't watch if you wish!) There was an episode where Kingfish sold Andy a house. There was NO HOUSE. Just a mansion-looking front, propped up for a movie set! Kingfish drove Andy past the house, & Andy bought it based on how the front looked! Some PEOPLE are like that, PROPPED UP FRONTS...RECOGNIZE!

January 30
Why We Need the Solid Rock
Isaiah 64:6~ "But we are all as an unclean thing,
and all our righteousnesses are as filthy rags;
and we all do fade as a leaf; and our iniquities,
like the wind, have taken us away."

"The Solid Rock" has one of my favorite verses. "When he shall come with trumpet sound, oh may I then IN HIM be found. Dressed in HIS RIGHTEOUSNESS ALONE, faultless to stand before the throne." That's what Isaiah is telling us about our righteousnesses (plural) in Isaiah 64:6. He said our righteousnesses are as "used menstrual rags" (literal Hebrew)! I told you it's not about US, It's about JESUS!!!

January 31
It's the Little Things
Luke 12:7a ~ "But even the very hairs of your head are all numbered..."

Leviticus 13:48 ~ "...in warp or woof of linen or wool..." (ESV)

Psalm 56:8 ~ "You number my wanderings [also "tossing and turnings"];
Put my tears into Your bottle; Are they not in Your book?" (NKJV)

How much is God concerned about the "little" things in our lives? Let's see:

1. God has given every hair on our heads a NUMBER (Luke 12:7).
2. He knows what's on the vertical and horizontal THREADS of our CLOTHES (warp/woof - Leviticus 13:48).
3. He keeps track of each tear we shed, every trip we take, and our concerns that cause us to toss and turn (Psalm 56:8).I'd say He's a God who pays attention to DETAIL. If YOU were the ONLY person on planet earth, Jesus STILL would have died for your sins...GOD LOVES US, and He CARES!!!

February

February 1
The Best and the Appropriate
Colossians 3:23~ "And whatsoever ye do, do it heartily,
as to the Lord, and not unto men."

Before you tell a young person that they owe God their best in what they wear to church (and I AGREE), consider this. Some of the athletic shoes we have a problem with COST MORE than our entire outfit! So who's giving God THEIR BEST? Clothing should be appropriate. Pull your pants up, men, we don't need to see all of that! A BIT LOOSER, LADIES. Not SO TIGHT that we can tell what you had for BREAKFAST!

February 2
The Story of a Favorite Hymn
Matthew 10:29-31 ~ "Are not two sparrows sold for a farthing?
and one of them shall not fall on the ground without your Father.
But the very hairs of your head are all numbered.
Fear ye not therefore, ye are of more value than many sparrows."

In 1904, Mrs. Civilla Martin visited a sick friend and asked if she ever got discouraged because of her illness. The woman responded, "How can I be discouraged when God watches over each little sparrow and I know He loves and cares for me?" Civilla wondered why God would care about the MOST COMMON and LEAST VALUABLE of all birds. She wrote her feelings to us in a song, "His Eye Is On The Sparrow."

February 3
Chill!
Exodus 8:22-23 ~ "And I will sever in that day the land of Goshen,
in which my people dwell, that no swarms of flies shall be there;
to the end thou mayest know that I am the Lord in the midst of the earth.
And I will put a division between my people
and thy people: to morrow shall this sign be."

1) There are SOME things that Christians & non-Christians alike go through! The first three plagues God sent touched Egypt AND Israel. **2)** Whenever God chooses, He can make a "DISTINCTION" between US & THEM (vs. 23)! God can make it storm over your neighbor's house & the sun shine on yours! Trust Him when folk mistreat you. He can KEEP YOU SAFE, when all HELL breaks out around you! Chill: GOD'S GOT THIS!

February 4
From Slave to Millionaire
Deuteronomy 28:13 ~ "And the Lord shall make thee the head, and not the
tail; and thou shalt be above only, and thou shalt not be beneath;
if that thou hearken unto the commandments of the Lord thy God,
which I command thee this day, to observe and to do them."

God says He'll make HIS children the HEAD & NOT THE TAIL. Sarah Breedlove is an example of this. (Before you say these blessings are for Israel, read Galatians 6:15-16 & pretend like you KNEW that believers are the ISRAEL OF GOD)! Sarah went from being an orphan of slaves to the first FEMALE MILLIONAIRE in America! That's her in the profile, better known as Madame C.J. Walker!

February 5
Rest and (Holy) Refreshment
Isaiah 43:7 ~ "Even every one that is called by my name:
for I have created him for my glory,
I have formed him; yea, I have made him."

If you need another reason to treat your body as the Holy of Holies (see previous post), it says we were made for GOD'S GLORY! Is what you're doing with your body glorifying God? I don't expect much response to this, but I believe most of you come to this page for the TRUTH! Be careful WHAT you put in your body & WHO you give access to your body. And for God's Glory ...PLEASE REST YOUR BODY! ~ Mark 6:31

February 6
Get that Exercise!
1 Timothy 4:8 ~ "For bodily exercise profiteth little:
but godliness is profitable unto all things,
having promise of the life that now is,
and of that which is to come."

BODILY exercise profits literally "for a little time." Physical exercise is beneficial, but it's temporary. We need to ALSO exercise our SPIRITUAL muscles which profit us HERE & in the WORLD TO COME (end of the verse)! The word for exercise (gymnasia) is where we get our word GYMNASIUM. The root (gumnazo) means "NAKED"! Back in Bible days, people exercised without anything that would WEIGH THEM DOWN!

February 7
DON'T Leave It Like You Found It
Galatians 6:10 ~ "So then, as we have opportunity, let us do good to
EVERYONE ["men" is not in the original text],
and especially to those who are of the household of faith."

A lady went to a pet store and asked for 100 mice and 200 cockroaches! The store owner looked puzzled. The lady asked him if there was a problem. He said "NO, but do you mind if I ask why you need 100 mice and 200 roaches?" She said, "My husband is a pastor in this city, and has been called to pastor another church in another city. The deacons at the church here, told us to leave the parsonage... JUST LIKE WE FOUND IT!" Please DON'T leave this world like YOU FOUND IT! Touch some one's life. You may never have that particular opportunity again.

February 8
What MY Daddy Owns!
Psalm 24:1 ~ "The earth is the Lord's and the fullness thereof,
the world and those who dwell in it."

A group of children were walking home from a private school, when a rich boy in the group began to tease a poorly dressed girl he saw on the street. "Hey POOR girl!" he said. "See those CATTLE on that hill? My daddy owns them. And those PLANES in the sky are my dad's! Even those SHIPS out there on the water belong to MY daddy! What does YOUR DADDY own little poor girl?"The little girl didn't hesitate. She said, "You see those HILLS your daddy's cattle are standing on, they belong to MY FATHER. The SKY your daddy's planes fly in, and the WATER his ships float on... they ALL belong to MY FATHER!!!

February 9
Jesus Plays the Dozens
2 Corinthians 5:17~ "Therefore if any man be in Christ,
he is a new creature: old things are passed away;
behold, all things are become new."

Jesus playing the dozens? That's a Black term for trading insults, especially about parents ~ e.g. "Your mama's so stupid she sold her car for gas money!" The "dozens" has its origins in the OLD & DEFORMED SLAVES who were DEVALUED & sold by the DOZENS! Not funny, is it? Jesus called a particular group, "children of snakes" (Matthew 3:7-8). That would make THEM...? The Good News: ONE CAN CHANGE, IN CHRIST!

February 10
Just One Thank You
Luke 12:17~ "And Jesus answering said,
'Were there not ten cleansed? but where are the nine?'"

Jesus healed 10 LEPERS. ONLY one said THANK YOU! Jesus asked what happened to the other nine. When you don't say thank you, you're acting like you deserved that service, favor, or gift. You can change someone's day, no LIFE with a simple THANK YOU. That waitress you thought owed you service, could have had a bad day & gone "KIZZY" on you! (See "Roots" the miniseries!) Just say THANK YOU...JESUS!

February 11
Ain't Nothin' Like the Real Thing
John 14:6~ Jesus saith unto him, I am the way, the truth,
and the life: no man cometh unto the Father, but by me.

Some folks worked at a bank that taught its employees how to recognize counterfeit money. The supervisor made them count genuine bills until they got frustrated. Finally someone asked why they were wasting time counting real money. The supervisor said, "If you spend enough time with the REAL THING, you'll know a PHONY when you see one! JESUS is the REAL THING. Spend time with HIM!

February 12
Goodness and Mercy
Psalm 23:6~ "Surely goodness and mercy shall follow me,
all the days of my life,
and I will dwell in the house of the Lord, forever."

One day I turned past a corner store & a man jump in front of the van. Car Jacking came to mind. I put it in reverse & there was another man in back! The store owner was sitting out front so I got out, & saw FIRE under the van! The store owner helped put it out. I wanted to thank the two men but they were gone! The owner said he had been the ONLY one around, but the Lord told me their names ~ Goodness & Mercy! Angels?

February 13
He's on a Counter!
1 Peter 5:8~ "Be sober, be vigilant; because your adversary
the devil, as a roaring lion, walketh about,
seeking whom he may devour."

Satan can't get to God, so why not go after HIS CHILDREN! Remember when going through trials: **A)** The devil is defeated, per Revelation 12:11-12. **B)** He's on a COUNTER. There's a number that will be saved before Christ comes. You made Satan nervous when you came to Jesus! He doesn't know which one will set off the end times! ~ Romans 11:25 **C)** If the devil isn't bothering you, YOU'RE PROBABLY NOT BOTHERING HIM!!! ~

February 14 – Valentine's Day
Looking Good, Darling!
Proverbs 18:22~ "Whoso findeth a wife findeth a good thing,
and obtaineth favour of the Lord."

The profile is my beautiful wife of more than 30 YEARS! Solomon said whoever finds a wife finds a "good thing..." (Proverbs 18:22). Thank God for my "GOOD THANG!" Pardon the Ebonics. King Lemuel's mother taught him that a good wife (virtuous woman), makes her HUSBAND LOOK GOOD (Proverbs 31:23)! GOD gave me all that I have and has made me all that I am. NINA BAILEY makes all of that LOOK GOOD, Love You Sweetheart!

February 15
Way Out, Man
Luke 9:31~ "Who appeared in glory,
and spake of his decease which he should accomplish at Jerusalem."

Exodus: Greek = ex (out) + odos (way) = WAY OUT. EXODUS tells of Israel's WAY OUT of Egypt. Jesus spoke of his death (exodos) in Luke 9:31. We get our word EXIT. Exit signs in many public buildings are supposed to be wired to the city's power on the street. That way there's EXIT LIGHTS ON, even if you don't pay the bill! Your exit is on the city! Jesus provided US an EXIT from God's wrath, at Calvary. It's free, it's on HIM!

February 16
Keep Your Business YOUR BUSINESS
Ecclesiastes 10:20~ "Curse not the king, no not in thy thought;
and curse not the rich in thy bedchamber:
for a bird of the air shall carry the voice,
and that which hath wings shall tell the matter."

I remember wondering how parents knew when we had done wrong. They often said, "A little bird told me!" I found out MOST of the time that "little bird" was ME. I'd say or do something that told them I was guilty. Stop putting your VERY PERSONAL BUSINESS ON FACEBOOK! That "little bird" just might speak up at a courthouse or job interview! Think there's no verse for this? See Ecclesiastes 10:20!

February 17
What a Man!
1 Timothy 2:5~ "For there is one God,
and one mediator between God and men, the man Christ Jesus."

Ooh, ooh...all Facebook folk with your Q & A. Can I play? **Q:** Who is the man, that would risk his neck for his brother man? Who's the one that won't cop out, when there's danger all about? **A:** Not SHAFT! BEHOLD, THE MAN ...CHRIST JESUS! ~ 1 Timothy 2:5; John 19:5; John 15:13. Might I add "What a Man, What a Man, What a Man, What a Mighty GOOD MAN..."(In my Salt N Pepa/En Vogue voice!)

February 18
Oneness... and the Blåtand on Your Computer
John 17:21-23~ "That they all may be one; as thou, Father,
art in me, and I in thee, that they also may be one in us:
that the world may believe that thou hast sent me.
And the glory which thou gavest me I have given them;
that they may be one, even as we are one: I in them,
and thou in me, that they may be made perfect in one;
and that the world may know that thou hast sent me,
and hast loved them, as thou hast loved me."

Jesus prayed to his Father for "ONENESS" among believers.

Harald Blåtand was King of Denmark 940-985 AD. He UNITED Danish tribes into ONE Kingdom, converted the Danes to CHRISTIANITY, & conquered Norway. When 21st century entrepreneurs came up with a way to UNITE computers & telecommunication devices AS ONE, they gave the new technology Blatånd's English name. What? I'm sorry, it was BLUETOOTH :o)

February 19
One Letter Over
Psalm 119:18 – "Open thou mine eyes,
that I may behold wondrous things out of Thy law."

Little Johnny was to do a presentation at church on the omnipresent God, 15 letters on 15 cards that read GOD IS EVERYWHERE. His ATHEIST father decided to embarrass him. He made new letters for Johnny. To the surprise of the church, the letters read GOD IS NO WHERE! Johnny stood to read through his tears, then smiled and walked to the stage. He moved the "W" next to the "NO," then stepped back and said, "GOD IS NOW HERE!"

February 20
His Master's Voice
Psalm 95:7-8~ "For he is our God;
and we are the people of his pasture, and the sheep of his hand.
Today if ye will hear his voice,
harden not your heart, as in the provocation,
and as in the day of temptation in the wilderness."

Nipper was the real and famous RCA dog, head cocked to the side, listening to something through the cylinder of an old fashioned phonograph. That's a record player for you who are like some of my youth who thought records were GIANT CD'S! The trademark name of that (R)adio (C)orporation of (A)merica photo was "His Master's Voice"! Nipper was listening to a recording of "His Master's Voice!" Are you? ~ Psalm 95:7-8

February 21
Good Reading
James 1:22~ But be ye doers of the word, and not hearers only, deceiving your own selves.

James 1:22 tells us to be DOERS of the Word and not just HEARERS! The Greek word for "DOERS" is "POIETES," from which we get our English word "POET"! A good poet will make words come alive. A good Christian will make The Word come alive! Paul said we are LIVING LETTERS written in the heart & being read by men (2 Corinthians 3:2-3). Yes, people are READING YOUR LIFE! Question…is it GOOD READING? :o) ~ Pt. 2 Tomorrow

February 22
The Mirror and the Foundation
James 1:23~ "For if any be a hearer of the word, and not a doer, he is like unto a man beholding his natural face in a glass..."

God's Word is called a MIRROR in James 1:23 (KJV= glass = polished steel). James said to HEAR the word & not DO it is like seeing your "GENESIS" (birth) face in the mirror, flaws & all, then walking away the same! The mirror SHOWS you the problem. Now what? Look just below the mirror. THERE IS A FOUNTAIN! Cowper said it's filled with BLOOD DRAWN FROM IMMANUEL'S (Jesus') VEINS. Dive in, & lose all your guilty stains!

February 23
Transfer!
Leviticus 4:32-34 ~ "And if he bring a lamb for a sin offering, he shall bring it a female without blemish.
And he shall lay his hand upon the head of the sin offering, and slay it for a sin offering in the place where they kill the burnt offering.

And the priest shall take of the blood of the sin offering with his finger,
and put it upon the horns of the altar of burnt offering,
and shall pour out all the blood thereof
at the bottom of the altar."

Remember when the sinner brought a lamb to the priest as a sacrifice for his sin? The sinner laid his hand on the lamb's head, transferring his sins to the INNOCENT LAMB & the Lamb's INNOCENCE to HIMSELF! Then the INNOCENT LAMB was killed, NOT THE SINNER! The LAMB died for the SINNER! BEHOLD the Lamb of God, that takes away the sin of the world! His Name? JESUS! ~ John 1:29; 2 Corinthians 5:21

February 24
Forgiveness, Divorce, and What They Have in Common
Luke 23:34~ "Then said Jesus, Father, forgive them;
for they know not what they do.
And they parted his raiment, and cast lots."

What do the words "FORGIVE" & "DIVORCE" have in common? In the New Testament they're the SAME WORD, the Greek word "af-ee'-ay-mee". (Luke 23:34; 1 Corinthians 7:11,12,13) The connection? The word means to "send away" or "get rid of". In divorce, you get rid of the PERSON & hold on to the GRUDGE. In forgiveness, you get rid of the GRUDGE & hold on to the PERSON! THANK YOU LORD for getting rid of my SIN! ~

February 25
Forgiveness – LET THE THING GO
Hebrews 10:17~ "And their sins and iniquities will I remember no more."

God is the ONLY ONE who can "forget" wrong done (Hebrews 10:17 & more). If you cut my arm off I can forgive you. But whenever I look at the missing arm, or someone calls me Stumpy, I will remember what you did. If you forgive in the biblical sense of the word, you will LET THE THING GO, AFTER it's been dealt with! That would be treating it AS IF you forgot by NOT BRINGING IT UP! True FORGIVENESS is our "forgetting."

February 26
Think no Evil
1 Corinthians 13:5~ "[Love] Doth not behave itself unseemly,

seeketh not her own, is not easily provoked, thinketh no evil..."

1 Corinthians 13:5 says "...Love (charity in vs.4)...THINKETH no evil..." The word "thinketh" means not to keep an account or records! Yes, REAL LOVE will get rid of that list (real or mental) you've been keeping of all the WRONG DONE TO YOU! The psalmist asks, if GOD kept an record of sin, WHO WOULD BE ABLE TO STAND? ...But there is FORGIVENESS! ~ Psalm 130:3-4. Now, can you say ...JESUS?!

February 27
Don't Be Rabid
Galatians 5:15~ "But if ye bite and devour one another,
take heed that ye be not consumed one of another."

A woman listened as the doctor gave her the results of some tests. He said, "I'm afraid you have RABIES!" She began to cry & scream, then she asked for a pen & paper. He said, "It's NOT FATAL, you don't have to write a will. You're NOT going to die!" She said "Doctor, this isn't a will, it's a LIST of people I want to BITE BEFORE you give me those shots!" Be careful how you bite & devour one another!

February 28
All Things Work Together
Romans 8:28~ "And we know that all things work together
for good to them that love God,
to them who are the called according to his purpose."

During World War II, Jimmy Durante (famous for his large nose) did his song & comedy act for wounded servicemen. He had agreed to do 1 set because of other engagements. He did 3. Ed Sullivan asked him why he stayed. He pointed to 2 men in the front row. One had lost his left arm in service & the other his right arm, yet together they were CLAPPING each other's hand! ALL things work TOGETHER...

March

March 1
What's That Sticking Out of Your Eye?
Matthew 7:3-5~ "And why beholdest thou the mote
that is in thy brother's eye,
but considerest not the beam that is in thine own eye?
Or how wilt thou say to thy brother,
Let me pull out the mote out of thine eye;
and, behold, a beam is in thine own eye?
Thou hypocrite, first cast out the beam out of thine own eye;
and then shalt thou see clearly to cast out the mote
out of thy brother's eye.

A country pastor woke to find his bicycle missing. He told a deacon that he believed it was a member, and his next sermon would be the 10 COMMANDMENTS. "When I get to THOU SHALT NOT STEAL (#8), I'll get a CONFESSION!" That Sunday he got to #6, "Thou Shalt Not Kill," and STOPPED. The deacon asked, why? He said, "When I saw in my Bible, Thou Shalt Not Commit ADULTERY (#7), I remembered where I LEFT MY BICYCLE!" ~ Matthew 7:3-5

March 2
Israel or Jacob?
Exodus 3:6 ~ "Moreover he said, I am the God of thy father,
the God of Abraham, the God of Isaac, and the God of Jacob.
And Moses hid his face; for he was afraid to look upon God."

Why does God call HIMSELF the God of Abraham, Isaac & Jacob? Why not Abraham, Isaac & Israel since ISRAEL & JACOB are the SAME PERSON? (Genesis 32:27-28). Israel means "prince with God or a God-governed man." Jacob means "heel grabber, supplanter or a trickster" (Genesis 25:26)! Why identify with Jacob? It's simple: God still loves even the power grabbers & tricksters. He wants to be your God, REALLY!

March 3
EXTREME HOME MAKEOVER!
Matthew 12:43-45 ~ "When the unclean spirit is gone out of a man,
he walketh through dry places, seeking rest, and findeth none.

Then he saith, 'I will return into my house from whence I came out;
and when he is come, he findeth it empty, swept, and garnished.'
Then goeth he, and taketh with himself
seven other spirits more wicked than himself,
and they enter in and dwell there:
and the last state of that man is worse than the first.
Even so shall it be also unto this wicked generation."

Anyone who gets rid of the bad stuff in their lives should be OK, RIGHT? The problem is once that stuff is GONE, it has to be REPLACED. An empty house is dangerous. If you invite a "higher power" into your life, you open the door to ANY "god" that wants to move in. When JESUS moves into your life, all rooms will be FULL! Call it, "AN EXTREME HOME MAKEOVER!" (John 10:10; Psalm 16:11)

Comment ~ This post was inspired by the comments of my friend & member, Wink Bennett on the last post. Thank You Wink. ;o)

March 4 (originally posted in 2011)
John 10:9 ~ "I am the door: by me if any man enter in,
he shall be saved, and shall go in and out, and find pasture."

In EARTHQUAKE-prone areas we're told to stand in a doorway, get in a bathtub with a mattress over our heads, or get under a table! Why? STABILITY! You can't see behind doors or under tubs, but those AREAS ARE REINFORCED! Jesus said HE is the DOOR (John 10:9). BEFORE you panic, stand in THE DOOR, BATHE in THE WORD (Ephesians 5:26), & get under the protection of HIS TABLE (Psalm 23:5)! Now let's PRAY FOR JAPAN!

Comment ~ All of us who call on the name of Jesus should be praying for our brothers and sisters in Japan. We should also help in any OTHER way we can, when the LEGITIMATE calls come!

March 5
All Suffering Is Not Because of Sin
Job 42:7 ~ "And it was so,
that after the Lord had spoken these words unto Job,
the Lord said to Eliphaz the Temanite,
'My wrath is kindled against thee, and against thy two friends:

for ye have not spoken of me the thing that is right,
as my servant Job hath.' "

God rebuked Job's "friends" for telling Job that his trials were because of sin in his life! ALL suffering is NOT because of sin! If you're suffering because of sin, you'll KNOW IT! God doesn't "child train" (Hebrews 12:6-7) without us knowing why! A preacher told one of my hospitalized members that she was there because of some SECRET sin. I told her that was a LIE, because I WASN'T IN THE BED NEXT TO HERS!

Comment ~ @ Everybody - Some suffering is meant to strengthen us, and others are for God to get glory and joy from delivering and blessing us (1 Peter 5:10; Job 42:10; James 1:2-4)!

March 6
Set Free or Made Free?
John 8:32 ~ "...the truth shall FREE (Deliver) YOU."

Ever been to jail? OK, just to VISIT? Ever BAIL anyone out of jail & they ended up right BACK IN JAIL? That's because they were SET FREE & not MADE FREE! When JESUS is Lord of your life, HE'S the TRUTH that MAKES YOU FREE. That TRUTH is PERMANENT, & can keep you from going into bondage CONTINUOUSLY. Can you HANDLE THE TRUTH, or are you CONTENT with TEMPORARY PAROLE?

March 7
Favor Ain't Fair
Ephesians 2:8 ~ "For by grace are ye saved through faith;
and that not of yourselves: it is the gift of God."

Did you know "grace" & "favor" are the SAME New Testament word? It's the word "charis", from which we get "charisma" & "charismatic"! Since GRACE (Favor) is a GIFT, it's UNDESERVED! The root word emphasizes the JOY & PLEASURE that the GIFT brings! So when you say "Favor Ain't Fair," THANK GOD IT ISN'T! We're SAVED by God's FAVOR (Grace)! If God HAD GIVEN us what we DESERVED... ???

March 8
How to Love More than One Woman At a Time
Ephesians 5:25-26 ~ "Husbands, love your wives,
even as Christ also loved the church, and gave himself for it;☐ ☐
That he might sanctify and cleanse it
with the washing of water by the WORD..."

I may lose a few men with this post, but I guarantee you that the HOLY SPIRIT won't let you forget it! I'll give the men a moment to decide whether or not they want to read any further......OK. I know that the CONTEXT of these verses is marriage. But did you know that the word for "wives" in verse 25 can mean a wife, woman, virgin, or widow?!

We as men should be responsible for loving ANY women we are in relationship with (including friends, sisters, mothers, etc.), AS CHRIST LOVED THE CHURCH and made a SELF-sacrifice for her! WOW! Then it goes on to say how we should SANCTIFY (set apart, cover, cleanse, protect) the women in our lives, WITH OUR WORDS!

The Greek word for "WORD" in verse 26 is "rhema," which is SPECIFICALLY the SPOKEN word out of OUR MOUTHS! Can you imagine JESUS ever calling the CHURCH some of the things we as men call the women we are responsible for covering? Yet JESUS CHRIST and the Church is EXACTLY what these relationships are a PICTURE of, according to verse 32!

A non-Christian ought to be able to look at our relationships with the WOMEN in our lives, and see the relationship between Jesus and His Church! Much of HOW and WHO women are and become, has a lot to do with how we treat them ...especially how we TALK to them!!! I'm just saying. :o)

March 9
All Things
Romans 8:28 ~ "And we know that ALL things work together for good
to them that love God, to them who are the called according to his purpose."

This is a 'LIFE LESSON' verse for me. Almost every time I use this verse, I get several people who say, "Pastor Bailey, I just DON'T SEE how BAD THINGS can work out for my GOOD. Doesn't the verse say ALL THINGS work together for good...?"

Consider this horror story from MY very own life, or it could have been a Blessing, depending on how you look at it. This is an absolutely TRUE story.

In 2008, a man and a woman wounded me severely! I had never met them before that fateful day. I had never done ANYTHING to harm either one of them. Yet the man knocked me unconscious, and the woman took a KNIFE and CUT MY THROAT from one side to the other!

I was told that there was a chance I might not be able to talk again, let alone preach. I was also told that POTENTIAL injury to a particular muscle in my neck when the woman cut me, could hinder me from being able to lift my right arm!

Can you imagine how I was feeling at the possibility of not being able to preach or praise Him by lifting up my hands, ever again? It all depends on how you are conditioned to read stories!

You see, the man who knocked me out was an anesthesiologist. The woman was my surgeon! The knife was a scalpel. The two conspired to remove a potentially "deadly" cancerous thyroid from my neck! My surgeon was obligated to tell me all that COULD go wrong if they nicked my vocal cords or a muscle that helps me raise my arm. Even "HOW" they discovered the cancer in the first place is a TESTIMONY to this verse. I had an infection from an ingrown hair during SHAVING, that caused one side of my face to swell to the size of a softball. While draining my face, the doctor saw a DARK SPOT on my DARK NECK in the area of my thyroid. That's how they discovered the problem.

After close to 9 hours of surgery, I was told that the cancer was gone and nothing vital was damaged! And WE KNOW, that ALL THINGS... (Excuse me a minute....:o)

March 10
God Doesn't Change
John 3:16 (not Bailey 3:16) ~ For God so loved the world,
that he gave his only begotten Son,
that whosoever believeth in him should not perish,
but have everlasting life.

March is the month of the Pastor and Wife's Appreciation at our church. SO MANY WONDERFUL YEARS of serving these marvelous people of God in the same location!

I have friends who only believe in Pastor's Appreciations, NOT Pastor and Wife! I have to remind some of them where they would be ...WITHOUT THEIR WIVES! Nina is NOT the pastor, but I could NOT do my job effectively without her. As a matter of fact, if she didn't serve as a human anchor, consoler, and confidante in my life, John 3:16 would read like this: Bailey 3:16 ~ For Bailey so loved the world, that he gave them all he had one Sunday. But they made him mad on Monday, so he took it all back on Tuesday. But Bailey and the world RECONCILED on Wednesday, so he gave them everything back on Thursday. But they ticked him off AGAIN on Friday, and he sent them ALL TO HELL ON SATURDAY!

Now read JOHN 3:16 again, and BE GLAD that GOD DOESN'T CHANGE (Malachi 3:6) ...and I'M NOT HIM! Also THANK GOD that He gave me the wife that He did!!! :o)

March 11
The Best Choir Anywhere
Psalm 33:3 ~ "Sing unto him a new song; play skillfully with a loud noise."

May I lighten the moment for just a moment (pun intended)?

I know I'm prejudiced, but not in error, when I say I serve a church with one of the best choirs anywhere. (If you don't feel that way about yours, there's something wrong with you ...or them! :o)

I am a musician, and have been one LONGER than I've been a preacher. I have taught this verse on numerous occasions to numerous musicians! The word "skillfully" in the verse means to play well, joyfully, pleasingly, thoroughly, with ability, with preparation, etc. It also suggests that EVERYBODY isn't gifted in MUSIC, and probably shouldn't be in the choir!

I taught our choir, as well as my sons and God-son who happen to be the musicians, that you DON'T sing songs like, "I SHALL NOT BE MOVED" for the offering.

So imagine my surprise when the wife and I marched in Sunday to the choir singing, "I Shall Wear A Crown ...WHEN IT'S ALL OVER!" As my friend Minister Jewel M. London would say (Oxford Sermons Volume III), "It's NOT OVER ...Until God Says It's Over!" Now my wonderful and anointed choir, do what verse 3 says, and ...Sing Unto Him A NEW SONG! LOVE YOU!!! :o)

March 12
A Really "Down" Post
John 6:38 ~ "For I came down from heaven, not to do my own will, but the will of Him that sent me."

John 10:15 ~ "As the Father knows me, and I know the Father: and I lay down my life for the sheep."

44

Hebrews 1:3 ~ "Who being the radiance of his glory,
and the exact representation of His person,
and upholding all things by the word of His power,
when He had made purification of sins,
sat down on the right hand of the Majesty on high…"

1 Corinthians 15:24, 25 ~ "Then comes the end,
when He shall deliver up the kingdom to God the Father;
when He shall have put down all rule and all authority and power.
For He must reign, until He has put all His enemies under His feet."

Some English words have several meanings. DOWN is one of those words. I used to own a "down" comforter (blanket). It was made from the soft, fluffy under body feathers of a young bird. These feathers are called DOWN! You have really NOT known comfort until you've slept on a DOWN pillow or under a DOWN blanket, that is, if you are NOT allergic.

What does all of that have to do with those verses? I'm glad you asked! What is the COMMON THREAD in those verses? It's the word "DOWN." I just gave you a DOWN comforter for your soul! Jesus CAME DOWN from heaven, LAID DOWN His life, went back to heaven and SAT DOWN at the right hand of the Father, and will come back one day and PUT DOWN all His enemies! Go ahead and praise Him if that COMFORTS YOU! :o)

March 13
Don't Just Read It
Psalm 14:1~ "The fool hath said in his heart, 'There is no God.'
They are corrupt, they have done abominable works,
there is none that doeth good."

Read a FB page where a man said he preferred NOT to read the Bible. Guess what? I AGREE! Don't just read it, HIDE IT in your heart (Psalm 119:11)! Psalm 14:1 & 53:1 are STILL TRUE because GOD said it! There's a major airline that (unofficially) WON'T ALLOW a Christian pilot & co-pilot to fly the same plane. In case Christians are right about the RAPTURE, they need a non-Christian LEFT BEHIND to fly the plane! :o)

March 14
Lord, Is It I?
Matthew 26:21-22 ~ "And as they did eat, he said,

Verily I say unto you, that one of you shall betray me.☐ ☐
And they were exceeding sorrowful,
and began every one of them to say unto him,
Lord, is it I?"

Many of you will probably NOT RESPOND to what I'm about to say, but it needs to be said. How many of us, when things go wrong in the church (or life in general), start looking for someone ELSE to blame; e.g. the preacher, the choir, a member, an auxiliary or ministry leader, employer, co-worker, politician, mother, father (or lack thereof), children, weight, finances, etc.?

Now how many of us do what Jesus' disciples did when he told them, "One of you will betray me?" They didn't say "Uh Uh, NOT ME LORD!" EVERYONE of them said, "LORD, IS IT I ?" That is, all EXCEPT for Judas. He said, Teacher (Greek word is Rabbi. KJV says Master), is it I (verse 25)? Judas had a teacher-student relationship with Jesus, and NOT a Lord-servant relationship!

If Jesus is Lord of your life, when things go wrong don't point the finger at others. Ask this question, "LORD, is it I?"

March 15
God Hears
Isaiah 65:24 ~ "And it shall come to pass,
that before they call, I will answer;
and while they are yet speaking, I will hear."

I've come to the conclusion over the years that not only does God love me, but He loved me FIRST, just as His Word says (1 John 4:19). I use to try and take credit for loving Him, but He constantly reminds me that I love Him, BECAUSE He first loved ME!

God reminded me again a little over a week ago when I took my two favorite girls in the whole world, my wife Nina and the baby girl, to a restaurant. I told my 7-year-old to let me know when our waiter, Steve, was in the area. I wanted to ask for more napkins, but within seconds, Steve walked by, dropped napkins on the table and kept going.

When he came back near our table, Shamira said, "Daddy, there he is!" I told her to look on the table. She spotted the napkins and asked, "HOW did he do that, daddy?" I used the situation as an opportunity to teach, and paraphrased the verse above as well as Matthew 6:32.

I said, "Sweetheart, Steve knew what we needed, BEFORE WE ASKED! That's the way God is. He said ...before you call, I will answer!"

46

You know what came across her mind, don't you?

"Well daddy, if God knows what we need BEFORE we ask, then WHY ASK!"

Here was my answer: "Baby, God loves us SO MUCH, that He just LOVES TO HEAR OUR VOICE!!!"

Have you talked to your Heavenly Father today? He already knows what you need, He just wants to HEAR YOUR VOICE! :o)

March 16
The Crab Mentality
Philippians 2:3-5 ~ "Let nothing be done through strife or vainglory;
but in lowliness of mind let each esteem other better than themselves.
Look not every man on his own things,
but every man also on the things of others.
Let this mind be in you, which was also in Christ Jesus..."

Do you have a CRAB MENTALITY? Ever dealt with LIVE CRABS? Put them in a bucket, & walk away. NO COVER required on the bucket. When you come back, you'll have the SAME number of crabs that were there WHEN YOU LEFT! Why? Because when one crab tries to climb OUT of the bucket, ANOTHER CRAB will REACH UP & PULL it back DOWN! Please don't let that be you. Let's LIFT ONE ANOTHER UP!

March 17
All About Saint Patrick
Hebrews 9:14~ "How much more shall the blood of Christ,
who through the eternal Spirit offered himself without spot to God,
purge your conscience from dead works to serve the living God?"

1 Peter 1:2~ "Elect according to the foreknowledge of God the Father,
through sanctification of the Spirit,
unto obedience and sprinkling of the blood of Jesus Christ:
Grace unto you, and peace, be multiplied."

Matthew 28:19 ~ "Go ye therefore, and teach all nations,
baptizing them in the name of the Father, and of the Son, and of the Holy Ghost."

If you don't read the entire post, you will MISS what for SOME of you will be a REVELATION! :o)

I know there are differing stories about who Saint Patrick was and what he did, so I'll pull from a couple of things common to each story. We know he is the patron saint of Ireland. The only Catholic Church that I was Blessed to preach at (every February for several years) is called SAINT PATRICK'S, named after this man. He was actually born in Britain (depending on who you ask) around A.D. 390 to a wealthy Christian family. His family had a country villa, a townhouse and quite a few slaves! As a boy, Patrick had NO INTEREST in Christianity. Around the age of 16, he was kidnapped and sent overseas to tend sheep AS A SLAVE in the cold, mountainous countryside of Ireland for 7 years.

Classics professor Philip Freeman, of Luther College in Iowa, says that Patrick got a RELIGIOUS CONVERSION while he was there and became a very deeply believing Christian. According to folklore, a voice came to Patrick in his dreams and told him to escape. He found passage on a pirate ship back to Britain, and was reunited with his family. Then the voice told him to go back to Ireland!

"He gets ordained as a priest by a bishop, and goes back and spends the rest of his life trying to convert the Irish to Christianity," Freeman said.

Patrick's work in Ireland was extremely hard. He was constantly beaten and harassed. It's IRONIC that we honor him on the day that he died, MARCH 17 (c. 461).

Patrick was largely forgotten after his death. But slowly, mythology grew up around Patrick. Centuries later he was honored as the patron saint of Ireland, Freeman noted. Part of the myth surrounding Patrick is that he DROVE THE SNAKES out of Ireland. While there are NO SNAKES in Ireland, it's because there NEVER WERE ANY! It's TOO COLD there!

The reason for the scriptures and the post brings me to something more believable. The SHAMROCK in the profile picture is the SYMBOL of Ireland! You can find this three-leaf clover shape in a box of Lucky Charms Cereal or in the Logo of the NBA's Boston Celtics. All have IRISH connections.

The greatest connection says that Patrick USED THE SHAMROCK to teach the HOLY TRINITY to the Irish people!!! The scriptures above bring all three persons together at work in our atonement, salvation and baptism. Now you know ...THE REST OF THE STORY! Happy SAINT PATRICK'S DAY. :o)

March 18
Which Way You Went
John 14:5-6 ~ "Thomas saith unto him, '
Lord, we know not whither thou goest;

and how can we know the way?'
Jesus saith unto him, 'I am the way, the truth, and the life:
no man cometh unto the Father, but by me.' "

Some funerals can feel like an Alfred Hitchcock movie. The ending is unclear! John 14:5 and 6 says you can be SURE of your final destination. A tombstone in an English cemetery read: "Remember man, as you walk by, as you are now, so once was I. As I am now, so shall YOU be - Prepare my friend, to follow me!" ~ A note left on the stone by a stranger read: "To follow you, I'll not consent, until I know WHICH WAY YOU WENT!"

March 19
Real Abstinence
Romans 14:16~ "Let not then your good be evil spoken of."

"I don't care what they think." You should! If you invite vegetarian friends for lunch, DON'T serve HAM SANDWICHES! We know the Word says we have liberty in Christ, but God said "don't let your GOOD be EVIL spoken of" & "abstain from all APPEARANCE of evil" (Romans 14:16; 1 Thessalonians 5:22). Maybe that's why that famous SOFT DRINK company took the COCAINE out of their COCA COLA around 1902.

March 20
Ever Feel Like an ATM?
1 Samuel 22:1-2~ "David therefore departed thence,
and escaped to the cave Adullam:
and when his brethren and all his father's house heard it,
they went down thither to him.
And every one that was in distress,
and every one that was in debt,
and every one that was discontented,
gathered themselves unto him;
and he became a captain over them:
and there were with him about four hundred men."

Ever feel like the Bank of _ (insert your name)? People come to you & withdraw some of YOUR strength, wisdom, courage, hope & yes, MONEY! That must be how David felt in 1 Samuel 22:1-2 when he was hiding in a cave from Saul! People in distress, in debt, & discontent found him in the cave & asked him to lead them. Q) Where do YOU go when YOU NEED

HELP? A) David encouraged HIMSELF, IN THE LORD! ~ 1 Samuel 30:6

March 21
The Mud Man
Jeremiah 18:1-6~ "The word which came to Jeremiah from the Lord, saying,
Arise, and go down to the potter's house,
and there I will cause thee to hear my words.
Then I went down to the potter's house,
and, behold, he wrought a work on the wheels.
And the vessel that he made of clay
was marred in the hand of the potter:
so he made it again another vessel,
as seemed good to the potter to make it.
Then the word of the Lord came to me, saying,
O house of Israel, cannot I do with you as this potter?
saith the Lord. Behold, as the clay is in the potter's hand,
so are ye in mine hand, O house of Israel."

A boy shaping a MUD MAN finished it except for ONE arm. Mom called him to go with her to get his dad from work. He left the MUD MAN in the yard. While walking with mom downtown he saw a VETERAN with ONE ARM leaning on a wall. He grabbed the empty sleeve of the missing arm & said, "Why did you leave before I got FINISHED WITH YOU???!!!" That's what THE POTTER (God) is asking US (the clay) TODAY! ~

March 22
Go To Church
Psalm 73:1-3~ "Truly God is good to Israel,
even to such as are of a clean heart.
But as for me, my feet were almost gone; my steps had well nigh slipped.
For I was envious at the foolish, when I saw the prosperity of the wicked."

Ever feel like "bad" people are doing better than God's children? You're struggling to make ends meet & they're doing well! In Psalm 73, Asaph said he almost stumbled at how well the wicked were doing (vs. 2-3). They don't seem to go through what we do (5). They're arrogant, evil & rich (6-12)! But he went to God's house, & God showed him how they'd end up (17-18)! Go to church! Some things you can't learn at HOME!!!

March 23
"My Heart Leaps Up, When I Behold a Rainbow in the Sky"
Genesis 9:16 ~ "And the bow (rainbow) shall be in the cloud;
and I will look upon it, that I may REMEMBER
the everlasting covenant between God
and every living creature of all flesh that is upon the earth."

Three (3) things about A RAINBOW that everyone should know:

1) It takes RAIN and CLOUDS to SEE it! A rainbow is the refraction (bending) of the light waves of the sun when they pass through rain drops or mist. It may NOT be raining where you are when you see it, but there are water drops SOMEWHERE nearby! You can not see a rainbow on a bright sunny day. It takes a background such as clouds or overcast, to see a rainbow. God's promises show up best, when it starts to get DARK in our lives!
2) The inside color of the rainbow closest to us, is PURPLE. It was (and still IS in some circles) the color worn by ROYALTY. When we look up, we remember Jesus as the KING of kings! The outermost color on top of the arc closest to God, is RED! God looks down and "remembers" the BLOOD that His Son Jesus shed for us!
3) God calls it a "bow" as in the WEAPON (bow and arrow). That's why the bow is pointed UPWARD, AT HIMSELF! Remember Calvary? God took out His anger against sin on His SINLESS Son (Isaiah 53:10; 2 Corinthians 5:21), instead of US! If Jesus is your Saviour, God ain't mad at ya! :o)

March 24
Let the Past Stay Buried!
Philippians 3:13-14~ "Brethren, I count not myself
to have apprehended: but this one thing I do,
forgetting those things which are behind,
and reaching forth unto those things which are before,
I press toward the mark for the prize
of the high calling of God in Christ Jesus."

A man found a dead rabbit in his yard & concluded that his dog went into the neighbor's yard & killed it! He washed & dried the rabbit, sneaked over the fence & put it back in the neighbor's hutch. One day his angry neighbor came to the house & said, "I buried a rabbit a few days ago. Some

SICK person dug it up, cleaned it up, fluffed it up, & put it BACK IN THE HUTCH!" Let the PAST STAY BURIED!

One of my mentors, Warren Wiersbe, said, "DON'T EMBALM THE PAST IN ORDER TO ESCAPE THE FUTURE!!!" :o)

March 25
Favor Ain't Earned

Ephesians 2:8-9~ "For by GRACE you have been saved □□through faith,
and that not of yourselves; □it is the gift of God,
not of □works, lest anyone should □boast." (NKJV)

You can't WORK for God's FAVOR! The "manna" God sent to feed his people in the wilderness fell AT NIGHT, when they were SLEEP (Numbers 11:9)! You can't work when you're SLEEP! If you trust HIM, he'll rain down favor on you! When you get up each morning, take a spiritual look around. Bread from heaven (Exodus 16:4), daily (Matthew 6:11; Lamentations 3:22-23), as much as you can handle (Exodus 16:8)!

March 26
For the Birds

Matthew 10:16~ "Behold, I send you forth as sheep in the midst of wolves: be ye therefore wise as serpents, and harmless as doves."

Football is an AGGRESSIVE sport. That's why their teams are named after AGGRESSIVE birds such as Falcons, Eagles & Ravens! When it comes to CHRISTIANS, Jesus said BE HARMLESS as DOVES (Matthew 10:16)! Doves are NON-AGGRESSIVE birds. The CORPUS CHRISTI (Body of Christ) RAVENS? God has more resources than you, so stop trying to fight your own battles. The battle is NOT YOURS, it's the LORD'S! ~ 2 Chronicles 20:15

March 27
FM or AM

Luke 11:23~ "He that is not with me is against me: and he that gathereth not with me scattereth."

A man lived on the BORDER of the North & the South during the Civil War. He wanted no part of the war, so he wore a Union BLUE coat & Confederate GRAY pants! When the two armies met on his property the Confederate Army shot him in his Union coat, & the Union Army shot him in his Confederate pants! Jesus said you're either FM or AM, (F)or (M)e or (A)gainst (M)e! CAN'T serve two MASTERS! ~ Luke 11:23; 16:13

March 28
Sleeping in the Storm
Isaiah 41:10~ "Fear thou not; for I am with thee:
be not dismayed; for I am thy God: I will strengthen thee;
yea, I will help thee; yea, I will uphold thee
with the right hand of my righteousness."

Going through life's storms? Here's a lesson from Birdland on dealing with storms. Why does a bird up in a tree, out on a limb, in the dark, in a storm, go to sleep WITHOUT FEAR OF FALLING? Because God put a tendon in the legs of the bird that cause the talons (claws) to close & lock when the bird bends it's knees! When you find yourself UP A TREE IN A STORM, BEND YOUR KNEES & lock into God's promises!

March 29
Whack-a-Mole, Whack-a-Sin
Colossians 3:5 ~ "Mortify (put to death)
therefore your earthly members (body parts)…"

People often say to me, "Pastor, I know I'm saved, but how do I deal with a particular sin in my life?" I remind them of the scripture up top, and the game in the profile picture. Have you ever been to a fair or a carnival and played the game "Whack-A-Mole?" That's the game in the profile. During this game, toy moles (rodent like creatures) pop up through random holes for a second or two. The object of the game is to hit the mole in the head and knock it back into the hole before it dips out of sight.

Even though you are a "new creation" in Christ (2 Corinthians 5:17), we still reside in this old flesh. That old flesh will "pop up" from time to time! The flesh wants what it wants! But greater is He that is IN YOU… (1 John 4:4)! Paul says in the verse to "put to death" the deeds of the flesh. In other words, "whack-a-sin" in the head BEFORE it gets a toe-hold in your life! How do you do that? By using those ESCAPE doors God has provided. 1 Corinthians 10:13 says that God WILL NOT allow you to be tempted (to sin) beyond what you are able to handle, without providing a WAY OUT!

For example… if you find yourself in the back seat of a car with someone and things get a little "hot", God has provided at least TWO ways of escape. They are called… CAR DOORS! The words "no" and "let's wait until we are married" are also ways of escape!

I know, I know! If I enabled that new "Dislike" button that Facebook is supposed to have, many of you would click it right now. I'm just trying to save some of us some HEARTACHE down the road! Now go WHACK some of that old fleshly stuff upside the head... before you HURT YOURSELF! :o)

March 30
Be Patient
James 1:2-4 ~ "My brethren, count it all joy
when ye fall into divers temptations;
knowing this, that the trying of your faith worketh patience.
But let patience have her perfect work,
that ye may be perfect and entire, wanting nothing."

The last time I took off in a plane, I saw a line of cars waiting at a RAILROAD CROSSING for a train to pass. No one in the cars knew when the train would end. From the AIR, I could see the BEGINNING & the END of the TRAIN! I tried to tell the cars in line to be patient, but they didn't hear me. God SEES the BEGINNING & the END of trials in your life. Be Patient, THIS TRAIN SHALL PASS! ~ Ecclesiastes 7:8; James 1:2-4

March 31
Thaw the Chicken!
2 Chronicles 25:2~ "And he did that which was right
in the sight of the Lord,
but not with a perfect heart."

The FAA tests windshields on jets for bird strikes with a SPECIAL GUN. It fires DEAD CHICKENS at jet speed! When the British borrowed it to test windshields on their new high-speed trains, the chicken went THROUGH the windshield & the engineer's chair! The British informed the FAA, who had one suggestion: "First, THAW THE CHICKEN!" You can cause DAMAGE doing the RIGHT THING with a HARD HEART!

April

April 1
Don't Be the One This Day is For
Psalm 51:10 ~ "Create in me a clean heart, O God;
and renew a right spirit within me."

A facility in our area for those with MENTAL PROBLEMS has a UNIQUE way of determining when a patient is ready to go home. They put them by a bathtub of RUNNING WATER & give them a choice of a BUCKET or a SPOON to get the water out of the tub. GUESS who are candidates to go home? The ones who TURN OFF THE WATER! That's the ROOT of the problem! We OFTEN FOCUS on the FRUIT (sin) & not the ROOT (the heart).

April 2
He Sees the BLOOD
Exodus 12:13 ~ "For the Lord will pass through to smite the Egyptians;
and when he seeth the blood upon the lintel, and on the two side posts,
the Lord will pass over the door,
and will not suffer the destroyer to come in unto your houses to smite you."

God sent ONE LAST PLAGUE to force Pharaoh to let HIS people go. God went through Egypt killing the first born of man & beast that didn't have the BLOOD of a SLAIN LAMB over the doorposts. God DID NOT say, "When I look in your window & see what you're doing, I'll judge you." He DID SAY, "When I SEE THE BLOOD, I will PASS OVER YOU!" Jesus is OUR SACRIFICIAL LAMB …and PASSOVER. ~ 1 Corinthians 5:7

April 3
Who's Throwing Them In?

Exodus 1:22 ~ "And Pharaoh charged all his people, saying,
'Every son that is born you shall cast into the river,
and every daughter you shall save alive.' "

1 Peter 5:8 ~ "Be sober, be vigilant; because your adversary the devil,
as a roaring lion, walks around, seeking whom he may devour."

When Nina and I had returned from our trip to England in 2011, we found that more of our friends had lost children to violence, and this reminded me of a story I have shared with you all before...

Two men were fishing in a boat when they saw a baby float by. One of the men jumped in the water and saved the baby. A few minutes later, another baby floated by! The other man jumped in and swam... UPSTREAM PAST THE BABY! "What about the baby?" the man in the boat shouted. "You get it," he said. "I'm going to find out WHO'S THROWING THEM IN!"

We most certainly need to save our children and our young people, but let's find out why they're in this mess in the first place!

April 4
I'll Be Back

John 20:7 ~ "And the napkin, that was about his head,
not lying with the linen clothes,
but wrapped together in a place by itself."

Go with me into the empty tomb of OUR LORD & notice something interesting in this verse. The head napkin that was placed on Jesus' face, was folded neatly & setting aside by itself. Jesus had evidently taken time to fold it before he left the tomb! If you left a folded napkin at the table BACK THEN it meant, "I'LL BE BACK!" I won't insult your intelligence, you connect the dots! He WILL be back! :o)

April 5 (Easter Sunday in 2015)
He's STILL Up

Luke 24:5-6 ~ "And as they were afraid, and bowed down their faces to the
earth, they said unto them, 'Why seek ye the living among the dead?
He is not here, but is risen:
remember how he spake unto you when he was yet in Galilee.' "

I don't mean to mess up our "Easter" song "He AROSE," but consider this. I AROSE this morning from sleep, but I intend to go BACK TO SLEEP at some point in time. When the Bible says "HE IS RISEN" (& it does in several places), the aorist tense of "risen" suggest an action the happened in the PAST, the RESULTS of which STILL STAND IN THE PRESENT. In other words, He got up, & HE'S STILL UP! HE IS RISEN!!!

April 6
Are You Where You're Supposed to Be Right Now?
Ephesians 6:12 ~ "For we wrestle not against flesh and blood,
but against principalities, against powers,
against the rulers of the darkness of this world,
against spiritual wickedness in high places."

Has anyone read the first verse of the story that led to David's sin with that married woman Bathsheba? 2 Samuel 11:1-2 says it was the time of year when kings GO TO BATTLE! David, THE KING, should have been at war with his army. He was at home in bed! Where should YOU be right now? Don't be in BED (yours or anyone else's), when you ought to be in BATTLE!

April 7
Don't Be an Easy Target
1 Peter 5:8 ~ "Be sober, be vigilant;
because your adversary the devil, as a roaring lion,
walketh about, seeking whom he may devour."

I was sitting down minding my own business when a question came up and sat down beside me and told me to ask you, "Are you an easy target for the ENEMY?" If you are not KEEPING up in your prayer life, Bible study, fellowship with other saints ...then you are lagging behind. God reminded Israel that the ENEMY picks off the weak & weary! Those LAGGING BEHIND. Are you a STRAGGLER? (Also see Deuteronomy 25:17-18: "Remember what Amalek did unto thee by the way, when ye were come forth out of Egypt; how he met thee by the way, and smote the hindmost of thee, even all that were feeble behind thee, when thou wast faint and weary; and he feared not God.")

April 8
YOU Ask Him!
1 Peter 3:15~ "But sanctify the Lord God in your hearts:
and be ready always to give an answer to every man
that asketh you a reason of the hope that is in you
with meekness and fear."

An atheist sitting next to a woman reading her Bible on a plane decided to have some fun. He asked if she believed the Bible. She said, "Every word!"

Atheist: Even that tale about Jonah in a fish for 3 days?
Christian Woman: Yes.
Atheist: How can a man can live in a fish for 3 days?
Christian Woman: When I get to heaven I'll ask him!
Atheist (sarcastically): Suppose Jonah's NOT IN HEAVEN?
Christian Woman: Then YOU ASK HIM!!!

April 9
Move On Up a Little Higher
Job 39:27-30 ~ "Doth the eagle mount up at thy command,
and make her nest on high?
She dwelleth and abideth on the rock,
upon the crag of the rock, and the strong place.
From thence she seeketh the prey, and her eyes behold afar off.
Her young ones also suck up blood: and where the slain are, there is she."

An eagle swoops down & picks up small animals in its talons, & takes it to high heights where the animals SUFFOCATE! A pilot discovered mice eating at the hydraulic system of his plane. Having NO time to land, he decided to try something. He pointed the plane upward & took it to a level where the mice SUFFOCATED! When your enemies are eating at you, move up to ANOTHER LEVEL! Don't live on their level!

April 10
Already Defeated
Revelation 12:10-11 ~ "And I heard a loud voice saying in heaven,
'Now is come salvation, and strength,
and the kingdom of our God, and the power of his Christ:
for the accuser of our brethren is cast down,
which accused them before our God day and night.
And they overcame him by the blood of the Lamb,
and by the word of their testimony;
and they loved not their lives unto the death.' "

My grandmother in Texas made fried chicken from chickens raised IN

HER YARD. She took one by the neck & with a flick of the wrist, snapped its neck! Then she cut off the HEAD & tossed the chicken in the yard! The chicken flopped around the yard, WITH NO HEAD! I said, "Momma Mandy LOOK, the CHICKEN!" She said, "It's DEAD, baby, it just doesn't know it yet!" Sounds like the DEVIL, already DEFEATED!

April 11
Giants, Grasshoppers, God ... and Binoculars
Numbers 13:33~ "And there we saw the giants, the sons of Anak,
which come of the giants: and we were in our own sight
as grasshoppers, and so we were in their sight."

10 Israeli spies saw their enemies as GIANTS & themselves as grasshoppers. They forgot about the 3rd "G", GOD, the great EQUALIZER! When you look at an object through a set of binoculars, it gets LARGER! Now turn the binoculars around & that SAME OBJECT GETS smaller. Next time you look at your problems & they seem TOO LARGE, turn those spiritual binoculars around, & see them the way GOD sees them.

April 12
Less Snorkeling, More SCUBA
1 Corinthians 2:9-10~ "But as it is written,
'Eye hath not seen, nor ear heard,
neither have entered into the heart of man,
the things which God hath prepared for them that love him.'
But God hath revealed them unto us by his Spirit:
for the Spirit searcheth all things, yea, the deep things of God."

Ever been snorkeling? You're limited by the length of the tube in your mouth (snorkel) as to how far underwater you can go. Scuba-diving requires a separate tank for breathing & allows you to go MUCH DEEPER than a snorkel tube! SCUBA is an acronym for (S)elf (C)ontained (U)nderwater (B)reathing (A)pparatus. When it comes to God's Word, be DILIGENT (2 Timothy 2:15). Less snorkeling, more SCUBA!

April 13
New and Dependable
Lamentations 3:21-22 ~ "This I recall to my mind, therefore have I hope.
It is of the Lord's mercies that we are not consumed,

because his compassions fail not."

Anyone going through something & wondering, where's God? Jeremiah spent 20 verses in Lamentations 3 on how badly he was treated by God! Then he says, something came to his mind that gave him hope (vs 21). If all of that happened to me & I'm NOT DEAD, it has to be because of HIS loving kindness (vs 22). In verse 23 he made another observation, that mercy is NEW & DEPENDABLE each day WE wake up! ~ INSERT SHOUT HERE...

April 14
Awesome God
Psalm 124 ~ "If it had not been the Lord who was on our side,
now may Israel say;
If it had not been the Lord who was on our side,
when men rose up against us:
Then they had swallowed us up quick,
when their wrath was kindled against us:
Then the waters had overwhelmed us,
the stream had gone over our soul:
Then the proud waters had gone over our soul.
Blessed be the Lord,
who hath not given us as a prey to their teeth.
Our soul is escaped as a bird out of the snare of the fowlers:
the snare is broken, and we are escaped.
Our help is in the name of the Lord,
who made heaven and earth."

I'm having a moment. I was looking out of my window at well-defined gray & white clouds against a clear powdered blue sky and thinking about how AWESOME GOD IS! Psalm 124 (for me) is explained so beautifully in a song written by my friend Allowyn Price. The City Wide Revival Choir recently blessed our hearts with the song, "Look Where The Lord Has Brought Me From, He's Brought Me From A MIGHTY LONG WAY!"

April 15
We'll Leave the Light On For You
1 John 1:5 ~ "This then is the message which we have heard of him,
and declare unto you, that God is LIGHT,
and in him is NO DARKNESS at all" (KJV)

Simple message. Are you living in darkness, without Christ? This verse is GOD'S WAY of saying the SAME THING that the MOTEL 6 commercials are saying, centuries later ..."We'll leave the LIGHT ON FOR YOU!!!"

April 16
Ain't Going To Let Nobody Steal My Joy
2 Corinthians 5:21~ "For he hath made him to be sin for us,
who knew no sin;
that we might be made the righteousness of God in him."

Once you're saved, the devil causes you to doubt your righteousness in Christ. That's called GUILT! God forbid you should sin AFTER you're saved! Have you ever noticed WHAT DAVID asked God (in Psalm 51:12) to restore, AFTER he had sinned with Bathsheba? Not SALVATION, but the JOY of salvation! Don't let the devil STEAL YOUR JOY. If Christ is Lord of your life, You're OK ...in God's eyes!

April 17
Barabbas... and Bailey
Mark 15:6-15 ~ "Now at that feast
he released unto them one prisoner, whomsoever they desired.
And there was one named Barabbas,
which lay bound with them that had made insurrection with him,
who had committed murder in the insurrection.
And the multitude crying aloud began to desire him
to do as he had ever done unto them.
But Pilate answered them, saying,
'Will ye that I release unto you the King of the Jews?'
For he knew that the chief priests had delivered him for envy.
But the chief priests moved the people,
that he should rather release Barabbas unto them.
And Pilate answered and said again unto them,
'What will ye then that I shall do unto him
whom ye call the King of the Jews?'
And they cried out again, 'Crucify him.'
Then Pilate said unto them,
'Why, what evil hath he done?'
And they cried out the more exceedingly,

'Crucify him.'
And so Pilate, willing to content the people,
released Barabbas unto them, and delivered Jesus,
when he had scourged him, to be crucified."

Remember when Pilate tried to get out of crucifying Jesus (whom he found to be innocent) by giving the people a choice of releasing one prisoner? They chose to release a murderer named Barabbas (John 18:40 says he was also a thief)! You'll find the story in Mark 15:6-15; Matthew 27:15-26; Luke 23:13-25; John 18:39-40.

Can I tell you about an imaginary conversation I had with this man Barabbas? I imagined that I was part of the murderous gang that Barabbas hung around with BEFORE he was sentenced to die on a cross. After his release, he came back to the pre-planned hideout we had designated in case anything went wrong during one of our crimes. We all were shocked to see him. Then we worried about whether or not he had led the authorities to our hiding place.

Bailey: "Barabbas! What are you doing here, man?"
Barabbas: "I don't know!"
Bailey: "Did anyone follow you?"
Barabbas: "I don't know!"
Bailey: "Weren't you scheduled to be crucified for some of the stuff WE'VE done?"
Barabbas: "Yep."
Bailey: "Did you escape?"
Barabbas: "Nope."
Bailey: "They let you go???!!!"
Barabbas: "Yep!"
Bailey: "Are you SERIOUS? How did THAT happen?"
Barabbas: "I really don't know. All I do know is that, somebody named JESUS was hung on the cross ...IN MY PLACE!!!"

Excuse me, people. I need a PRAISE BREAK.....GLORY!!!

April 18
Where He Laid His Head
Luke 9:58 ~ "And Jesus said unto him, Foxes have holes,
and birds of the air have nests;
but the Son of man has no place to LAY HIS HEAD."

John 19:30 ~ "When Jesus therefore had received the vinegar,
he said, 'It is finished:'
and he BOWED HIS HEAD, and gave up the ghost."

What do you see that is common to both verses?

It's the position of JESUS' HEAD! The words for "lay his head" and "bow his head" come from the exact same Greek word, "klino"! The roots of our English word "recline" are found in the word "klino."

In Luke 9:58, Jesus says to a scribe who claims he will follow Jesus anywhere (Matthew 8:19-20), "Foxes have holes to live in, birds have nest to live in, but I don't own a home! I don't even have a place of my own in which to lay my head!" Would you STILL want to follow Jesus? In other words, Jesus was saying, "I don't have a RESTING PLACE!" Grandma would have said, "Boy, you don't have a pot to _____ , or a window to throw it out of!" (I'll let YOU fill in the blank, even though it's a word you will find in your BIBLE!)

My subject on two messages I have preached on this is "A RESTING PLACE." Guess what? Jesus FOUND that resting place ...ON CALVARY! John 19:30 says he reclined his head on the cross, then He EXHALED (ekpneō in Luke 23:46)! Why is it when SOME women (or men for that matter) exhale, they burn up your clothes? When Jesus exhales, the WHOLE WORLD has access to salvation! Jesus found HIS REST, in SAVING US! Now, I've found in HIM ...a RESTING PLACE!

April 19
How to (and How Not to) Give

I Timothy 6:17-19~ "Charge them that are rich in this world,
that they be not highminded, nor trust in uncertain riches,
but in the living God, who giveth us richly all things to enjoy;
That they do good, that they be rich in good works,
ready to distribute, willing to communicate;
Laying up in store for themselves
a good foundation against the time to come,
that they may lay hold on eternal life."

Boy 1: My dad DRAWS A LINE on the floor & throws his money in the air. What lands on the left goes to the Lord, what lands on the right he keeps for himself.

Boy 2: My father does the same thing. What comes down HEADS he gives to the Lord. TAILS, he keeps for himself.

Boy 3: My dad throws his money in the air. What STAYS in the air he gives to the Lord! What comes down, he keeps for HIMSELF."

April 20
Get Out of Those Grave Clothes!
John 20:4-7~ "So they ran both together:
and the other disciple did outrun Peter, and came first to the sepulchre.
And he stooping down, and looking in,
saw the linen clothes lying; yet went he not in.
Then cometh Simon Peter following him,
and went into the sepulchre, and seeth the linen clothes lie,
And the napkin, that was about his head, not lying with the linen clothes,
but wrapped together in a place by itself."

These verses tell us that Jesus CHANGED HIS CLOTHES before He left the tomb! The original language also suggests that the clothes were laying neatly in one place like a COCOON, still retaining the SHAPE of the Lord's body even though there was NO BODY in them! The head wrap (napkin) was neatly folded in another place in the tomb. These clothes were NOT just left thrown all over the tomb as THIEVES do when they steal (Matthew 28:12-13). As a matter of fact, a thief would NOT have taken the time to TAKE OFF the clothes!

Jesus didn't want to be seen wearing His GRAVE CLOTHES! Too many of God's people are still wearing the "grave clothes" they had on when they got saved! Still wearing the same old bad habits, same sins, same fears, same frustrations, same worries, etc.

There is a brand new wardrobe available FREE OF CHARGE to the Christian! When you see the words "Put on" in the Bible, it is the word "enduo." It means to be "clothed with"!

1. Be clothed with the armor of light... ~ Romans 13:12
2. Be clothed with the Lord Jesus Christ... ~ Romans 13:14
3. Be clothed with the full armor of God... ~ Ephesians 6:11
4. Be clothed with the new self... ~ Colossians 3:10
5. Be clothed with a heart of compassion, kindness, humility, gentleness and □patience... ~ Colossians 3:12

Now GO, get out of those old dirty clothes!!! :o)

April 21
Have You Seen Him?

1 Corinthians 15:5-8 "And he appeared to Cephas (Peter), then to the twelve.
Then he appeared to more than five hundred brothers at one time,
most of whom are still alive, though some have died.
Then he appeared to James, then to all the apostles.
Last of all, as to one untimely born, he appeared also TO ME."

Why is it so difficult for some to believe that Jesus Christ IS RISEN from the dead? Paul told the church at Corinth that Jesus had been seen AFTER He got up from the grave. He had been seen by Paul himself, Peter and the disciples, as well as the apostles (verses 5-8). In the verse before us, Paul tells them that more than 500 brothers (in the Lord) at one time saw Jesus AFTER His resurrection! I know what some of you are thinking, "Well, Paul could have just been SAYING that!"

Consider this. Paul said something else in that same verse. He told the church at Corinth that many (or most) of the more than 500 who had seen Him, were STILL ALIVE at the time. In other words, "You can go check with them if you don't believe me!" Paul made a statement that was VERY EASY to verify at the time! Paul saw Him. Peter saw Him. The rest of the disciples and apostles saw Him. Over 500 MEN ALONE saw Him.

The question is, if you'll allow me to paraphrase an old song by the Chi-lites, "Have YOU Seen ...HIM?"

April 22
Just Do YOU!

Genesis 1:27; 2:24 ~ "...male and female created he them.";
"and they shall be one flesh."

Did you notice that Genesis 2:24 DID NOT say that they would become ONE BRAIN?! That verse has to do with physical intimacy.

I apologize to all of you Steve Harvey fans, but remember he's a comedian, and I do believe he is a Christian, albeit a very new one. Take his work for what it is. It's mostly comedy, NOT THEOLOGY! In the popular movie which was loosely based on the book he authored, he tells women to "Think Like A Man." The title of his book is, *Act Like A Lady, Think Like A Man*.

I have a sermon entitled, "Think Like A Lady, Act Like A Lady; Think Like A Man, Act Like A Man!" I believe we are confused enough as it is, and we DON'T need to try to THINK like someone we are not. Actually, you CAN'T do that! At best, you would be guessing. We don't all think alike. Men and Women don't think like each other, because they AREN'T EACH OTHER! If you take a poll you'll find that every woman is unique, and often doesn't even think like ANOTHER WOMAN! Same goes for men.

Dr. L.K. Curry asked a series of profound questions at the Citywide Revival in recent years. Allow me to loosely paraphrase a few of them in my own words. Have you ever asked yourself why the thoughts in YOUR head (which are NOT tangible) don't DRIFT into the head of the person next to you? Why didn't I wake up this morning thinking exactly what YOU THOUGHT? Why are my thoughts self-contained in my own head? Why didn't you act on what your partner was thinking today? Why can surgeons operate on your BRAIN, but NOT the SIN in your head? It's because your thoughts are unique and often personal TO YOU!

I'm a Christian, yet God says that HIS THOUGHTS are not OUR thoughts (Isaiah 55:8).

I was inspired to do this post by a comment from a former member, Helen Gill-Smith. She and her husband moved away, but we keep up on Facebook. She said, "I don't want to think like a man, I just want to know... WHAT MEN THINK!" That makes more sense. Now ladies, don't try to THINK like a man. Just find out, as best you can, what they are thinking... AND JUST DO YOU! :o)

April 23
Worth Your Salt
Colossians 4:6~ "Let your speech be always with grace,
seasoned with salt,
that ye may know how ye ought to answer every man."

Salt makes food taste better. NO SALT can leave food tasting BLAND or BITTER. Salt was so valuable that soldiers in years past were paid with it. That's where we get the word "SAL-ARY"! Are you "Worth Your Salt"? So it is with GRACE. Our words can leave people feeling BETTER or BITTER! Is there GRACIOUSNESS or GRUMPINESS in how you talk to people? (I'm just a messenger saying what GOD SAID! :o)

April 24
Set Up to Be Blessed
Revelation 13:8~ "And all that dwell upon the earth shall worship him,
whose names are not written in the book of life
of the Lamb slain from the foundation of the world."

We've been SET UP by God to be BLESSED! If God KNOWS ALL (& He does), then He knows what I will do BEFORE I do it! Adam didn't put HIMSELF, the TREES, or the SNAKE in that garden, GOD DID! (Genesis 2:8-9; 3:1). God knew that WE would make WRONG CHOICES! That's why Jesus is the "Lamb slain from the FOUNDATION of the world" (Revelation 13:8). Jesus' death FOR US was PLANNED BEFORE we got here. Can you say, SET UP? :o)

April 25
Shout Right HERE
Genesis 42:36 ~ "And Jacob their father said unto them,
'Me have ye bereaved of my children:
Joseph is not, and Simeon is not, and ye will take Benjamin away:
all these things are against me.' "

WHY do we often ASSUME THE WORST when we should know that GOD DESIRES THE BEST for us? Jacob thought that TWO of his sons in this verse were dead. Little did he know that WHERE they were, (Egypt where there was FOOD), was where God was trying to get HIM! And one of those sons that Jacob thought was dead (Joseph), was IN CHARGE of the food distribution! Yes, you can shout right .....HERE!

April 26
As Far As the East is From the West
Psalm 103:12 ~ "As far as the east is from the west,
so far hath he removed our transgressions from us."

FOOTBALL players don't drop balls due to the SUN in their eyes because football fields are designed to run NORTH/SOUTH (the sun rises in the East)! Psalm 103:12 says, "As far as the East is from the West, that's how far he's removed our sins from us!" Since there is NO EAST or West pole, EAST NEVER MEETS WEST! Want to get rid of your sins forever? Run East/West, with the RISEN SON IN YOUR EYES! (John 1:29)

(Inspired by my son Aaron Bailey who when playing collegiate football explained to me why he never dropped a ball because of the sun!)

April 27
The Son Is as Old as His Father...
Genesis 1:26~ "And God said,
'Let us make man in our image, after our likeness:
and let them have dominion over the fish of the sea,
and over the fowl of the air,
and over the cattle, and over all the earth,
and over every creeping thing that creepeth upon the earth.' "

Linda Clark Myrick said in a comment on Wednesday's post that her study in the Trinity started in Genesis 1:26, "And God said, Let "US" make man..." Might I add that the same "US" shows up in Gen. 11:7 at the tower of Babel. HIS name in Hebrew (EL) is written in PLURAL form (ELOHIM), yet ALWAYS translated singular in English (GOD)! The Father, Son & Holy Ghost have ALWAYS BEEN CO-EQUAL. The Son is as old as His FATHER!

April 28
... And Older Than His Mother!
Psalm 110:1-4 ~ "The LORD said unto my Lord,
Sit thou at my right hand ..."

Was God on Prozac or was He schizophrenic & talking to himself? NEITHER! When you see all CAPITALS on the word "LORD" in the Old Testament, it's the Hebrew word YAHWEH which is the Father's Covenant name. Capital "L", small "ord" is "Adonay" which is Master/Owner. The Father was talking to HIS SON! I told you Jesus was OLDER than His MOTHER! HE IS GOD!

April 29
Calm Down, Men
Judges 16:7-8~ "And Samson said unto her,
'If they bind me with seven green withs that were never dried,
then shall I be weak, and be as another man.'
Then the lords of the Philistines brought up to her
seven green withs which had not been dried,
and she bound him with them."

I shared with a class here in Bakersfield the need for Bible students to scrutinize their versions of the Bible for proper application to today's generation. In Judges 16:7-8 (NIV-New International Version), Delilah asked Samson the secret to defeating his strength. Samson said, "Just tie me up with 7 THONGS!" CALM DOWN, MEN! Go look up "THONG" in a good English dictionary, & then put leather strips in those verses!

April 30
Twelve Gates

Isaiah 53:5~ "But he was wounded for our transgressions,
he was bruised for our iniquities:
the chastisement of our peace was upon him;
and with his stripes we are healed."

Revelation 21:21 ~ "And the twelve gates were twelve pearls:
every several gate was of one pearl:
and the street of the city was pure gold, as it were transparent glass."

Since we know that a PEARL is the result of a "WOUNDED OYSTER," these verses should have DEEPER meaning for us. When God's children get to heaven, we will enter through ONE of TWELVE GATES made of ONE PEARL EACH. That's a HUGE PEARL! As we pass through & BEYOND the gates, we can look back & be reminded that all of our hurts & afflictions are BEHIND US because of what Jesus did FOR US!

May

May 1
Even When You Lose Your Head
Hebrews 13:5~ "Let your conversation be without covetousness,
and be content with such things as ye have,
for he hath said, 'I will never leave thee, nor forsake thee.' "

Our 6-year-old had a doll that was filthy & broken! I promised her a new one. She said NO! I said it would be EXACTLY the same doll. Again she said NO! Though the old doll kept losing its head & hair, she insisted on keeping it. I asked why? She said, "Daddy, she's been with me from the beginning, I just can't throw her away NOW!" Teach, BABY! God won't desert you, even if you LOSE YOUR HEAD on occasion.

May 2
More from the Chi-Lites
John 12:20-21~ "And there were certain Greeks among them
that came up to worship at the feast:
The same came therefore to Philip, which was of Bethsaida of Galilee,
and desired him, saying, 'Sir, we would see Jesus.' "

While the Jews looked for signs (Matthew 12:38; 1 Corinthians 1:22-24), these Gentiles wanted a FACE-to-FACE interview with JESUS! The reason I teach the way I do, (using the mundane), is in my audacious use of the Chi-Lites' hit song. My desire is that you would SEE HIS FACE EVERYWHERE YOU GO! On the street, and even at the picture show! Have you seen him? Tell me have you seen HIM? :o)

May 3 (written in 2011)
Osama Bin Laden's Distant Relatives
Proverbs 24:17-18~ "17 Rejoice not when thine enemy falleth,
and let not thine heart be glad when he stumbleth:
Lest the Lord see it, and it displease him,
and he turn away his wrath from him."

My celebration of JUSTICE is tempered today because a human

slipped into ETERNITY WITHOUT JESUS & his punishment will last MUCH LONGER than our anger! Osama Bin (son of) Laden was the 17th of 57 children, & the ONLY CHILD of his father's LEAST favorite of 11 wives. He NEEDED attention! My concern is for some of his distant family who attend our churches: BEEN LYING, BEEN STEALING, BEEN BACKSTABBING...etc!

May 4
Three Tests
Titus 1:10-11~ "For there are many unruly and vain talkers
and deceivers, specially they of the circumcision:
Whose mouths must be stopped, who subvert whole houses,
teaching things which they ought not, for filthy lucre's sake."

With many FALSE TEACHERS around, who should I trust & believe? I get that question most often from non-believers. 1) Does what they say line up with God's Word? 2) Is it for PROFIT? 3) Is what they're telling you, working for them? Would you buy height or hair growth products from Pastor Bailey? I'm all of 5'7" & balding fast! If what I'm telling you ISN'T WORKING FOR ME, why should you invest in it?

May 5
Comprehend vs. Apprehend
Ephesians 3:17-19 ~ "That Christ may dwell in your hearts by faith;
that ye, being rooted and grounded in love,
May be able to comprehend with all saints
what is the breadth, and length, and depth, and height;
And to know the love of Christ, which passeth knowledge,
that ye might be filled with all the fulness of God."

What's the difference/similarities in the words "comprehend" & "apprehend"? A monkey is said to have a PREHEN(SILE) TAIL which can GRAB HOLD of things like tree branches. When you COMPREHEND, you grab hold with your mind. The word COMPREHEND in verse 18 should be APPREHEND! When you APPREHEND, you take possession of the thing FOR YOURSELF! Don't just COMPREHEND GOD'S LOVE for you, APPREHEND IT!

May 6
Boundaries
Proverbs 22:28 ~ "Do not move the ancient landmark
that your ancestors have set."

I wonder – am I the only one who remembers when our parents had BOUNDARIES set for us? That's what this verse is about. Landmarks were BOUNDARY markers that showed where your property line was. Often times a man would MOVE the landmark in order to give himself property that DIDN'T BELONG TO HIM! The Bible speaks at least six times against removing landmarks. That was considered STEALING!

Many of us have stolen HEARTACHE and TROUBLE for ourselves by removing the BOUNDARY MARKERS that GOD has set for us! Yes, some of us had boundaries as children. But we also had fun, and survived within the rules that our GOD and our parents set for us. Many of us today would call that OLD FASHION, but they were BOUNDARIES that taught us how to RESPECT one another!!!

May 7
Are You a Dipper, or an Abider?
James 5:11~ "Behold, we count them happy which endure.
Ye have heard of the patience of Job,
and have seen the end of the Lord;
that the Lord is very pitiful, and of tender mercy."

The word "endure" = to "abide under" a BURDEN. Dr. Tony Evans told us in Dallas a few years ago about two types of TEA drinkers, "Dippers" & "Abiders"! Those who DIP their tea-bag in & out, and those who leave it in the hot water. Those who let their bag ABIDE in the water, have STRONGER TEA than the Dippers. If you find yourself in HOT water, ABIDE until God takes you out! Are you a DIPPER, or an ABIDER?

May 8
Mono, or Stereo?
Colossians 2:5-7~ "For though I be absent in the flesh,
yet am I with you in the spirit, joying and beholding your order,
and the stedfastness of your faith in Christ.
As ye have therefore received Christ Jesus the Lord, so walk ye in him:
Rooted and built up in him, and stablished in the faith,
as ye have been taught, abounding therein with thanksgiving."

HOW do I "ABIDE" (last post) in hot water? The verses say be STEADFAST in your faith! The Greek word for "steadfastness" here is STEREMA, from which we get our word STEREO! It means to be stable, strong, solid like STEREO! You're NOT in your furnace alone (MONO). Jesus is in it with you (Balanced Stereo)! The Holy Ghost will give you strength to Abide (Rom. 8:26). NOW, are you MONO (Lone Ranger), or STEREO?

May 9
A Good Exchange
Isaiah 40:31~ "But they that wait upon the Lord
shall renew their strength;
they shall mount up with wings as eagles;
they shall run, and not be weary;
and they shall walk, and not faint."

Isaiah 40:31 teaches more than just the RENEWING OF OUR strength. The Hebrew word for "renew" is "chalaph". It means to exchange, substitute, change for something better! There is a picture here of taking off an old set of clothes and putting on NEW CLOTHES. Now let's try it. "They that wait upon the Lord shall EXCHANGE THEIR strength for something better..." Might that be, HIS STRENGTH? ~ 2 Corinthians 12:9-10

May 10
Happy Mother's Day
2 Timothy 1:5~ "When I call to remembrance the unfeigned faith that is in thee, which dwelt first in thy grandmother Lois, and thy mother Eunice; and I am persuaded that in thee also."

Happy Mother's Day. I am thinking of my PRECIOUS MOTHER, whose COMMITTED LOVE I couldn't begin to express. She's with the Lord now, but I'll never forget Clemmie Lee Bailey!

May 11
Can YOU See a Difference in YOU?
2 Corinthians 5:17~ "Therefore if any man be in Christ,
he is a new creature: old things are passed away;
behold, all things are become new."

Paul says in this verse (under inspiration of the Holy Spirit), If ANYONE ("tis" = male or female) be in Christ, he or she is a new CREATION (building, something established): old things are passed away; BEHOLD = LOOK (there is a VISIBLE difference in how we act towards GOD & PEOPLE). Why? Because the OLD has become NEW! Can YOU see a difference in YOU?

May 12
Avoid the Flypaper
Luke 12:15~ "And he said unto them,
'Take heed, and beware of covetousness:
for a man's life consisteth not in the abundance
of the things which he possesseth.' "

Some years ago another of my mentors, Dr. Haddon Robinson, gave a group of us the BIBLE definition of COVETOUSNESS. It's WANTING MORE of what you have ENOUGH of already! It has to do with GREED, not need! It's OK to have THINGS, as long as they don't have you! Dr. Robinson said it's like a FLY landing on flypaper & saying, "MY FLYPAPER!" Then the flypaper says, "MY FLY!!!" Then the fly dies!

May 13
Can You Hear Me Now?
James 1:19-22~ "Wherefore, my beloved brethren,
let every man be swift to hear, slow to speak, slow to wrath:
For the wrath of man worketh not the righteousness of God.
Wherefore lay apart all filthiness and superfluity of naughtiness,
and receive with meekness the engrafted word,
which is able to save your souls.
But be ye doers of the word, and not hearers only,
deceiving your own selves."

Want to be a DOER of the Word & not just a HEARER (vs.22)? James says, LISTEN more than you TALK (vs.19)! Jewish Rabbis point out that we have 2 ears exposed & 1 tongue HIDDEN! Should we be doing TWICE as much listening? James says you become a DOER when you remove the "superfluity" (King James Version) of wickedness. SUPERFLUITY in it's original language meant EXCESSIVE EARWAX! Can you HEAR ME NOW?

May 14
Public Service Announcement
2 Corinthians 11:14-15~ "And no marvel;
for Satan himself is transformed into an angel of light.
Therefore it is no great thing if his ministers also be transformed
as the ministers of righteousness;
whose end shall be according to their works."

YOU CANNOT find out who saw your profile. Jordan DOESN'T make high heels. YOU WON'T KNOW what that man saw when he walked in on his daughter. YOU WON'T see pictures of Osama Bin Laden's dead body. There are NO free iPads. You'll NEVER know WHY that baby is laughing. NOT ON FB. Stop clicking those SPAM LINKS. You expose yourself, & OTHERS! I'll return to my regularly scheduled post shortly!

Comment to my friend April Wright: Thank you for this post. We need to learn not to be so GULLIBLE. We are ALL susceptible if we're not careful. Clicking on these links may cause you to have to delete your account and start over. The devil can make things LOOK GOOD or INTERESTING. He IS a liar ...and he has plenty of children!!! ~ John 8:44 :o)

May 15
Praying about Weeds
Philippians 4:6~ "Be careful for nothing;
but in every thing by prayer and supplication with thanksgiving
let your requests be made known unto God."

Years ago, WEEDS blocked the BAY view from our new home. My spirit wouldn't let me cut them, so I PRAYED! We left the house one day & told the kids NOT to go outside. We returned to find weeds lying flat in front of the back door. Had our kids disobeyed? My son had been in his 2nd floor bedroom window talking to a friend. He FELL HEAD FIRST. The WEEDS broke his fall. PRAY about EVERYTHING, even WEEDS!

May 16
Learning How To Walk
Ephesians 5:15~ "See then that ye walk circumspectly,
not as fools, but as wise."

Paul doesn't just tell the church at Ephesus to WALK IN LOVE (vs. 2), he tells them to walk CIRCUMSPECTLY (vs. 15 - KJV)! The Greek is "AKRIBOS," from the same word we get our English word ACROBAT! It means to walk STRAIGHT, ACCURATELY & CAREFULLY! If you were walking along the top of a fence & there was a Pit Bull in one yard & a Rottweiler in the other, you WOULD have to walk CIRCUMSPECTLY!

May 17
Leave the Noise Outside
1 Kings 6:7~ "And the house, when it was in building,
was built of stone made ready before it was brought thither:
so that there was neither hammer nor axe nor any tool of iron
heard in the house, while it was in building."

WOW! When the TEMPLE was being built, the hammering, chiseling & fitting of the stones was done OUTSIDE of the area. There was a spirit of reverent worship (QUIET) on the building site! At the temple site, the STONES just FIT TOGETHER! Jesus was CRUCIFIED OUTSIDE of the city, to the SOUND of axes & hammers. Let's leave the DRAMA (noise & stuff that's not worship) OUTSIDE, & come TOGETHER to worship HIM!

May 18
Thermometer or Thermostat?
Matthew 5:13~ "Ye are the salt of the earth:
but if the salt have lost his savour, wherewith shall it be salted?
it is thenceforth good for nothing, but to be cast out,
and to be trodden under foot of men."

"The church was not merely a thermometer that recorded the ideas and principles of popular opinion; it was a thermostat that transformed the mores of society". ~ (Dr. M.L. King Jr., Letter from Birmingham Jail, April 1963). Are you a thermometer or a thermostat? One just MEASURES CHANGE, the other CAUSES IT! That's the difference between food with or without SALT. Now will you pass the SALT, PLEASE? ~

May 19
Make It Plain
Habakkuk 2:2~ "And the Lord answered me, and said,
'Write the vision, and make it plain upon tables,
that he may run that readeth it.' "

A new pastor noticed the sanctuary had only one light in the ceiling. He asked a deacon to order a chandelier. The man agreed. Weeks passed & NO chandelier. The pastor asked the deacon what happened. He said, "Pastor, we tried to order it but no one could SPELL it. Then we realized that no one knew how to PLAY it. We decided that what this church needs, is MORE LIGHT!" Whatever your vision, make it PLAIN!

May 20
Double Blessing
Deuteronomy 28:3~ "Blessed shalt thou be in the city,
and blessed shalt thou be in the field."

BARAK is the most used Hebrew word for BLESSED (Deuteronomy 28:3ff). God's people are BLESSED & NO ONE can change that (Numbers 23:20)! No demon or witch can curse you! God HIMSELF won't allow a curse on what He has Blessed (Genesis 9). The Latin word for bless is "beatus". That's why we call Matthew 5 the "Beatitudes". The Greek word there, "makarios" is PLURAL! DON'T say Blessed, Everybody say, I'M BLESSED BLESSED!

May 21 (originally written in 2011)
Take Heed
Matthew 24:4~ "And Jesus answered and said unto them,
'Take heed that no man deceive you.' "

Matthew 24:36~ "But of that day and hour knoweth no man,
no, not the angels of heaven, but my Father only."

Matthew 24:44~ "Therefore be ye also ready:
for in such an hour as ye think not the Son of man cometh."

Harold Camping is the 89-year-old broadcaster & president of Family Radio Network. He's behind the posters & broadcasts that say Judgment Day (Rapture) is TODAY - May 21, 2011! Read what JESUS says in Matthew 24. Stop worrying & selling your stuff (what will you do with the money IF...?) Jesus said BE READY, WHEN HE DOES COME! Now, if it's THE LORD'S WILL ...I'll talk to you all TOMORROW!
P.S. For those who believe the world will end today & for the rest of us, PLEASE read Ephesians 4:14 carefully! The "wind" in this verse is a

STRONG WIND! A child is no match for that. The word "sleight" of men (KJV) means trickery or dice playing. It's the Greek word "KUBEIA" from which we get the word CUBE. It literally is a picture of one who CHEATS PLAYING DICE (Cubes)! KNOW WHEN you're being deceived!

May 22
Under His Feet
Ephesians 1:15-23~ "Wherefore I also,
after I heard of your faith in the Lord Jesus,
and love unto all the saints,
Cease not to give thanks for you,
making mention of you in my prayers;
That the God of our Lord Jesus Christ, the Father of glory,
may give unto you the spirit of wisdom and revelation
in the knowledge of him:
The eyes of your understanding being enlightened;
that ye may know what is the hope of his calling,
and what the riches of the glory of his inheritance in the saints,
And what is the exceeding greatness of his power
to us-ward who believe,
according to the working of his mighty power,
Which he wrought in Christ,
when he raised him from the dead,
and set him at his own right hand in the heavenly places,
Far above all principality, and power, and might,
and dominion, and every name that is named,
not only in this world, but also in that which is to come:
And hath put all things under his feet,
and gave him to be the head over all things to the church,
Which is his body, the fulness of him that filleth all in all.

The verses say that the SAME POWER that raised JESUS from the dead, is AVAILABLE to us (vs. 19, 20)! Are you shouting yet? If I'm in Christ, and ALL things have been placed UNDER HIS FEET, guess where my problems ought to be (vs. 21, 22)? NOT STRESSING ME OUT, but UNDER these size 10 & a halves, or whatever YOU WEAR!

P.S. ~ HIS FEET are BIGGER than yours!

May 23
Great Expectations
Hebrews 11:1 ~ "Now faith is the substance of things HOPED for,
the evidence of things not seen."

Biblical HOPE is not a wish, but an EXPECTATION OF GOOD! I learned TRUE FAITH from a mentally challenged youth who took a shop class. The class was asked by the teacher to bring a BROKEN small appliance from home to the shop, and try to repair it. The teacher told the students that they might NOT be successful, and to expect FAILURE. Everyone came to class with a small broken appliance. The teacher's mouth dropped when the young mentally challenged boy came with a BROKEN TOASTER under one arm... and a LOAF OF BREAD under the other! That's FAITH! If you pray for rain, take an umbrella when you leave the house ...even if it's 100 degrees outside! That's TRUE FAITH...with EXPECTATION! Do YOU have the type of faith that takes the BROKEN pieces of your life to God with a smile on your face, because you're EXPECTING things to be FIXED when you're in His PRESENCE? :o)

May 24
Hold Fast
Hebrews 4:14 ~ "Seeing then that we have a great high priest,
that is passed into the heavens, Jesus the Son of God,
let us HOLD FAST our profession."

Petty Officer Jon Tumilson was one of 22 Navy SEALS and 16 others, who were killed when their helicopter was shot down in Afghanistan in August of 2011. Tumilson's dog, a Labrador retriever named Hawkeye, had been loyal to him in life, and would NOT leave the casket during the memorial! Dr. Joel C. Gregory asked our class at the American University in Paris, France, "If a dog can be that LOYAL to a dead soldier, can't WE HOLD FAST to a LIVING SAVIOR?" Don't give up. As the late Dr. Carl J. Anderson would say... "HOLD ON OLD SOLDIER!!!" (Someone NEEDED to hear that today! :o)

May 25
Not Exactly a Kind Farewell
Genesis 31:49~ "The Lord watch between me and thee,
when we are absent one from another."

Beautiful benediction, right? No, a sign of DISTRUST between 2 people! Uncle Laban had tricked his nephew Jacob out of a wife & wages. Jacob tricked Laban out of cattle. They now live close to each other & DON'T TRUST one another! Laban says, "Lord, keep your eyes on Jacob WHEN I'M AWAY!" (& vice versa). Read the whole story!

May 26
Hallelujah!
Psalm 146:1~ "Praise ye the Lord. Praise the Lord, O my soul."

Hallelujah is NOT the highest praise. It's NOT A PRAISE AT ALL! It's a request for you to join in & PRAISE GOD! It means, "You All Praise The LORD!" Here's why you should CONTINUE to say it. 1) It encourages others to JOIN you in praise. 2) It reminds the devil of what his NAME WAS (LUCIFER in Isaiah 14:12 is "Helel"), & what his JOB USED TO BE (Ezekiel 28:13-15). Want to make the devil mad? Say It...:o)

May 27
The TRUE Highest Praise
Psalm 149:6 ~ "Let the high praises of God be in their mouth, and a two-edged sword in their hand."

If Hallelujah isn't the highest praise, what is? The Bible DOES NOT SAY, but it's easy to figure out. The phrase "high praises" is in this verse. "Praises" is in ITALICS. It's NOT in the original verse! It speaks of the HIGH PLACE, or HEAVENS, where our praise (vs 1-5) gets deposited! Nehemiah 9:5 & Philippians 2:9-11 tell us that GOD'S NAME is ABOVE any PRAISE or OTHER NAME. Can you say ...JESUS? :o)

May 28
Communication!
Deuteronomy 24:5b ~ "...he shall be free at home one year, and shall cheer up his wife which he has taken."

I know, I know! Yes this is the LONGEST POST by far that I have done to date, but I'm determined to at least try and help. That's why I put something "quick" over the top of this so some of you will have something to read and move on. This may or may not be your issue. I understand. But if you need help with at least "understanding" your relationship with your "significant other," stay with me.

Since so many of you ladies mention it to me, I feel the need to address the lack of "communication" with the men in your lives. I used to believe that men didn't communicate, until I found out what the word really contains (excuse me while I put on my word-smith hat :o).

Now this may take a few minutes. Do you have the time to work with me? If you're getting bored already you might want to do something else right now, because I'm starting to feel this issue that I'm about to share with you.

Look at the word communicate in English. Do you see any cognates (similar sounding, looking and/or related words)? How about "common," "commune," "communion," "commute," etc. The central theme running through all of those words is SHARING! That's what the New Testament word "KOINONIA" means when you see the word COMMUNICATE!

Here's the problem. Most people think that the only way to COMMUNICATE is through our "words." However, a man is actually COMMUNICATING with you when he buys you a box of candy, flowers, dinner, or takes you for a walk on the pier or a ride anywhere, and yes ...sex, even if he doesn't say a word.

I know, stay with me! I've been married to my "segulla" (jewel - Malachi 3:17) of a wife for 36 years this coming August. I told you once that when I first met her, she was washing clothes on a WASHBOARD. For sake of time and space, you senators (seniors) please explain what a washboard is to your children and grandchildren. :o)

Nina was raised by her grandfather, who is a man of VERY few WORDS. Yet, I have learned SO MUCH about being a real FAMILY MAN ...from him! Now he doesn't talk anywhere near as much as I do, but I would settle any day for being the man he is in taking care of his family.

When Nina and I were struggling financially early in our marriage, he would always pop up to the house, often unannounced, come as far as the front door with an envelope for the kinds as well as Nina and I. "Hi, this is for you and the kids." Then he would just go back to the car, which may still be running, and go home. No fanfare, not a lot of words if any, no explanation. It's the way he and MANY OTHER MEN are wired.

Nina's grandfather is the reason that our kids, as they grew older, got allowances from Nina and I. He also bought our first washing machine. You don't think my WIFE loves that man? :o) If you talk to him on the telephone, be prepared for a very, very SHORT conversation. That's just who he is. Yet there is NO DOUBT in the mind of anyone that knows him that "Grandpa Adam" is a Christian, and he deeply LOVES the Lord and his family and friends.

If my wife asks me how my day was, I'll usually say simply, "OK," no matter how it went. However, I make sure that I have a bit of time when I ask Nina how HER day was. "Well, I got up this morning and got my coffee, then I showered and woke Shamira up. I did her hair and got her dressed. Then I fixed breakfast and got a call from so and so wondering what time I was going to pick them up..." Are you getting the picture? She hasn't even left the house yet in this conversation!

Men are usually HEADLINE-oriented, while women are DETAIL - oriented. "Sweetheart, I just wanted to know if your day was OK. Just the HEADLINES!"

Now women, don't stop talking because of what I just said. Details are what make you the unique and WONDERFUL WOMEN that you are. You often see and hear things that we as men don't. You are concerned when we come home in our dirty clothes, and plop down on your clean couch. Is it wrong for us to do that? YES. But remember, we men were MADE from dirt (Genesis 2:7)! Dirt doesn't bother many of us as much as it bothers you ladies. You came from man's side, not the dirt.

Do you know that the Bible even uses DIFFERENT words to describe how men and women were created? Men were "squeezed" ("formed" in Genesis 2:7) into shape as a potter squeezes clay through their fingers. You know, a rough (and rugged) draft. The beauty in pottery is in its rugged differences.

Women were "built" or "fashioned" according to the Hebrew word for "made" in 2:22. You all are FINELY CRAFTED! (YES LORD! :o).

Your question now probably is, Why are some (if not most) men the way they are? It's because of the differences that God created in each gender to compliment and often contrast with the other. What some (if not many) of you have heard is TRUE. Don't get mad at me, men, because this is an issue we can actually DO SOMETHING ABOUT! The "average woman" has a MUCH LARGER vocabulary that the "average" man!!! Why, you ask?

I can only speak for my generation, but I see the same traits in today's children. When you were little girls, ladies, HOW did you "communicate" when (or if) you played with your dolls? You talked to that doll like she was a human being. Some of you had ENTIRE CONVERSATIONS with "Chatty Cathy," "Barbie," "Susie Walker," and "Tammy Tears"!

Now, remember that the "KEN" (male) dolls did not exist yet. The toys that boys played with gave us this type of vocabulary, "BANG... ZOOM... POW... GET EM'...!" Action toys and games don't require a whole lot of verbal skill.

Now are you starting to understand, ladies, why YOU have more to say?

Now keep in mind that I'm talking to women with GOOD and GODLY men who don't talk much. If you hooked up with anyone other than who

God had for you, you cannot blame God, and should NOT be surprised about anything that happens. He does, however, have a word for you. My advice to you is to PRAY and read 1 Corinthians chapter 7, especially verses 13-16. (There's plenty there for you men as well.) Much of this CAN work on unsaved men if you are willing to sacrifice and put up with some stuff (not abuse).

Am I boring you? I hope not because I have just a little bit more. I taught a "couples class" from a book I highly recommend by Bill and Pam Farrel entitled, "Men Are Like Waffles, Women Are Like Spaghetti." Here's the bottom line, and I'll let you go for the day. Like intertwined spaghetti, most woman can NATURALLY do more things at one time. Some call that "multi-tasking." You can be ironing with one hand, cooking with the other, have the phone under your chin, kick the door closed with one foot and the dog out with the other! You do that well.

Most men on the other hand, when we get into a particular "box" such as waffles have, we are THERE UNTIL we leave it! That's the reason why your man REALLY doesn't hear you when you try to talk to him while he's in that T.V. box watching (or playing) a game! It's NOT that he doesn't care or that he doesn't love you. We're just focused on THAT BOX. One thing at a time. As I close, because this was long enough to be a sermon, remember that a waffle has MANY "boxes." Working on the car, fixing something around the house, even his worship in church are just a few of those boxes. That's why when you ask him to take you out, he may do it to keep down confusion in the house (or not), but he is STILL in the "TV BOX," because the GAME is still on!

The answer? Try getting in (not forcing your way in) the box that he may be in at the time, and people like Pastor Bailey will keep working on them from the other end by teaching them their responsibility to work at KEEPING YOU HAPPY …every day of your life (Deuteronomy 24:5). If I can do it for a year as the verse says, I can do it for a LIFETIME! Thank you all for listening to me ramble on. I love you all so much, IT HURTS! At least my FINGERS DO! :o)

May 29
Freed in the Fire!
Daniel 3:24-25 ~ "... Did we not cast three men bound into the fire?
They answered and said to the king, True, O king.
He answered and said,
But I see four men unbound, walking in the midst of the fire,
and they are not hurt…"

I heard something on the radio today that caught my attention, and caused me to re-read this story. There is SO MUCH in the DETAILS of God's Word! Three Jewish men by the name of Shadrach, Meshach, and Abednego, refused to compromise THEIR belief in the ONE TRUE GOD! They WOULD NOT worship a golden idol set up by the ruler of the "then known" world, king Nebuchadnezzar of Babylon. The punishment was to be DEATH in a burning fiery furnace (Daniel 3:6)!

Some Babylonian "HATERS" noticed that the three Hebrew men were not worshiping the golden image, so they told the king (3:8-12). Nebuchadnezzar got angry (3:13), ordered the furnace to be heated 7 times hotter than normal (3:19), and the three to be TIED UP and thrown into the furnace... clothes and all (3:20-21)!

Now watch how GOD can work when WE go through the fires of this world! The flames were SO HOT, they KILLED the king's men that threw Shadrach, Meshach, and Abednego into the fire (3:22)! The three Hebrew men fell down into the flaming inferno TIED UP, according to verse 23. When king Nebuchadnezzar check on them, he was alarmed! He asked his governors (verse 24), "Didn't we throw 3 men tied up into this furnace?"They answered, "Yes." "LOOK! I see four MEN walking around LOOSE in the middle of the fire! And the FOURTH ONE reminds me of somebody!!!"

If you aren't shouting yet, it's probably because you missed what I have missed in the many times I have read this. We have taught over the years that NOTHING on the three Hebrew men was burned (verse 27). According to the above verses, that's NOT TRUE. The one thing on them that was burned was the ROPES THAT BOUND THEM! They went INTO the fire TIED UP. When king Nebuchadnezzar saw them, they were walking around LOOSE!

Sometimes you will not be TRULY FREE of the things that HAVE YOU BOUND in this world, until you have gone through the FIRES of this world! What you're going through now may be intended to FREE you from some stuff! And there is a FOURTH person in that fire with you! His name... is JESUS! :o)

May 30
We're In a Fixed Fight!
1 John 4:4 ~ "You are of God, my little children, and have overcome THEM
(false prophets with the spirit of antichrist):
because greater is HE that is IN YOU (God),
than he that is in the world (the devil)."

As a young man years ago, I once had great seats to a pro-wrestling match. I was closer than I should have been to the ring. I discovered something! (If you don't want to know THE TRUTH, get thee to ANOTHER PAGE)! PRO WRESTLING IS A FIXED FIGHT! Fake BLOOD, chairs that stop INCHES BEFORE they hit the person, and crushing blows that NEVER actually hit the throat, are EASILY seen UP CLOSE! Ahhh, the days of Pepper Gomez, Pat Patterson, Ray Stevens, Kinji Shibuya, Mitsu Arakawa, and Bobo Brazil (You all DO remember his famous Coco [head] Butt)?... but I DIGRESS!!! The participants in those matches knew the winner, BEFORE they set foot in the ring! They just went through the motions. It's the same thing with our DAILY STRUGGLES against the devil! Did you know that WE woke up this morning as participants in a FIXED FIGHT? Satan may knock us down a time or two, but OUR VICTORY has already been PREDETERMINED!

May 31
Saints or Sinners?
1 Corinthians 1:2~ "Unto the church of God which is at Corinth,
to them that are sanctified in Christ Jesus,
called to be saints, with all that in every place
call upon the name of Jesus Christ our Lord, both theirs and ours."

In 1 Corinthians 1:2, Paul addresses the SAINTS at Corinth. IN chapter 5 he addresses their sin, but still DIFFERENTIATES between THEM & the GENTLES (5:1)! Are you still calling yourself a SINNER SAVED BY GRACE? If so, would you do me a favor? Find a scripture, ANY SCRIPTURE, where God calls a SAINT a sinner once they have been saved! Sinful though we may be. Inbox me. I'll wait! We are SAINTS, who sin on occasion.

June

June 1
HONESTY
Romans 14:16~ "Let not then your good be evil spoken of."

1 Thessalonians 5:22 ~ "Abstain from all appearance of evil."

Years ago, Pastor Manuel Scott Jr. came to town to preach a revival. He told me he'd gone to the bank that week & the teller had given him too much money. He counted his money & told her she'd made a mistake. She said, "No, I gave you too much on purpose. I've been at the revival each night. You've preached about HONESTY. I just wanted to see if you practiced what you preached!"

June 2
You've Been Blessed for a LONG Time
Ephesians 1:3-4~ "Blessed be the God and Father of our Lord Jesus Christ, who hath blessed us with all spiritual blessings in heavenly places in Christ, according as he hath chosen us in him before the foundation of the world, that we should be holy and without blame before him in love."

The verses coupled with the past participle "HAS BLESSED" say that God has BLESSED ME IN CHRIST in ETERNITY PAST! That means "BLESSINGS CAME DOWN LONG BEFORE PRAISES WENT UP!" Sorry to mess up another one, but think about it. Aren't you GLAD that our BLESSINGS don't depend on our PRAISE?! Remember those times you didn't feel like, were too busy, or couldn't praise Him, & He STILL BLESSED YOU?

June 3 (originally written in 2011)
Costly and Valuable
Psalm 116:15 ~ "Precious in the sight of the Lord is the death of his saints."

The Church lost a great warrior this past weekend, Gladys L. Medearis. She was the wife of Pastor Victor Medearis of the Double Rock Baptist Church of San Francisco. I took time to mention this couple because this should have made FRONT PAGE NEWS! They had been married 69 YEARS!!! The verse says her death was COSTLY & VALUABLE IN GOD'S SIGHT. Those who die in Christ do NOT die worthless or alone!

June 4
Keep the Line Open
1 Thessalonians 5:17 ~ "Pray without ceasing."

PRAY WITHOUT CEASING. How? When Nina & I were dating, we spent hours on the phone. We didn't want to hang up! "You hang up, ...no YOU hang up, ...you first!" Nina would fall asleep. I'd wait until she woke up. I loved knowing she was on the OTHER END of an OPEN LINE, & hearing the sound of HER VOICE when she woke up. Let GOD HEAR from you when you wake up, & KEEP THE LINE OPEN ...TO HIS VOICE!

June 5
Remember, We're a Team
Romans 12:3-5 ~ "For I say, through the grace given unto me,
to every man that is among you,
not to think of himself more highly than he ought to think;
but to think soberly, according as God
hath dealt to every man the measure of faith.
For as we have many members in one body,
and all members have not the same office.
So we, being many, are one body in Christ,
and every one members one of another."

A TURTLE, trying to get across an ALLIGATOR POND, saw a piece of ROPE lying near two BIRDS. He asked, "Could EACH OF YOU put one end of this rope in your mouths, I'll BITE DOWN on the middle, & you can FLY me across this pond?" As they were IN THE AIR over the pond, an ALLIGATOR looked up & said, "WOW, I wonder WHOSE BRILLIANT IDEA that was?" The TURTLE said, "Mi..........!" Remember CHURCH, we're a TEAM!

June 6
On One Condition...
John 3:16~ "For God so loved the world,
that he gave his only begotten Son,
that whosoever believeth in him should not perish,

but have everlasting life."

Agape is COMMITTED LOVE. It is NOT UNCONDITIONAL LOVE. John 3:16, has a CONDITION. WHOSOEVER BELIEVETH! (also John 3:18; John 14:21-23) Agape is NOT GODLY LOVE because SINNERS can do it! John 3:19 says "men LOVED darkness..." It's the SAME word for love as John 3:16, 2 Pet. 2:15; 2 Tim 4:10 (agapao - the verb form of the noun "agape"). God is COMMITTED to us because of Jesus, as sinners are committed to darkness!

June 7
Don't Be Deceived
2 Corinthians 11:13-15 ~ "For such are false apostles,
deceitful workers, transforming themselves
into the apostles of Christ.
And no marvel; for Satan himself
is transformed into an angel of light.
Therefore it is no great thing if his ministers
also be transformed as the ministers of righteousness;
whose end shall be according to their works."

My son in ministry Anthony Scott & his wife Maya have a PARROT named Ray Ray in their home. Ray Ray can DANCE, TALK & IMITATE sounds! During a stay there, I woke up through the night thinking my cell phone was ringing. Ray Ray was IMITATING my cell phone ring! Don't be deceived by every POTENTIAL leader, partner, or spouse that may speak like an angel. It may be the devil himself, or Ray Ray!

June 8
Need a Change?
Psalm 23:1 ~ "The Lord is my shepherd; I shall not want."

Pastor Mervin Redmond told a story about two sheep having a CONVERSATION. One was complaining to the other, "I'm getting really sick of this. Look at my wool. Full of FLEAS & TICKS and always MATTED!" The other sheep said, "Well, look at ME. My wool is FLUFFY, CLEAN and always shining & glistening." Then he said to the other sheep, "You might want to CHANGE SHEPHERDS!" Who's taking CARE of YOU?

June 9
Use Your Heads, Gentlemen

1 Peter 3:7 ~ "Likewise, ye husbands, dwell with them according to
knowledge, giving honour unto the wife, as unto the weaker vessel,
and as being heirs together of the grace of life;
that your prayers be not hindered."

A husband & wife were having an argument. Neither would admit they
were wrong. Finally the wife said, "I'll admit I'm WRONG, if you'll admit
I'm RIGHT." He agreed, & like a gentleman he insisted she go first. "I'm
wrong," she said. With a twinkle in his eye, he responded, "YOU'RE
RIGHT!" Use your HEADS, men, NOT YOUR FISTS! That's what that
"WEAKER VESSEL" is all about. She's NOT your PHYSICAL equal!

June 10
Redeemed, Redeemed

1 Corinthians 6:19-20 ~ "What? know ye not that your body
is the temple of the Holy Ghost which is in you,
which ye have of God, and ye are not your own?
For ye are bought with a price:
therefore glorify God in your body,
and in your spirit, which are God's."

Johnny made a TOY BOAT & took it to a lake. Once in the water, the
boat drifted away. It was LOST. One day while downtown with his dad, he
saw HIS BOAT in the window of a pawn shop! He asked his dad for all the
money he had saved, & he bought the boat. Johnny looked at it & said,
"You're mine TWICE. Because I MADE you, & because I BOUGHT
YOU!" God MADE us. We drifted away. JESUS BOUGHT US BACK!

June 11
GO!

Acts 1:8 ~ "But ye shall receive power,
after that the Holy Ghost is come upon you:
and ye shall be witnesses unto me both in Jerusalem,
and in all Judaea, and in Samaria,
and unto the uttermost part of the earth."

A BABY CAMEL asked his mother why he had huge feet. "To help you stay on top of SOFT SAND when crossing the desert," she said. "Why the LONG EYELASHES?" "To keep sand out of your eyes." she said. "Why two HUMPS?" he asked. "To STORE WATER for long trips." "So we are WELL-EQUIPPED FOR THE DESERT, but Mom ...Why are we IN THE ZOO?" "GOD DIDN'T EQUIP US, to STAY where we are!" GO, be a WITNESS & HELP SOMEBODY!

June 12
God Can Bless You Through Your Enemies
Proverbs 13:22~ "A good man leaveth an inheritance
to his children's children:
and the wealth of the sinner is laid up for the just."

An ATHEIST heard a woman praying for God to feed her family. He bought food, left it on her porch & hid. She saw the groceries & began to PRAISE GOD. He came out laughing & told her it was HIM, NOT HER GOD! She said, "THANK YOU JESUS! I knew You could do it, but I didn't know You could get the DEVIL HIMSELF to drive to the store, buy the food & drop it off!" God can use your ENEMIES, to BLESS you!

June 13
Don't Trip!
Psalm 55:12-14 ~ "For it was not an enemy that reproached me; then I could
have borne it: neither was it he that hated me
that did magnify himself against me;
then I would have hid myself from him:
But it was thou, a man mine equal, my guide, and mine acquaintance.
We took sweet counsel together,
and walked unto the house of God in company."

We EXPECT betrayal from enemies, NOT from CLOSE FRIENDS! David says about a close friend (probably Ahithophel), "I could have handled this from an enemy. You & I were close friends. We talked & went to CHURCH TOGETHER!" Ahithophel gave advice to David's son on how to DETHRONE David (2 Samuel 16:20ff)! Ever been betrayed by a FRIEND? Don't trip! READ how they end up ~ 2 Samuel 17:23; Matthew 27:1-5

June 14
Just Slides Right Off
Psalm 23:5 ~ "Thou preparest a table before me
in the presence of mine enemies:
thou anointest my head with oil; my cup runneth over."

Shepherds SATURATE their sheep with oil so that if attacked by SNAKES & WOLVES, the enemy just SLIDES right off! God's children are anointed by HIS SPIRIT. Attacks, lies & labels CAN'T STICK! GOD HAS LABELED YOU AWESOME, MARVELOUS & PRECIOUS (Psalm 139:14; Lamentations 4:2)! It doesn't matter if someone switches labels. The VALUE of the product has ALREADY been SET, BY THE MANUFACTURER! :o)

June 15
The Triple "J" Man
2 Corinthians 6:14ff ~ "Be ye not unequally yoked
together with unbelievers:
for what fellowship hath righteousness with unrighteousness?
and what communion hath light with darkness?"

MY SINGLE SISTERS IN CHRIST, TRUST GOD to provide the "RIGHT MAN" for you. You're waiting (sort of :o) for the one man YOU think God has for you! THAT one guy might be in CHINA right now! If a man meets GOD'S QUALIFICATIONS, GOD won't contradict His Word! You'll have SEVERAL SINGLE, TRIPLE "J" MEN to CHOOSE from! A TRIPLE "J" MAN is one who has JESUS, JOY... & A JOB!

June 16
Everything Has an Expiration Date
Psalm 30:5 ~ "For His anger□□ endures but for a moment;
His favor lasts for a lifetime:
weeping may SPEND THE NIGHT,
but JOY comes in the morning."

Are you going through a STORM right now? Do yourself a favor. Whenever you're going through something that is not so pleasant, go to your refrigerator or pantry and find any item in ITS ORIGINAL PACKAGE. Somewhere on that package is an EXPIRATION DATE. When you find it, run around the house and THANK GOD that EVERYTHING, including your TRIALS, HAS... you got it, AN EXPIRATION DATE! Say it with me now, "Weeping may SPEND THE NIGHT, but joy will be checking in... AFTER THE WEEPING CHECKS OUT!" :o)

June 17
Morning Prayer
Proverbs 3:5-6 ~ "Trust in Jehovah with all your heart,
and lean not upon your own understanding:
☐In all your ways acknowledge him,
And he will direct your paths."

I saw this prayer on a friend's page some time ago: "Dear God, so far today I've done OK. I HAVE NOT gossiped or lost my temper. I HAVE NOT been greedy, crabby, mean, nasty, selfish, or overindulgent, and I'm very grateful for that. But dear God, in a few minutes I'm gonna GET OUT OF BED... and then I'm probably gonna need a LOT MORE HELP! Amen."TRUST GOD, even after you BREAK your nighttime FAST! (BREAKFAST :o)

June 18
Gray Hair and Why It's There
Matthew 7:3 ~ "Why do you see the speck
that is in your brother's eye,
but do not notice the log that is in your own eye?"

One day a little girl asked her mother, "Mama, why do you have so much GRAY HAIR?" Her mother said, "Each gray hair represents YOUR DISOBEDIENCE to me. Every time you disobey, I get another gray hair!"The little girl looked puzzled, and then asked, "So mama, are YOU the reason GRANDMA has so much gray hair too?" Let's be careful how we judge others. If rebellion really caused gray hair, someone somewhere has gray hair ...BECAUSE OF US!

June 19
Mind Your Own Business
1 Thessalonians 4:11 ~ "...and that you study to be quiet,
and to do your own business, and to work with your hands,
even as we charged you..." (ASV)

Have you ever wondered why it is so difficult for some folk to MIND THEIR OWN BUSINESS as the verse says? Because as Paul said to the church at Thessalonica, "It takes work to SHUT UP!" That's what the word "STUDY" in the verse means. It means to "aspire, be ambitious, strive or labor" to be calm, quiet, silent...! Now does this mean that we should not attempt to RESTORE a fallen brother or sister (Galatians 1:1-2) when they are OBVIOUSLY and ADMITTEDLY wrong? Of course not! It means that we should not be "busy-bodies" in other folks' business.

Let's admit it. MUCH of what people do is NOT for your correction. It's either to get into your Kool-Aid (business), or to lift themselves up by making YOU look bad. God KNOWS who those people are, and He will deal with them accordingly. In the meantime, GET TO WORK minding your own business! I used to lead a song as a child in the church choir where I grew up. I believe it's still on a reel-to-reel tape somewhere. I remember it well because of the length of the title and the lyrics of the song. The name of the gospel song was, "I've Got Six Months To Mind My Own Business, & Six Months To LEAVE YOURS ALONE!!! :o)

June 20
You Don't Have to Look Like What You've Been Through
Matthew 6:16-18 ~ "And when you fast,
do not look gloomy like the hypocrites, '
for they disfigure their faces that their fasting may be seen by others.
Truly, I say to you, they have received their reward.
But when you fast, anoint your head and wash your face,
that your fasting may not be seen by others,
but by your Father who is in secret.
And your Father who sees in secret will reward you."

These verses teach that we should not purposely try to LOOK RELIGIOUS in order to impress folk! Oh what a list of things that "Christians" do in order to APPEAR more religious. I know it doesn't happen in YOUR church, but at the churches down the street and around the corner from yours, there are people who come late ON PURPOSE and walk to the front of the church!Many of them just want to be seen! It's the same with those people who wait until the offering period is OVER, and then decide to stand and announce their giving and the amount. Jesus says in the verses that when HYPOCRITES would fast, (or give and pray as in verses 1-8), they wanted to make sure that people SAW THEM. Their MOTIVES were wrong. Did you know you can do the RIGHT thing for the WRONG reasons?These "hypocrites" made sure their hair was out of place and their faces were so disfigured that they LOOKED HUNGRY. Everyone would know that they had been fasting and would talk about how RELIGIOUS they were for doing so! Jesus said when you exercise a ritual that is connected to what you believe (such as prayer, giving, fasting), as much as IS POSSIBLE ...keep it between You and God! He told them to wash themselves and stop walking around looking like they were starving, just to illicit religious sympathy (16-18). People will KNOW you are a Christian by the way you conduct yourself. Have you ever had someone tell you how good or how happy you look, when on the inside you were going through a storm? The JOY OF THE LORD will do that for you! When all HELL is breaking out in your life, you can still SMILE and treat people like a child of God would. Aren't you glad that because of the GLORY OF GOD over your life, you DON'T LOOK LIKE what you've BEEN THROUGH? Bless the Lord ...at ALL TIMES! ~ Psalm 34:1 :o)

June 21
God Can Use Whatever He Has Put Into Your Hand
Exodus 4:2 ~ "And the LORD said unto him,
'What is that in your hand?' And he [Moses] said, 'A rod.' "

Moses was concerned about how to approach Pharaoh about letting God's people go (Exodus 4:1). God gave Moses POWER and AUTHORITY to deal with Pharaoh by telling him to use what was already IN HIS HAND, his shepherd's stick (staff, rod). Doesn't seem like much, does it? I read about a 24 year old man named Danny Simpson from Ottawa, Canada. In 1990, he robbed a bank of $6,000. Unknown to him at the time, the gun Danny used to commit the robbery was a vintage 1918 Colt .45 semi-automatic revolver. Danny Simpson's gun is in a museum now, and is worth up to $100,000 on the collectors market! The GUN in his hand was worth over 16 times what he stole!!! If Danny Simpson had only KNOWN what was IN HIS HAND, he would NOT have had to spend 6 years in jail! Now STOP worrying about what you DON'T HAVE, take what God has put in YOUR HAND (given you), put it in HIS HAND and remember ..."Little becomes MUCH, when you place it in the Master's Hand!"

June 22
Enjoy Your Present from God
Matthew 6:34 ~ "So don't worry about tomorrow,
for tomorrow will bring its own worries.
Today's trouble is enough for today." (NLT)

Dr. F.G. Sampson use to say, "Yesterday is a CANCELED CHECK; you can't get it back. Tomorrow is PROMISSORY NOTE that may never get fulfilled. All you have is TODAY!" TODAY is a gift from God (Psalm 119:23). I wonder if that's why it's called... the PRESENT? Live your life in the PRESENT! ONE DAY at a time. Someone put a SIGN up in their gas station that said, "FREE GAS... TOMORROW!" THINK about it. Some of you will catch that on BART or in your car later on! :o)

June 23
The Spirit Will Lead You – Sometimes with a Stop Sign
Acts 16:6-7 ~ "Next Paul and Silas traveled
through the area of Phrygia and Galatia,
because the Holy Spirit had told them not to go
into the province of Asia at that time.
Then coming to the borders of Mysia,
they headed for the province of Bithynia,
but again the SPIRIT OF JESUS [the original actually says that]
did not let them go." (NLT)

I am a firm believer that God knows PRECISELY what He is doing... AT ALL TIMES. The verse up above RELEASED me from the why, when, where and ifs of God's will for my life. I'm THOROUGHLY convinced that the Holy Spirit will BLOCK MY agenda in order to protect me, and/or to direct me to where God wants me to be at any given time. This Facebook ministry is a PERFECT example of that! This was NOT MY original intention when I signed up for this media!

Did you catch the fact that IT WAS GOD HIMSELF, in the person of the Holy Spirit, who PREVENTED Paul, Silas and Timothy from PREACHING THE WORD in Asia Minor at that particular time? God wanted them to go preach in Macedonia (verses 9-10)! Now if you are constantly BUMPING YOUR HEAD into a wall trying to go where YOU want to go, MAYBE the SPIRIT OF JESUS is directing you somewhere else! God will NOT always give you a PREVIEW of what He's doing, but HE WILL often stop you from doing... what YOU'RE DOING!!!

June 24
The Beginning and the End, and the Dash in the Middle
Revelation 22:13 ~ "I am Alpha and Omega [what He says],
the beginning and the end [what He does],

the first and the last [who He is]."

Hebrews 12:2 ~ "Looking unto Jesus, the author☐ and finisher
[or perfecter] of our faith; who for the joy that was set before him
endured the cross, despising the shame,
and is seated at the right hand of the throne of God."

In Revelation 22:13, Jesus says that He is the Alpha (first letter of the Greek Alphabet) and Omega (last letter of the GREEK alphabet. In Hebrew (which we believe Jesus spoke to His Jewish brothers and sisters), He would have said, "I am the Aleph-Tau" which are the first and last letters in the HEBREW alphabet. You'll find those 2 letters together several times in the Old Testament... UNTRANSLATED! They just pop up in some very STRATEGIC places, but translators don't know why! I believe it's JESUS putting His signature throughout the Hebrew Scriptures! Now if He's A & Z (English), it stands to reason He's got EVERTHING between (A-Z) under control!!!

Hebrews 12 tells us in its very first verse that we are in a race. My question to you, "Do you know how to run the GRAVEYARD DASH?" Let me explain. My beloved brother, Sherwin Clement Bailey, lived from 1955-2008. He had NO CONTROL over the 1955, or the 2008. The part of his life that he had some say over, was the DASH (-) in the middle of those 2 numbers on his headstone. He's with the Lord now. Remember that GOD ALONE has the FIRST and the LAST words. He even REIGNS over the DASH in the middle. He will, however, ALLOW you to determine its outcome. Having trusted Jesus Christ as Lord and Savior during the DASH (his life), Sherwin kept his eyes on Jesus, who Hebrews 12:2 says was, "The 1955 and The 2008 of his FAITH!" The dash he ran in between, he ran with love for Jesus! Jesus PERFECTED Sherwin's faith on June 25, 2008. When I was in school, what is now called the 100 meter race was called the 100 YARD DASH. It was called a DASH because like a dash (-) , it was short compared to the other races. Life is SHORT compared to ETERNITY! Have you learned how to run your DASH trusting Jesus?

One last question: Does your dash look like this - or like this ~ ? :o)

June 25
Love (GRACE) Lifted Me
Romans 8:3 ~ "For God has done what the law,
weakened by the flesh, could not do.
By sending his own Son in the likeness of sinful flesh and for sin,
he condemned sin in the flesh..."

The Bible says that Jesus came to FULFILL the law (Matthew 5:17)! He fulfilled the Law by paying the debt WE owed (and couldn't pay) at CALVARY. The verse says that the law was WEAK because of OUR FLESH, which couldn't keep it (see Romans 3:19-20). Have you ever OVERCOOKED a roast? Try getting it out of the pan with a MEAT FORK, and it will fall apart! Think of the FORK as the LAW. The problem is NOT with the Fork (the Law), it's the MEAT (our flesh) that's weak! Now watch this! If you use a SPATULA (Grace), you can now LIFT the meat from the pan!!! God's LOVE (Grace) LIFTED ME! How about YOU? :o)

June 26
Honesty is STILL the Best Policy

Hebrews 13:18 ~ "Pray for us, for we are sure that we have a clear conscience, desiring to act honorably (honestly) in all things." (ESV)

It's not always easy for people, EVEN CHRISTIANS, to be honest all of the time. But DISHONESTY can only lead to grief! A Charlotte, North Carolina man purchased a box of 24, very rare and very expensive cigars. He insured them against several things, including theft and fire. He then preceded to smoke his entire inventory of cigars within a month! He had NOT even made his first premium payment on the policy.He decided to file a claim against the insurance company. In the claim, the man stated that the cigars were lost "in a series of SMALL FIRES." The insurance company refused to pay, citing the obvious reason: that the man had consumed the cigars in the normal fashion. The man sued the insurance company... AND WON!!!

While delivering the ruling in the case, the judge agreed that the claim was petty and frivolous. He said nevertheless that the man held a VALID POLICY from the company which said that the cigars were insurable and also guaranteed that it would insure against fire. The judge also said that the insurance company failed to define what was considered to be "unacceptable fire," and was obligated to pay the claim.

Instead of going through a long dragged out and costly appeal process, the insurance company accepted the ruling and paid the man $15,000.00 for the rare cigars he had lost in the "fires."When the man cashed the check, the insurance company had him ARRESTED... on 24 counts of ARSON!!! With his own insurance claim and testimony from the previous case being used AGAINST HIM, the man was convicted of intentionally burning his insured property and sentenced to 24 months in jail and a $24,000.00 fine. TRUE STORY! :o)

June 27
Remember Where Your Strength Comes From
2 Chronicles 26:5 ~ "...and as long as he (Uzziah) sought the LORD,
God made him to prosper." (KJV)

Uzziah has gotten a BAD RAP! He was NOT a bad king (26:4). He DID NOT keep Isaiah from seeing God (Isaiah 6:1). Important events (like the death of a king) WAS simply a way of DATING other events .2 Chronicles 26:5-7 says as long as Uzziah sought the Lord, GOD caused him to PROSPER! But when UZZIAH BECAME STRONG (26:16), his own heart caused his downfall! Don't forget who BLESSES YOU EVERYDAY!

June 28
We Must Protect This House
Ephesians 6:16 ~ "In all circumstances take up the shield of faith,
with which you can extinguish
all the flaming darts of the evil one..." (ESV)

I have a serious concern about the direction in which our FAMILIES are headed. At any given time you can turn on the news and see the violence, drugs and even the redefinition of the family itself. Satan has mounted an all out ASSAULT on THE FAMILY!I love how Dr. R.A. Vernon explained the "fiery darts" (KJV) of the wicked (or wicked one ~ the devil) in the verse. In Paul's day the fiery darts were arrows that had been dipped in a flammable substance and lit on fire before being shot at an object. Can you imagine the damage that would do? Dr. Vernon reminded us of how the Indians in the old TV westerns would dip their arrows in something flammable, and then shoot those flaming arrows. Watch this. Do you remember that they DID NOT shoot those arrows at the men, but at THE WAGONS! Why? I'm glad you asked. The Indians knew that the food, the wife, and the children were in the wagons! In other words, they made the man CHOOSE between himself, and his FAMILY. Don't allow Satan's attacks on your family to be successful. Protect your family with the WHOLE ARMOR OF GOD (verses 10-18).

One more thing. The next time your CHILD (I don't care how old he or she is) tells you what they will or won't do, just remember... That's YOUR HOUSE, I THINK?

June 29
Sometimes, Oil is Just Oil

Matthew 25:1~ "Then shall the kingdom of heaven be likened unto ten
virgins, which took their lamps,
and went forth to meet the bridegroom."

Don't SPIRITUALIZE EVERYTHING in the Bible. When I was in
Bible college, one of my professors would always say, "If the PLAIN
SENSE makes GOOD SENSE, then it's NONSENSE to look for any
OTHER SENSE!" Often times scripture just IS, what it IS!

In Matthew 25:1-13 for example, I've heard it taught that anytime you
see OIL in the Bible, the oil represents the Holy Spirit! How can the OIL in
the lamps represent the HOLY SPIRIT if they RAN OUT OF IT? It was also
being BOUGHT and SOLD! None of that suggests the Holy Spirit, because
you CANNOT buy, sell or run out of The Spirit! Sometimes, OIL IS JUST
OIL! Now if the Bible says that God can Bless you BEYOND your ability to
ask or think (Ephesians 3:20)... stop trying to spiritualize, allegorize or
figure it out, and JUST BELIEVE IT!!! :o)

June 30
Get off the Lettuce Diet
Genesis 11:4 ~ "Then they said,
'Come, LET US build ourselves a city and a tower
with its top in the heavens,
and LET US make a name for ourselves,
or else we will be dispersed over the face of the whole earth.'"

Many of you recognize this verse from the Biblical story of the Tower
of Babel. Dr. Maurice Watson shared this scripture with us one Monday
evening at the Fairmont Hotel in Dallas, Texas. It was NOT a message
AGAINST wanting to do great things. It' was a message against wanting to
do great things... FOR THE WRONG REASONS!!!

The postdiluvian world (people who lived AFTER the flood that
happened in Noah's time), consisted of a group of megalomaniacs (Look it
up. I don't want you to get lazy :o). These were people on a LETTUCE
DIET! All you have to do is read the verse, "LET US build a city and tower
that reaches into the heavens." WHY? It's in the same 4th verse, "LET US
make a NAME FOR THEMSELVES!" There's more LET US (lettuce) in
11:3-4. Do you DO what you do for CHRIST, or do you do it in order to
make A NAME FOR YOURSELF? It's also obvious that they DID NOT
believe God when He said that He wouldn't destroy the world by WATER
any more (Genesis 9:15). Why else would they want to build a structure that
HIGH?

One more thing. Isn't it ironic that the very thing they were trying to avoid, (being scattered over the earth), is what GOD told them TO DO in Genesis 1:28. He told man to be fruitful, multiple and fill or cover (replenish) the entire earth. Some of you may not know how the story ends. Genesis 11:1 teaches that BEFORE the Tower of Babel was built, everybody in the world spoke the SAME LANGUAGE! After the people started to build the tower, God had some LET US of His own! It's in 11:7. God said (no doubt to the other TWO persons in the Godhead), "LET US go down there and MIX UP (confuse) their language so they won't be able to understand one another. When that happened, people ended up SCATTERING with those who spoke the same language, as God had instructed them to do in Genesis 1! Now you know how you got WHERE you are, speaking the LANGUAGE that you speak!

Before you implement those great plans for your life, ask yourself the question they used to ask in that Sprite commercial, "What's My MOTIVATION?" Deacon Al Carter asks us that question at the church on a regular basis. It keeps us on our toes! You're probably not going to like this final question, but here it goes anyhow. Has God ever messed up YOUR PLANS, in order to accomplish HIS OWN PLANS??? :o)

July

July 1
Pilate's Wash Basin
Matthew 27:24 ~ "When Pilate saw that he could prevail nothing,
but that rather a tumult was made, he took water,
and washed his hands before the multitude, saying,
'I am innocent of the blood of this just person: see ye to it.'"

One of the best sermons I've ever heard was taken from this verse. The preacher was Dr. C.A.W. Clark and his sermon was, "What Happened To Pilate's Wash Basin?" Clark had us on the edge of our seats waiting for the LOCATION of the basin so that we might visit it. Then he said that it was in "MY HOUSE and YOUR HOUSE!" Whenever we fail to acknowledge JESUS in our lives, WE'RE USING PILATE'S WASH BASIN!

July 2
Making It To the Other Side
Romans 3:23 ~ "For all have sinned,
and come short of the glory of God."

As children, we tried to jump the roofs of the bungalows of a near-by school. They were about 7-8 feet high & a few feet apart. One day, a boy missed by INCHES. He hit the opposite bungalow & split his head open! I missed by several feet & landed on the ground in between. We BOTH MISSED the other side! Stop comparing someone else's sins to yours. WITHOUT JESUS, NONE OF US will make it to the other side!

July 3
Question to Ponder...

Forgive me, but I'm going into "teacher mode" and asking a question. In September of 2010, I did a post on the subject coming up tomorrow. I'll give you a chance to answer the question, then I'll do an EDITED repost. ~ Where, in the BIBLE, is there a verse or teaching that there is no such thing as BIG SIN & little sin?

July 4
And the Answer Is...
John 19:11 ~ "Jesus answered,
'Thou couldest have no power at all against me,
except it were given thee from above:
therefore he that delivered me unto thee hath the greater sin.'"

There ARE BIG SINS & little sins; JESUS SAID SO! (Jeopardy Theme Song is playing while you look it up!). Raping a 6-month-old (that really happened) is a GREATER SIN than a lie. Without the BLOOD of JESUS that keeps on cleansing (literal translation) us from our sins, a lie & a rape will keep you out of heaven! (Romans 3:23 & 6:23) Short is short, be it by 1 inch or 1 mile. That's why WE ALL NEED JESUS!

July 5
At the Source
John 2:1-11 ~ "And the third day there was a marriage in Cana of Galilee;
and the mother of Jesus was there:
And both Jesus was called, and his disciples, to the marriage.
And when they wanted wine,
the mother of Jesus saith unto him, 'They have no wine.'
Jesus saith unto her, 'Woman, what have I to do with thee?
mine hour is not yet come.'
His mother saith unto the servants,
Whatsoever he saith unto you, do it.
And there were set there six waterpots of stone,
after the manner of the purifying of the Jews,
containing two or three firkins apiece.
Jesus saith unto them, 'Fill the waterpots with water.'
And they filled them up to the brim.
And he saith unto them, 'Draw out now,
and bear unto the governor of the feast.' And they bare it.
When the ruler of the feast had tasted the water
that was made wine, and knew not whence it was:
(but the servants which drew the water knew;)
the governor of the feast called the bridegroom,
And saith unto him, 'Every man at the beginning
doth set forth good wine; and when men have well drunk,
then that which is worse:
but thou hast kept the good wine until now.'
This beginning of miracles did Jesus in Cana of Galilee,

and manifested forth his glory;
and his disciples believed on him."

The FIRST MIRACLE in the Bible done BY JESUS was done AT A WEDDING! He can STILL work WONDERS IN OUR RELATIONSHIPS! The key is in what Mary said to the servants in verse 5, "Whatever He (Jesus) tells you to do, DO IT!" I also learned that the original language in verse 9 suggests that the water was changed... AT THE SOURCE (the well) and NOT in the pots! GOD fixes things AT THE SOURCE. Anyone up for a spiritual HEART TRANSPLANT? :o)

July 6
REAL Sowing and Reaping
Galatians 6:7 ~ "Be not deceived; God is not mocked:
Whatever a man sows, that shall he also reap!"

That verse has been used as a weapon to MAKE FOLK act right. Here's the truth & the context. VERSE 6 says, "Let YOU who are TAUGHT in the WORD, SHARE with those who TEACH YOU in ALL GOOD THINGS!" Now read VERSE 7! THANK YOU TO ALL who SHARE (sow) with the one who has tried to teach you. I am often OVERWHELMED!

July 7 (written in 2011)
All You Need
Philippians 4:19 ~ "But my God shall supply all your need
according to his riches in glory by Christ Jesus."

500+ gave me what I needed on one of the most difficult days of my life, ENCOURAGEMENT! I returned from Texas that Thursday night. Attended a Homegoing Service that Friday. Another Saturday, and was on my way to Vallejo to another one when I saw what y'all had done! After thanking the Philippians for taking care of him (vs. 10-18), Paul says to them, "MY GOD shall supply ALL YOUR NEED..." Why? Because they had supplied HIS! I pray GOD supplies ALL YOU NEED, today!

July 8
One More Confirmation...
Exodus 5:1~ "And afterward Moses and Aaron went in, and told Pharaoh,
'Thus saith the Lord God of Israel, Let my people go,

that they may hold a feast unto me in the wilderness.' "

Exodus 8:1~ "And the Lord spake unto Moses,
'Go unto Pharaoh, and say unto him, Thus saith the Lord,
Let my people go, that they may serve me.' "

Exodus 9:1~ "Then the Lord said unto Moses,
'Go in unto Pharaoh, and tell him,
Thus saith the Lord God of the Hebrews,
Let my people go, that they may serve me.'"

Have you noticed how the Old Testament prophets usually introduced what God was saying with, "Thus saith the Lord...?" (Over 400 times). Jesus DID NOT use that phrase. He would say, "Verily, Verily, I SAY UNTO YOU!" (Truly, Truly or Amen, Amen in Greek or Put a PERIOD right after this!) Why didn't He say, "Thus saith The Lord?" Because JESUS CHRIST IS LORD! :o)

July 9
The Sting(er)
1 Corinthians 15:55~ "O death, where is thy sting?
O grave, where is thy victory?"

Dr. F.G. Sampson & his daughter were in his car when a BEE appeared. His daughter panicked! He took one hand off of the steering wheel & caught the bee in flight! A few seconds later the bee flew out of his hand. He said, "Baby, it CAN'T hurt you now!" "Why, daddy?" He opened his hand, & the bee's STINGER was there! Jesus took the STING(ER) out of death at Calvary! Death can't hurt God's child!

July 10
Lovingkindness
Psalm 51:1 ~ "Have mercy upon me, O God, according to thy
lovingkindness: according unto the multitude of thy
tender mercies blot out my transgressions."

Lovingkindness (*chesed*) is an important word in Biblical Hebrew. It's the idea of LOYALTY or DEVOTION. God is DEVOTED to loving us, even when we mess up. David called on a LOVE HE COULD TRUST, when he LEAST DESERVED IT! I asked my awesome wife for a FRIED

BALONEY sandwich. She made it without bringing up my faults. That's KINDNESS. But she also put a FRIED EGG ON IT for me! That's LOVINGKINDNESS, in abundance!

July 11
"Of" vs. "From"
Matthew 11:29~ "Take my yoke..."

Hook Up With JESUS! If you're in a BURNING high-rise & a fireman appears on a ladder to save you, DON'T ask him for his qualifications. LET HIM carry you to safety FIRST! Then the King James version says, "...learn OF me." The Greek word "apo" is actually "FROM" me! You can learn "OF" me by asking someone who knows me. You can only learn "FROM" me by having a RELATIONSHIP WITH ME!

July 12
Endure to the END
Ecclesiastes 9:11; Matthew 10:22 ~ "The race isn't given to the swift or to the strong, but to those who endure to the end."

We've heard that many times. I tried for years to find that verse in the Bible. I couldn't find it. Then while reading through the entire Bible for the first time many years ago, I discovered it was a COMBINATION of the 2 verses up above.

There is a BLESSING in seeing things through to the end! Consider this: A contractor worked building houses for 40 years. He built some of the most magnificent homes in his area. early one year, he told his employer that he would be retiring later that year. That day finally came. This man had been the BEST at his job. NO ONE else in the area could build a house like he could. The houses he built were always FABULOUS, with STATE-OF-THE-ART features and the SAFEST materials. The employer asked the man if he could build ONE MORE house in the BETTER part of town for a very important client. The man told him NO, it was time to quit. After much coaxing, the contractor agreed to do ONE MORE house before he retired. His boss told him that this house needed to be his MASTERPIECE. "Spare NO EXPENSE," he said. "I want people to drive by this house and say, "That home was built by the greatest contractor in the region!"The man began work on the house, but his HEART WASN'T IN IT. He was thinking about RETIREMENT! He did something he had NEVER DONE in 40 years. He cut costs and got poor quality concrete for the foundation! Then, in order to finish quickly, he ALSO cut corners and built with cheaper and unsafe materials. He figured that with the money he would save, he'd be set for retirement. He finished WEEKS ahead of schedule. The house looked beautiful, ON THE OUTSIDE. But in the UNSEEN places within the walls and underneath the house, the contractor KNEW it WASN'T his best work. When his boss came to see the house and get the keys from the contractor, he marveled at the SPECTACULAR home that he saw before him, NOT KNOWING about the poor construction. The employer got the keys from the man and told him, "This is indeed your finest work!" The contractor was starting to FEEL GUILTY because he knew it wasn't! Imagine how he felt when his boss said, "The company wanted to THANK YOU for 40 years of excellent service. Here are the keys ... TO YOUR NEW HOME!"

You never know when YOUR boss (or GOD) may be setting you up for a RAISE or a PROMOTION! Work every day as if there is a BLESSING in it for YOU! There actually is, because what MAN doesn't see, GOD DOES! He will reward you accordingly. Now have a PRODUCTIVE day at work, people! :o)

July 13 (written in 2011)
Tragedy and Treasure

Matthew 6:19-21 ~ "Do not lay up for yourselves treasures on earth,
where moth and rust destroy and where thieves break in and steal,
but lay up for yourselves treasures in heaven,
where neither moth nor rust destroys
and where thieves do not break in and steal.
For where your treasure is, there your heart will be also." (ESV)

My heart is heavy and my prayers go out to the families of those lost and injured in the recent tragedy in Aurora, Colorado. The reason MY HEART is burdened as verse 21 suggests, is because I have TREASURE THERE! I have FRIENDS in and around the Aurora, Colorado area. I have NEVER set foot in Aurora, yet I have an INVESTMENT in Aurora. Several of my Facebook friends are in and around the area for one thing. Also, in 1997 I received an Honorary Doctor of Divinity Degree from a Bible College and Seminary in of all places, AURORA, COLORADO!

Here's my point. Make an INVESTMENT of prayers, friends, and/or finances etc., in cities and/or countries OUTSIDE of your own. Why? Let me ask you a question. Did you PRAY for Trelew, Argentina today? Why not? Probably because you have NO TREASURE THERE!

July 14
God Makes Changes
Malachi 3:6 ~ "For I am the Lord, I change not;
therefore ye sons of Jacob are not consumed."

It's true, GOD DOES NOT CHANGE! But He does MAKE CHANGES! Do you deal with your 22-year-old the way you deal with your 2-year-old? Of course not! That doesn't mean YOU have changed what you believe about parenting. You have MADE CHANGES to fit the maturity of that son or daughter! If God had not MADE CHANGES, we'd still be offering bulls & goats! According to Leviticus 11 you could not eat bacon, ham, crab, lobster, shrimp, or catfish! Aren't you GLAD GOD MADE CHANGES in Acts 10:9-15?

July 15
Don't Turn Your Nose Up
Ephesians 5:2 ~ "And walk in love, as Christ also hath loved us,
and hath given himself for us an offering
and a sacrifice to God for a sweet-smelling savour."

What does perfume & the sacrificial death of JESUS CHRIST have in common? One is SWEET smelling to us, and THE OTHER is a SWEET smelling savor to God! The two important ingredients in BOTH, are costly & repulsive. Jesus' BLOOD in salvation, & AMBERGRIS in perfume. Ambergris STABILIZES perfume so it smells sweet longer. Perfume is so expensive because ambergris is WHALE VOMIT! Don't turn your nose up at the NASTY things in life ...THEY'RE NECESSARY for a good outcome! Remember Romans 8:28?

July 16
I Am Who I Am
Exodus 3:14 ~ "God said to Moses, 'I AM WHO I AM.'
And he said, 'Say this to the people of Israel,
I AM has sent me to you.' " (ESV)

Many of you recognize this as being God's answer to Moses, after He told Moses to deliver the children of Israel from Pharaoh. Moses had asked God, "What shall I say to the children of Israel when they ask me who the God of their fathers is, that sent me?" God's response was, "Tell them 'hayah' (pronounced haw-yaw) sent you." "I AM" in English does not convey the full meaning of the Hebrew word. As I have studied that ONE WORD answer from God, let me give you as best I can, what God said. Are you ready? You sure? OK, fasten your seat belt because here goes: HAYAH means, "I was what I was, I was what I am, I was what I will be, I am what I was, I am what I am, I am what I will be, I will be what I was, I will be what I am, I will be what I will be!!!Did you get all of that? Because I'm not sure I can say that again! In other words, GOD'S GOT THIS. Got what? WHATEVER IT IS! Whether past, present, or future, no matter how, when or where... you can RELAX because He's GOT THIS, REALLY! :o)

July 17 (written in 2011)
Our Healer
Matthew 8:17 ~ "...that it might be fulfilled
which was spoken through Isaiah the prophet, saying:
'Himself [Jesus] took our infirmities, and bare our diseases.' " (ASV)

My reason for this post is for those who have a hard time believing that Jesus Christ is still a Healer. At the present, I am dealing with a lot of sickness in and around the congregation. May I share something with you? When you or your loved ones are sick, call on a child of God, who has more than just a medical opinion, to pray for you!

Now listen carefully. Doctors are NECESSARY, and most of them do know their business. Are they always wrong in their diagnosis and prognosis? Of course not! But GOD has the last say so in what He created! I've seen and heard about enough arrogant doctors (and other professionals) to last me a lifetime. I only ask ONE THING of them. Remember that GOD & PRAYER ARE an option! Please let your patients know that.

About six years ago I started teaching what I believe the Bible teaches to be HEALING in one of the elements of the Lord's Supper, namely The Bread! We've got The Blood down. We know that The Blood was shed by Jesus Christ for our sins, and we've written MANY songs about The Blood! What about the Bread?The Bread, which represents Jesus' body, was broken (no matter what some are teaching these days) for us, so that our bodies would not have to be! I have several posts on the subject of the bread and Jesus' broken body as it relates to physical healing. It's straight out of the Word of God. You'll have to check the archives of these posts, or wait for the book!

The reason I mention it today, is because the niece of one of our female members will be visiting our church tomorrow from Paris, Texas. When I first taught the healing power in the BREAD of the Lord's Supper (1 Corinthians 11:29-30; Isaiah 53:4-5; Matthew 8:14-17), a member came to me after church and told me that a hospital was going to "pull the plug" on her brother the following day. Mortuary staff had even come to the hospital and told the family how "good" they would make him look for the service! I told Sis. Thelma Lucas to take the Lord's Supper on her brother's behalf, and I did the same. The doctors DID "pull the plug" some 6 years ago, and I'll be EXCITED to hear how he's doing tomorrow from his daughter! Remember once again, doctors DON'T have the last word! A GOOD DOCTOR will tell you that.

Let me finish this post with a story that Pastor. A.B. Sutton shared with us a couple of weeks ago in Dallas, Texas, from his own life. Dr. Sutton was visiting a member's relative, that was sick in a hospital. On the way up the elevator in the hospital, an "arrogant doctor" began to speak without being prompted. With his name on his smock and his stethoscope around his neck, he proceeded to tell those on the elevator who he was. He listed his credentials and schools, and ended by telling them that he was the SPECIALIST that the hospital called, when OTHER doctors had failed. Then the doctor looked at Rev. Sutton and asked him who he was. Pastor Sutton said, "I'm the one they call...WHEN YOU FAIL!!!" :o)

July 18
His Hands Are Bigger
Philippians 4:19 ~ "But my God shall supply all your need according to his riches in glory by Christ Jesus."

A mother & son were in line at a grocery store. A clerk asked the mom if her son could have some candy. She agreed. The clerk held out the jar. The boy didn't move. The clerk said, "Take as much as you want." The boy said, "I want YOU to give it to me." The clerk reached in the jar & handed him some candy. In the car, mom asked her son why he wouldn't take the candy. He said, "Because HIS HANDS were BIGGER than mine!" Not only does GOD have BIGGER HANDS, HIS JAR is bigger too!

July 19
Look Up
2 Corinthians 5:7 ~ "Purge out therefore the old leaven, that ye may be a new lump, as ye are unleavened. For even Christ our passover is sacrificed for us."

E.V. Hill shared about a cartoon he had seen. The 1st frame is an EGG. The egg is CRACKED in the 2nd frame. A BABY CHICK sticks its head out & looks around in the next frame. Finally, the chick pulls its head back into the egg, & CLOSES IT UP! What did it SEE, that made it go BACK into the egg? Was it the HUMAN CONDITION? Looking at the world's condition can DEPRESS you. It's why there was only one window in the TOP of Noah's Ark. It's also why we walk by FAITH, NOT BY SIGHT!

July 20
Job Hunting?
Genesis 15:1 ~ "After these things the word of the Lord
came unto Abram in a vision, saying, 'Fear not, Abram:
I am thy shield, and thy exceeding great reward.' "

WOW! I saw a NEWS CLIP on television of a church encouraging their members to bring their RESUMES to the altar so the priest can pray over them. I pastor a church & have NO problem with that, but I CAN save you some time. Genesis 15:1 says, "Chill Out" (Fear not), & know that "GOD is your VERY GREAT SALARY" (literal translation of "reward" is salary or wages)! Now have a talk with GOD (Pray), TRUST HIM & go get THE JOB HE KNOWS is BEST for you! :o)

July 21
The Fork vs. the Spatula
Romans 8:3 ~ "For what the law could not do,
in that it was weak through the flesh,
God sending his own Son in the likeness of sinful flesh,
and for sin, condemned sin in the flesh:"

Jesus came to FULFILL the law (Matthew 5:17)! He fulfilled the debt WE owed the law (& couldn't pay) at CALVARY. The verse says the law was WEAK because of OUR FLESH, which couldn't keep it. Have you ever overcooked a roast? Try getting it out of the pan with a MEAT FORK, & it will fall apart. Think of the FORK as the LAW. No problem with the Fork, it's the Flesh (meat) that's weak! If you use a SPATULA (Grace), you can now LIFT the meat from the pan. God's LOVE (Grace) LIFTED ME!

July 22
And He Shall Purify
Malachi 3:3 ~ "And he shall sit as a refiner and purifier of silver:
and he shall purify the sons of Levi,

and purge them as gold and silver,
that they may offer unto the Lord an offering in righteousness."

A lady watched a SILVERSMITH at work to get insight on this verse for a class. She asked, "Why did you put it in the fire?" He said, "To purify it." She asked, "How long do you watch the silver?" "He said, "As long as it's in the fire. Too LITTLE heat and it won't be pure. Too MUCH heat will destroy it. I keep my eye on it constantly." She asked, "How do you know when it's READY?" He said, "When I can SEE MYSELF IN IT!" Now I KNOW why God allows us to go through some fire!

July 23
Precious Lord, Take My Hand
Psalm 139:10 ~ "Even there shall thy hand lead me,
and thy right hand shall hold me."

In 1932 while singing at a revival in St. Louis, Thomas Dorsey got a telegram that his pregnant wife had DIED! He rushed back to Chicago to find she had given birth to a boy, but the baby died that night! He buried both of them in the same casket & decided GOD WAS UNJUST. While alone one day in a room with a piano, a song came into Thomas Dorsey's head that changed his life, "Precious Lord, Take My Hand!" No matter how bad things get, God's got HIS SHEEP safely in His hand. ~ John 10:28-29

July 24
From the Narrow End
Matthew 7:13-14 ~ "Enter ye in at the strait gate:
for wide is the gate, and broad is the way,
that leadeth to destruction,
and many there be which go in thereat:
Because strait is the gate, and narrow is the way,
which leadeth unto life, and few there be that find it."

Jesus was talking to anyone who was trying to imitate the scribes & Pharisee's SELF-RIGHTEOUS way of life (Matthew 5:20). When I was in England, many of the streets were EXTREMELY NARROW but often led to LARGE & BEAUTIFUL open Courtyards, Castles & Cul-de-sacs! That's the way this Christian life is. ONE NARROW WAY IN. That would be JESUS (John 14:6)! But OH the JOY & BEAUTY that awaits at the end of this NARROW WAY! Sort of like traveling through a FUNNEL …from the

NARROW END!

July 25
Do You Need an Explanation?
Ephesians 3:20 ~ "Now unto him that is able to do exceeding abundantly above all that we ask or think, according to the power that worketh in us..."

I love the 1943 movie "Song of Bernadette." It's about Saint Bernadette Soubirous' vision at Lourdes, France of the Virgin Mary (whom my Catholic friends call Our Lady of Lourdes not Lords!) I LOVE THE PROLOGUE after the opening credits, "...For those who believe in God, no explanation is necessary. For those who DO NOT believe in God, NO EXPLANATION IS POSSIBLE." I'm neither confirming or denying the vision, but affirming a VERSE that teaches GOD is STILL WORKING MIRACLES!

July 26
No Double Jeopardy
1 Thessalonians 5:9 ~ "For God hath not appointed us to wrath, but to obtain salvation by our Lord Jesus Christ."

My son in ministry, Anthony Scott, recently had a dry grass fire burn within INCHES of his home! The fire started in the empty lot next to his house. I told him he could sleep well now, KNOWING that fire could NOT BURN GRASS that has already been burned! God had ALREADY reminded him of that! God poured out the FIRE OF HIS WRATH on His Son JESUS CHRIST at Calvary! If you are in Christ, it won't happen again! That would be DOUBLE JEOPARDY. God is TOO JUST for that!

July 27
Don't Be Arrogant
Romans 12:3~ "For I say, through the grace given unto me, to every man that is among you, not to think of himself more highly than he ought to think; but to think soberly, according as God hath dealt to every man the measure of faith."

1 Corinthians 15:10 ~ "But by the grace of God I am what I am: and his grace which was bestowed upon me was not in vain; but I laboured more abundantly than they all: yet not I, but the grace of God which was with me."

112

Don't be an ARROGANT Christian! OUR GREATNESS COMES FROM BEING IN CHRIST JESUS. Clint Eastwood (Dirty Harry) said, "A man's got to know his limitations!" Boxer Muhammad Ali was on a plane years ago when a flight attendant asked him to BUCKLE his seat belt. He refused! She KNEW who he was, but was NOT INTIMIDATED! She asked him again. Ali said, "SUPERMAN don't need no seat belt." She looked Ali dead in the eye & said, "SUPERMAN DON'T NEED NO AIRPLANE, EITHER!"

July 28
Uninvited
Job 1:6 ~ "Now there was a day when the sons of God
(unfallen angels) came to present themselves before the LORD,
and Satan☐ came also among them."

In the 1993 movie "Poetic Justice," Janet Jackson, Tupac Shakur, Regina King, and Joe Torry traveled from South Central Los Angeles, California to Oakland, California in a mail truck. In one scene, they pulled off the side of the road into a park area where a FAMILY GATHERING was going on. They ACTED like part of the family by mingling and helping themselves to the food! Some of us have enemies, friends, friends of friends, or even relatives who are just like that. They have this tendency to just show up, even if not invited! Beware of the DEVIL, who likes to SHOW UP in your family… UNINVITED, and help himself to your stuff!

July 29
Look Ever to Jesus
Hebrews 12:2 ~ "Looking unto Jesus,
the author and finisher of our faith;
who for the joy that was set before him endured the cross,
despising the shame,
and is set down at the right hand of the throne of God."

I remember that the most difficult thing for me to get used to in England was NOT the time difference. It was being on buses driving on the LEFT side of the street! In America we drive on the RIGHT side of the street (not including 1-way streets). It's STRESSFUL to see another BUS coming at you on the side of the street you're used to driving on! Here's the secret. Until you get oriented, FOCUS on the DRIVER and NOT THE ROAD!

That song means MORE now ~ "LOOK ever to JESUS, He will CARRY YOU THROUGH!"

July 30
A BREECH Delivery
Colossians 1:18 ~ "And he is the head of the body, the church:
who is the beginning, the firstborn from the dead;
that in all things he might have the preeminence."

Colossians 2:10 ~ "And ye are complete in him,
which is the head of all principality and power."

Most pregnant women know that when a baby's head is not in the proper position, it's called a "BREECH" position! That's when the feet or the buttocks of the baby is trying to come out first. Most doctors will wait until the HEAD is in the proper position, or try to "turn" the infant to be born HEAD FIRST! A breech delivery produces a LOT OF PAIN, and the possibility of NO LIFE! If you are experiencing a LOT of pain, and NO DELIVERANCE or NEW LIFE, maybe YOUR HEAD ...is in the WRONG POSITION! :o)

July 31
God's Workmanship
Psalm 139:14 ~ "I will praise thee;
for I am fearfully and wonderfully made:
marvellous are thy works;
and that my soul knoweth right well."

Suffering from low self esteem? David said God made you so well, people should stand in AWE of you (Yare = fearfully)! You are unique and distinct from anything else ever created (Palah = wonderfully)! What's needed for OTHERS to see the "You" GOD CREATED? The LOVE OF GOD in and around your life will make people stand back, look at you and go WOW! It doesn't matter how YOU THINK you look! By the way, Psalm 23:5 says God soaks you with oil! That means LABELS won't stick either!

August

August 1
The Contagious Jesus
Luke 5:12-14 ~
"And it came to pass, when he was in a certain city,
behold a man full of leprosy:
who seeing Jesus fell on his face, and besought him, saying,
'Lord, if thou wilt, thou canst make me clean.'
And he put forth his hand, and touched him, saying,
'I will: be thou clean.'
And immediately the leprosy departed from him.
And he charged him to tell no man:
'but go, and shew thyself to the priest, and offer for thy cleansing,
according as Moses commanded, for a testimony unto them.' "

Dr. Joel Gregory asked a profound question in his message about "The Contagious Jesus!" In this scripture about Jesus' encounter with a LEPER, Dr. Gregory asked us, "Who was more CONTAGIOUS? The leper, or JESUS?" Think about it. OF ALL the SICK & NEEDY PEOPLE Jesus met, He NEVER CAUGHT what THEY had. Yet THEY CAUGHT what HE HAD ...healing, hope, wholeness, deliverance, salvation, peace, etc.! Try hanging with Jesus. You'll probably catch what HE HAS! Yes, you can INSERT SHOUT HERE!

August 2
Boomerangs
Psalm 7:15-16 ~ "He made a pit, and digged it,
and is fallen into the ditch which he made.
His mischief shall return upon his own head,
and his violent dealing shall come down upon his own pate."

Why do we who are Christians worry about people who MISTREAT US? In these verses, God says that the wicked may dig a ditch for you, but they are going to FALL in the very ditch that they dig FOR YOU (verse 15)! Verse 16 really blesses my soul. It says that whatever EVIL my enemies try to do to me, will BOOMERANG and smack them in their own head! Now make sure YOU are NOT the one throwing those BOOMERANGS!!! :o)

August 3
LOOSE THEM!
John 11:44 ~ "And he that was dead came forth,
bound hand and foot with graveclothes:
and his face was bound about with a napkin.
Jesus saith unto them, 'Loose him, and let him go.' "

How many of us have read this verse and thought Jesus was talking to THE GRAVE CLOTHES? I've heard sermons preached that Lazarus couldn't do anything still bound in grave clothes (old habits), so Jesus told them (the grave clothes) to "loose him!" Well the "THEM" in the verse is THE same PEOPLE he told to move the stone! Many times it's not the PAST (old habits) holding them back. It's WE who won't help them DEAL WITH & FORGET their past! Now LOOSE THEM ...so they can function!

August 4
What God Forgets
Hebrews 8:12 ~ "For I will be merciful to their unrighteousness,
and their sins and their iniquities will I remember no more."

Hebrews 10:17 ~ "And their sins and iniquities
will I remember no more."

In 1850, an American novelist and short story writer by the name of Nathaniel Hawthorne wrote what has become a classic called *The Scarlet Letter*. A woman by the name of Hester Prynne conceives a daughter through an adulterous affair. Set in Puritan Boston in the 17th century, Hester was ridiculed by the townspeople and forced to wear a scarlet piece of cloth with the letter "A" (for Adulterer) sown to the chest of her gown! Can you imagine walking around the city with that reminder of your sin always with you? Imagine what church would be like if there were "sin detectors" (like metal detectors) at the entrance of every church.Imagine that whenever someone walked into the church, the SIN DETECTOR hollered out your sin. Beeeeep..."LIAR!" Beeeeep... "FORNICATOR!" Beeeep... "MURDERER!" How many people do you think would be in church if this were the case? Just ONE! The FIRST one to get to church and look inside to make sure NO ONE ELSE was there! Aren't you glad that when you become a truly repentant child of God, he says... "I won't REMEMBER your sins anymore?"

Interestingly, Hester REFUSED to say who the father of her daughter Pearl was. Ironically the father just happened to be a preacher! As you go

116

through the day, remember this... YOU ARE FORGIVEN!!! :o)

August 5
A Special Treasure – a Segulla!
Malachi 3:17 ~ "And they shall be mine, saith the Lord of hosts,
in that day when I make up my jewels;
and I will spare them,
as a man spareth his own son that serveth him."

God says that His people are His "segulla" (jewels). That means a
SPECIAL or PECULIAR TREASURE! (Titus 2:14). In the times of
ABSOLUTE MONARCHS, kings owned EVERYTHING IN THE
KINGDOM! They kept a small bag of jewels IN THEIR POSSESSION (a
segulla), to REMIND them that they OWNED IT ALL. Dr. Gregory asked
us this question in class, "Would you rather HAVE a treasure, or BE A
TREASURE?" It's the reason I call you PRECIOUS (valued possession of
God) so often! :o)

August 6
More than I Can Bear
2 Corinthians 1:8-10 ~ "For we would not, brethren,
have you ignorant of our trouble which came to us in Asia,
that we were pressed out of measure, above strength,
insomuch that we despaired even of life:
But we had the sentence of death in ourselves,
that we should not trust in ourselves,
but in God which raiseth the dead:
Who delivered us from so great a death, and doth deliver:
in whom we trust that he will yet deliver us."

Can I set at least 2 people free? GOD WILL put more on you than YOU
CAN BEAR! 1 Corinthians 10:13 is about SIN, not burdens! 2 Corinthians
1:8-10 says that Paul & his group were pressed (burdened) WELL
BEYOND their ability (strength) to bear it. Why? So they'd have to TRUST
IN GOD & NOT THEMSELVES (9)! In Genesis 4:13 after killing his
brother Abel, CAIN told God "... My punishment is MORE THAN I CAN
BEAR!" If God only gave you stuff you could bear, why would you NEED
HIM?

August 7
When 2 or 3 Are Gathered In My Name...
Matthew 18:20 ~ "For where two or three are gathered together
in my name, there am I in the midst of them."

"For where 2 or 3 are gathered together in my name, there am I in the midst..." Have you heard this verse used to justify having a small crowd made up of the pastor's wife & kids? READ verses 1-20, especially 16 & 19. JESUS gives a WAY TO HANDLE SIN in the church. If we follow His plan & the offending party still won't listen, Jesus says when the 2 or 3 (along with the church) DIS-FELLOWSHIP that person (put them out of the local church - vs.17), He and the Father will BACK YOU UP!

August 8
WHY ARE YOU STILL HERE?????
Luke 13:6-9 ~ "He spake also this parable;
A certain man had a fig tree planted in his vineyard;
and he came and sought fruit thereon, and found none.
Then said he unto the dresser of his vineyard,
'Behold, these three years I come seeking fruit on this fig tree,
and find none: cut it down;
why cumbereth it the ground?'
And he answering said unto him,
'Lord, let it alone this year also,
till I shall dig about it, and dung it:
And if it bear fruit, well: and if not,
then after that thou shalt cut it down.' "

People have a tendency to focus on the FIG TREE in danger of being cut down, rather than GOD'S CARE FOR US (the tree) YEAR AFTER YEAR (verse 8)! JESUS was answering questions in Luke 13:1-5 about why CERTAIN people die. Has anyone close to you died recently? The question ISN'T, "Why do some people die WHEN they do & the WAY they do?" The question according to vs. 6-7 should be, "WHY ARE YOU STILL HERE?" The answer's in vs. 9? You're here to BEAR FRUIT! ~ Galatians 5:22-26

August 9 (originally posted in 2011)
Broken and Beautiful
Isaiah 53:5 ~ "But he was wounded for our transgressions,

he was bruised for our iniquities:
the chastisement of our peace was upon him;
and with his stripes we are healed."

Traci Rock is an awesome WOMAN OF GOD, radio show host &
friend. I heard her show for the first time last night! All I can say is WOW!
The title of the program is "Broken & Beautiful!" If you have experienced
ANY BROKENESS in your life, God wants you to know that Jesus was
PIERCED (wounded) for our transgressions & BROKEN IN PIECES
(bruised) for our iniquities. That's what the original language says. Jesus
knows JUST HOW YOU FEEL (Hebrews 4:15-16)! Remember that when
you talk to Him!

August 10
Unforgivable Sin
1 John 1:7 ~ "But if we walk in the light, as he is in the light,
we have fellowship one with another,
and the blood of Jesus Christ his Son cleanseth us from all sin."

Is there an UNFORGIVABLE SIN? Some would point to Luke 12:10;
Matthew 12:31. We can argue about what that sin is, or we can put it in it's
context. It doesn't matter if there WAS an unforgivable sin -- BEFORE Jesus
died! He died for ALL OF OUR SINS! I looked up the word ALL in the
verse. Write this down, it means ...ALL! IF you've trusted JESUS with your
life, don't worry about an unforgivable sin. Move that table or chair & shout
HALLELUJAH that you live ...on THIS SIDE OF CALVARY!

August 11
Rejection is Direction
Isaiah 53:3 ~ "He is despised and rejected of men;
a man of sorrows, and acquainted with grief:
and we hid as it were our faces from him;
he was despised, and we esteemed him not."

Why are we shocked, upset and down right depressed when people
REJECT us? JESUS was DESPISED AND REJECTED by human beings!!!
That's what the verse says. Yet JESUS never took Prozac, tranquillizers or
felt totally hopeless, helpless and discouraged because PEOPLE quit on Him
or left Him. What makes us think that we are NOTHING without certain
people in our lives? If GOD is FOR YOU, (and He IS) He's MORE than the

WORLD AGAINST YOU (Romans 8:31; Psalm 118:6)! The crowd around Jesus at His death, was much smaller that the crowds that followed Him during His life. He was REJECTED! Now look back over your life at the people who have REJECTED you. (I'll wait for some of you to stop shouting "Thank You JESUS!") Aren't you glad that some people are no longer in your everyday life? That man that rejected you is now in jail for domestic violence against the one he left YOU for. The boss that fired you PUSHED YOU into a BETTER job. That credit card company that said NO, kept you from going into debt that you would have had a hard time recovering from THIS TIME. Isn't GOD GOOD? Now treat that REJECTION as DIRECTION for a NEW PATH in your life. I'll tell you where to start …in the next post. :o)

August 12
Start With the Foundation
Ezra 3:1-3 ~ "And when the seventh month was come,
and the children of Israel were in the cities,
the people gathered themselves together as one man to Jerusalem.
Then stood up Jeshua the son of Jozadak,
and his brethren the priests, and Zerubbabel the son of Shealtiel, and his
brethren, and builded the altar of the God of Israel,
to offer burnt offerings thereon,
as it is written in the law of Moses the man of God.
And they set the altar upon his bases;
for fear was upon them because of the people of those countries:
and they offered burnt offerings thereon unto the Lord,
even burnt offerings morning and evening."

If you want a new start in life, let me tell you where the path starts. Actually the inspiration comes from these verses. Start with WORSHIP! That's right…WORSHIP! After around 70 years in Babylonian captivity, exiles (from the Southern Kingdom of Judah) were allowed to return home to Jerusalem where the city walls and Temple had been destroyed and BURNED by Nebuchadnezzar about 50 years earlier. Now notice what the exiles did when they got back home to Jerusalem, led by Zerubbabel. They DID NOT rebuild the walls (for protection) first. The DID NOT even rebuild the Temple (house of God) first. The FIRST THING they rebuilt was THE ALTAR …the place of WORSHIP! They rebuilt that altar within the Temple where they could resume sacrifices to GOD. They restored WORSHIP! Start your new life by being a WORSHIPER! Now watch this. According to verse 3, still there in the midst of the burned-out rubble of the Temple was the

FOUNDATION (base) of the ALTAR! They started building their NEW ALTAR ...on its OLD FOUNDATION! If you missed that, Google the words to the song "Take Me Back" (to the place where I first received you), by Andre Crouch. You STILL have a foundation. His name is JESUS! ~ 1 Corinthians 3:11. It doesn't matter what you have been through or how bad the RUINS of your life are. God will ALWAYS leave you enough, even amongst the burnt out rubble of your life, to START ALL OVER AGAIN! You may not have a job, but you have a RESUME! You have an education. You have bus fare, an interview and a smile. You have an old beat-up car, but it runs. A roof that leaks is a roof none the less! You have a FOUNDATION! At age 65, Harland Sanders took $105 from his first Social Security check and started what would become Colonel Sander's Kentucky Fried Chicken! Benjamin Ryrie was a missionary in China. At 80 years old he decided to learn New Testament Greek. He became proficient in New Testament Greek. At 90 he went to seminary for a refresher course. At 100 years old he was still getting around on public transport, practicing his Greek on the bus! It's NEVER too late to start ALL OVER AGAIN!

August 13
Haters
Psalm 81:15 ~ "The haters of the Lord
should have submitted themselves unto him:
but their time should have endured for ever."

I've noticed a lot of talk on Face Book about HATERS! The Bible has something to say about HATERS. The first thing we should know is that what happens to His children, is PERSONAL to GOD! (Acts 9:4). Psalm 81:15 says if the HATERS don't SUBMIT, God won't ACQUIT (...in my Johnnie Cochran voice)! "...STAND STILL and see the SALVATION of the Lord" (Exodus 14:13). Or in the words of the late James Brown, "Sit back, relax and watch GOD WORK!"

August 14 (posted originally in 2011)
Dialog, not Monolog
Psalm 46:1 ~ "God is our refuge and strength,
a very present help in trouble."

I would that YOU WOULD pray for Nina and I as we head across the ocean for Oxford (via London), England in a few hours. We are NOT worried about what's happening there (verses 1-2,5), because we know who

REIGNS THERE (verse 10)! And NO, it's NOT the queen ...it's THE KING! Nina wants to see the queen, I'm going to learn more about THE KING! When you pray, remember that PRAYER is a DIALOG and NOT A MONOLOG! So after you finish talking to Him, BE STILL ...and let HIM talk to YOU! :o)

August 15 (posted originally in 2011)
This Was Indeed the Lord's Doing
Psalm 118:23-24 ~ "This is the Lord's doing;
it is marvellous in our eyes.
This is the day which the Lord hath made;
we will rejoice and be glad in it."

We have arrived in England safe and sound! I can't believe that I am across the street from historic Oxford University where I will be studying the remainder of the week! This is INDEED the Lord's doing; and it IS WONDROUS & EXTRAORDINARY in our eyes. Do you know why? Because of verse 22! Guess who was rejected and has now become the Chief Cornerstone of our Faith (John 1:10-11)? His name is JESUS. He's the reason we can rejoice and be GLAD ABOUT TODAY! :o)

August 16 (posted originally in 2011)
Look Up, and Live
Isaiah 53:6 ~ "All we like sheep have gone astray;
we have turned every one to his own way;
and the Lord hath laid on him the iniquity of us all."

Numbers 21:8~ "And the Lord said unto Moses,
'Make thee a fiery serpent, and set it upon a pole:
and it shall come to pass, that every one that is bitten,
when he looketh upon it, shall live.' "

In August of 2011 during a bus ride from London's Heathrow Airport to Oxford University, I saw cows on one side of the freeway, and sheep on the other side. The cows would eat the grass, and LOOK UP from time to time. The sheep kept their HEADS DOWN the entire time they were eating the grass. They walked and nibbled, and nibbled and walked. I understand now how SHEEP can easily go ASTRAY. You can't keep walking through life with your HEAD DOWN, and not get LOST or DEPRESSED! LOOK UP, and LIVE!

August 17
MORE GRACE (in the Freezer)
Romans 5:20-21 ~ "Moreover the law entered,
that the offence might abound. But where sin abounded,
grace did much more abound:
That as sin hath reigned unto death,
even so might grace reign through righteousness
unto eternal life by Jesus Christ our Lord."

One day in PRESCHOOL, my son was running over kids with a tricycle. I promised JUSTICE if he did it again! He did. He ran over the TEACHERS! On the way home I bought candy & ice cream. With candy in my pocket & ice cream in the freezer, I dispensed JUSTICE! After one SWAT he yelled, "I'm sorry, Daddy!" As the TEARS flowed, MERCY stopped me! He deserved more. As TEARS of JUSTICE dried on his face, I reached in my pocket, & gave him some GRACE. I had MORE GRACE, in the freezer!

August 18 (posted originally in 2011)
The Lord is My Light
Psalm 27:1 ~ "The Lord is my light and my salvation; whom shall I fear?
the Lord is the strength of my life; of whom shall I be afraid?"

Some are concerned about our safety here (in England) during the riots. We're cautious, but NOT AFRAID because of this verse! The riots could be resolved if JESUS was the LIGHT who GUIDES the lives of those rioting AND those who are callous to the PLIGHT of the less fortunate. "Dominus Illuminatio Mea" is the MOTTO of the University where I am studying this week. The words are on the logo in the profile picture. The Latin words in the middle of the Bible on the logo read, "The Lord Is My Light!"

August 19
Grace Trumps Sin
Romans 5:20-21 ~ "Now the law came in to increase the trespass,
but where sin increased, GRACE abounded all the more,
so that as sin reigned in death,
GRACE also might reign through righteousness leading to eternal life
through Jesus Christ our Lord." (ESV)

GRACE isn't a LICENSE to sin (Romans 6:1-2, 15). GRACE is a

TRUMP WHEN you sin! Are there any BID WHIST players out there? Bid whist is a predominantly African American card game from which came the card game "BRIDGE".Those who play Bid Whist know that a well placed TRUMP (wild card so to speak), will stop a LOUD MOUTH on their way to that city called BOSTON... where all of the books are won (or as some say, all of the "tricks" are turned :o).In Romans 5:20-21, Paul teaches that GRACE will always TRUMP (break up and overpower) SIN! Don't try to help Jesus! Just believe that HIS BLOOD washed away all of your sins, and that His HOLY SPIRIT will empower you to LIVE like it...not YOUR WILL to do so. "O wretched man that I am! Who shall deliver me from the body of this death? □I thank GOD through JESUS CHRIST our Lord. So then with the mind I myself serve the law of God; but with the flesh the law of sin." ~ Romans 7:24-25

August 20 (originally posted in 2011)
Jesu (Jesus), Joy of Man's Desiring
Psalm 42:1 ~ "As the hart panteth after the water brooks,
so panteth my soul after thee, O God."

I loved CLASSICAL music BEFORE I knew how to play GOSPEL music. I listened to two songs over & over for the entire 7 & 1/2 hour trip from Atlanta to London! Beethoven's "Allegro" from his *Fifth Symphony*, & Bach's "Jesu (Jesus), Joy of Man's Desiring!" Beethoven is also known for a symphony he didn't finish. Symphony #10 is called his UNFINISHED SYMPHONY. LIFE IS UNFINISHED until JESUS becomes the JOY OF YOUR DESIRE! Does your soul PANT (desire) after HIM, as a DEER DOES FOR WATER?

August 21
THE LORD WILL TAKE CARE OF ME!
Psalm 27:10~ "When my father and my mother forsake me,
then the Lord will take me up."
Hebrews 13:5-6 ~ Let your conversation be without covetousness;
and be content with such things as ye have:
for he hath said, 'I will never leave thee, nor forsake thee.'
So that we may boldly say, 'The Lord is my helper,
and I will not fear what man shall do unto me."

SOMEONE needs to hear this today. Is there anyone out there still feeling guilty about how BAD, ABUSIVE or NON-SUPPORTIVE your parents, husband, wife, friend, child, boss, teacher, church, etc. are, or were toward you? Is it DICTATING how you live your life? Has it affected your relationships in a negative way?

Here's GOOD NEWS! Read Psalm 27:10. It says when MOTHER and FATHER forsake me, THE LORD WILL TAKE CARE OF ME! Hebrews 13:5-6 says that God will NEVER leave you or forsake you, so you don't have to fear what HUMANS DO TO YOU! Now, when you finish running around the house praising the Lord, WALK IN THAT PROMISE AND BE BLESSED! :o)

August 22 (originally posted in 2011)
Wobbly Bridge – Millennium Bridge in London, England
1 John 1:9 ~ "If we confess our sins,
he is faithful and just to forgive us our sins,
and cleanse us from all unrighteousness."

Nina & I took a cruise under the famous Millennium Bridge on the Thames River in London. It was nicknamed the WOBBLY BRIDGE because of problems that caused it to WOBBLE when people walked across it. After 2 DAYS it was CLOSED for the next 2 YEARS for repairs! The architect said his ENGINEERING DESIGN was NOT the problem. He said the problem was (get this)..."THE WAY PEOPLE WALKED ON THE BRIDGE!" At some point we need to STOP blaming others & take responsibility for our own actions!

August 23 (originally posted in 2011)
God Doesn't Call the Qualified; He Qualifies the Called
Romans 11:29 ~ "For the gifts and calling of God are without repentance."

God DID NOT make a mistake when He called you! Jacob was a cheater, Peter had a temper, David had an affair, Noah got drunk, Jonah ran from God, Paul was a murderer, Gideon was insecure, Miriam was a gossiper, Martha was a worrier, Thomas was a doubter, Sarah was impatient, Elijah was moody, Moses stuttered, Zacchaeus was short, Abraham was old, and Lazarus was dead.... Now WHAT'S YOUR EXCUSE? Can GOD USE YOU, or not? God DOESN'T call the QUALIFIED, He QUALIFIES the CALLED.

August 24
Al Carter at the Bank
Romans 8:28 ~ "And we know that God causes everything
to work together☐ for the good of those who love God
and are called according to his purpose for them." (NLT)

One of our deacons, Al Carter, was a bit upset about being late getting to his bank one day. By the time he got to the bank, he discovered that the bank had been ROBBED EARLIER!!! Did you ever stop to think that when we get to heaven, IF it were POSSIBLE to do so, we would have a HEART ATTACK over all of the stuff God DID NOT allow to happen to us? Think about the things we COULDN'T SEE, that God prevented!

I've told our congregation more than once, "If you go outside after service and trip at the curb and break your leg, THANK GOD all the way to the hospital! A MURDERER could have been waiting for you at your car around the corner!" If you're God's child, WHATEVER happens today will eventually work out in YOUR FAVOR... when GOD gets through with it! It may take a human minute or so, but it will... HE PROMISED! :o)

August 25
Paul and Eutychus
Acts 20:9 ~ "And a young man named Eutychus, sitting at the window,
sank into a deep sleep as Paul talked still longer.
And being overcome by sleep,
he fell down from the third story and was taken up dead." (ESV)

I think I'll have some fun with you today. I have a question. Is the teaching on my Facebook page page BORING YOU? Especially when I edit and REPOST some things that I have already said?

I asked that question because a gifted friend of mine, Carl Fortier, made the following comment on a post in which I apologized for reposting it so quickly. He said, "Your postings never get old Pastor Steve. Just like Paul, I'd listen to your same message over and over again!"

That statement made me chuckle because, "Lest I be exalted above measure..." (as Paul said in 2 Corinthians 12:7), God reminded me of the story of which the verse up above is a part. Did you know that Paul's preaching put a young man by the name of Eutychus to sleep? According to Acts 20:9, the sleep was SO GOOD, that the young man FELL out of a third story window, and DIED!

Now Paul was able to bring the young man back to life (Acts 20:10-12). I have a concern about boring you all, because I don't want you to

126

ZONE OUT and hurt yourselves! I CAN'T DO what Paul did!

One Sunday while in the middle of his sermon, a PREACHER told a young boy to WAKE UP his father, who was sleeping next to the boy on the pew. The boy look at the preacher and said, "YOU wake him up pastor! YOU put him TO SLEEP!!!"

Now for context sake, Paul's long-winded (Acts 20:7) message only exposed the real problem. What really put the young man into a deep sleep was the LACK OF OXYGEN in the room because of so many burning lights (torches) around him!You will come to that conclusion if you "exegete the white spaces" (read between the lines) of Acts 20:8. So maybe I'm NOT the problem. Maybe you're uninterested because there are TOO MANY things going on... AROUND YOU! I TOLD you I just felt like messing with you. :o) :o) :o)

August 26
Heart Knocks
Revelation 3:20 ~ "Behold, I stand at the door, and knock: if any man
(Greek word "tis" = "anyone") hear my voice, and open the door,
I will come in to him, and will sup with him..."

Don't let people put a GUILT TRIP on you, especially those who try to use GOD to do it!

A man tried to HOOK UP with a CHRISTIAN co-worker. He went to her home, but she didn't answer the door. He left a note that read, "Revelation 3:20 ~ Behold I stand at the door and knock: if any man hear my voice and open the door, I will come in!" The next day at work, the woman slid a note under the man's office door which read, "Genesis 3:10 ~ I heard thy voice in the garden and I was afraid, because I was naked; and I HID MYSELF!"

SOME women are SMARTER than they may appear, MEN!!! Keep up the good work, ladies (some of you anyhow), and tell that man that if he likes what he sees, "PUT A RING ON IT!!!" (In my best Beyonce voice! :o)

August 27 (originally posted in 2011)
Pussycat, Pussycat, Where Have You Been?
Matthew 5:16 ~ "Let your light so shine before men,
that they may see your good works,
and glorify your Father which is in heaven."

Old nursery rhyme: "Pussycat, pussycat, where have you been? I've been to London, to see the Queen. Pussycat, pussycat, what did you there? I frightened a mouse, UNDER A CHAIR." The Late Dr. F.G. Sampson asked why all that CAT could report was that it CHASED A MOUSE? It went there to SEE THE QUEEN! People come to church looking for THE KING, & get distracted by US ...CHASING MICE! Nina & I recently returned from London. Didn't see the Queen, but we did see the WONDERS OF THE KING!

August 28 (originally posted in 2011)
Man Making Contest
John 1:3 ~ "All things were made by him;
and without him was not any thing made that was made."

John 15:5 ~ "I am the vine, ye are the branches:
He that abideth in me, and I in him,
the same bringeth forth much fruit:
for without me ye can do nothing."

Please PRAY for a vendor we met in London who has concluded that God is nonexistent, or POWERLESS! An apocryphal story is told of a group of "intelligent" men who decided they no longer needed God! They went to God & told him they could NOW do anything HE could. God said, "Can you MAKE A MAN from dirt?" They said, "Yes!" God said, "SHOW ME." ONE of the men got a shovel & began digging up dirt. God said, "STOP ...GET YOUR OWN DIRT!" Without God (Jesus IS GOD!), you can do NOTHING!

August 29
Shoes on the Wrong Foot
Psalm 119:133 ~ "Order my steps in thy word:
and let not any iniquity have dominion over me."

Years ago our 6-year-old came into the room with a smile on her face. She had put her shoes on ALL BY HERSELF! I said, "Great job sweetheart! Just ONE problem. They're on the WRONG FOOT!" GUESS what she did? She smiled, looked me in my eyes ...and CROSSED HER FEET! I laughed & said, "OK baby. NEW problem. YOU CAN'T WALK!" Sound familiar? Rather than FIX the problem, we try to make it LOOK RIGHT! Now UNCROSS YOUR FEET, and let GOD ORDER YOUR STEPS TODAY!

HE can FIX YOUR PROBLEMS!

August 30
Orderly Creation
Genesis 1:1 ~ "In the beginning,
God created the heavens and the earth."

Still need MORE proof that GOD is REAL, His WORD is TRUE & CREATION was NO ACCIDENT? Those who believe that this ORDERLY universe came into existence through an explosion (Big Bang) have not understood the WORD. That would be like pouring a box of ALPHABET CEREAL on the floor & the letters forming a STORY! CREATION is an ORDERLY story. God created water, then fish. Earth & AIR, then trees & animals. Heavens, then stars & birds. By the time He created man, ALL WE NEEDED was already here! :o)

August 31
Proverbs 31 Woman
Proverbs 31:10~ "Who can find a virtuous woman?
for her price is far above rubies."

The chapter NUMBER was appropriate on August 31, 2011, because that was the 31st anniversary of the BEST DAY of my life, OTHER THAN the day Christ saved me. That day marked 31 years since Nina & I got married – and now I'm looking forward to year 35!!!!!!!

Read all of Proverbs 31 & know that I have a "Proverbs 31 Woman!" She's ALL THAT, a BAG OF FISH & CHIPS & a SIDE SALAD! Verse 28 is my verse. Her children & husband get up in the morning & realize how BLESSED they are. I know because I'm in that crowd! LOVE YOU SWEETHEART! ♥♥♥♥♥♥♥

September

September 1
The Queen of Mean
1 John 3:17 ~ "But whoso hath this world's good,
and seeth his brother have need,
and shutteth up his bowels of compassion from him,
how dwelleth the love of God in him?"

Dubbed "The Queen of Mean" by New York tabloids, real estate tycoon Leona Helmsley died at 87 in 2007 & left around 8 BILLION DOLLARS to save DOGS! With all of the poverty & suffering in the world, she LACKED the Love of God (according to the verse). She did do SOME charitable things in her life, but a wise person once said, "Painting the pump on occasion doesn't change the quality of the WATER!" Trustees for the estate kept it from going TO THE DOGS! God WILL have the last laugh!

September 2
Speak the Truth IN LOVE!
Ephesians 4:15 ~ "But speaking the truth in love,
may grow up into him in all things,
which is the head, even Christ:"

Speak the truth IN LOVE! A new pastor had two wealthy UNGODLY brothers in his church. One brother died. The other promised the pastor enough money to build a NEW CHURCH, if he'd say that the dead BROTHER was a SAINT at his funeral. The pastor thought about it, & AGREED. The brother wrote the church a large check. At the eulogy the pastor said, "We're here to eulogize an UNGODLY SINNER. He was UNFAITHFUL to his wife & ABUSED his children. But compared to his brother, HE WAS A SAINT!"

September 3 (originally posted in 2011)
Happy Birthday, Mother Mamie George
Psalm 14:1~ "The fool hath said in his heart, 'There is no God.'
They are corrupt, they have done abominable works,
there is none that doeth good."

Psalm 53:1 ~ "The fool hath said in his heart, 'There is no God.'
Corrupt are they, and have done abominable iniquity:
there is none that doeth good."

On this day in 2011 I spent the afternoon at the birthday party of one of the MOTHERS at our church. On that Saturday, Mother Mamie George made 100 YEARS OLD! This isn't the type of post that might get great response, but it's a WONDERFUL story for ME! All she talked about was Faith, Family & Friends. That's why I chose these verses that say, "The FOOL has said in his heart, there is NO GOD..." May I ask you a question? Do you know any 100-YEAR-OLD FOOLS?

September 4
An Extreme Home Makeover, Revisited
Matthew 12:43-45 ~ "When the unclean spirit is gone out of a man,
he walketh through dry places, seeking rest, and findeth none.
Then he saith, 'I will return into my house from whence I came out';
and when he is come, he findeth it empty, swept, and garnished.
Then goeth he, and taketh with himself
seven other spirits more wicked than himself,
and they enter in and dwell there:
and the last state of that man is worse than the first.
Even so shall it be also unto this wicked generation."

Have you ever noticed how when a person tries to clean him or herself up, it's usually TEMPORARY and it leaves them STILL feeling EMPTY? In this passage, when the DEMON left the man's body, he (the demon) got RESTLESS! Anyone who gets rid of the bad stuff in their lives should be OK, RIGHT? The problem is that once that stuff is GONE, it has to be REPLACED WITH SOMETHING! An empty house is dangerous. If you invite a "higher power" into your life, you open the door to ANY "god" that wants to move in. That's what happened to the man in this scripture. When the demon that had left him could FIND NO PEACE, he (the demon) FOUND some friends and went BACK into the man that DID NOT replace the demon with SOMETHING LASTING! The house (man's body) was cleaned and decorated (verse 44), but those things DON'T LAST! When JESUS moves into your life, all rooms will be FULL! The promises and peace HE BRINGS, will be FOREVER! You can call it, "AN EXTREME HOME MAKEOVER!" (John 10:10; Psalm 16:11)

September 5
The God of Abraham, Isaac, and Jacob
Exodus 3:6 ~ "Moreover he said, I am the God of thy father,
the God of Abraham, the God of Isaac, and the God of Jacob.
And Moses hid his face; for he was afraid to look upon God."

Why does God call HIMSELF the God of Abraham, Isaac & Jacob? Why not Abraham, Isaac & Israel since ISRAEL & JACOB are the SAME PERSON (Genesis 32:27-28)? The name ISRAEL means "Prince with God" or a "God-governed man." JACOB means "heel grabber, supplanter or a trickster", which is what JACOB WAS (Genesis 25:26)! So why does GOD identify Himself with Jacob? It's simple, God still loves even the power grabbers & tricksters. FAITH will change that. Any JACOB'S out there? God wants to be the GOD of ALL of us, REALLY!

September 6
Beautiful Letters and Pretty Pictures
Psalm 119:18~ "Open thou mine eyes,
that I may behold wondrous things out of thy law."

A social worker in a Southern town was headed home after a long days work. She saw a run-down shack & stopped to see who lived there. She worked her way past the 3 broken steps & knocked on the front door. An elderly woman answered the door & invited her in. She was horrified by the old lady's living conditions. She sat down on a worn out couch & asked the old lady if she lived there alone. She said yes. The worker asked, "Do you have family?" "Yes. I have a son who is a JUDGE in New York. I scrubbed & cleaned houses to put him through school." The worker replied, "And he let's you live like this?" The old lady said, "Well, he DOES send me BEAUTIFUL LETTERS & PRETTY PICTURES!" The worker asked, "May I see some of those Beautiful Letters?" The lady gave her one from a broken table. The social worker started reading & tears ran down her face. "May I see some of the Pretty Pictures?" The old lady led her to the 1 small bedroom in the house & POINTED TO THE WALLS. The worker understood what happened. The son wrote LETTERS during the few months he had been gone, telling his mother how much he loved & appreciated her for what she had done for him, and that he was still searching for a reputable contractor to fix the house. She called them "Beautiful Letters". He sent money for her to live on, but because he didn't want anyone to take advantage of his poorly educated mother, he NEVER sent her cash. The mother had mixed water & flour to make a glue, & pasted over $90,000 worth of Bonds & Certificates over the cracks in her bedroom walls. She didn't know. She called them ...PRETTY PICTURES! God has sent us some Beautiful Letters & Pretty Pictures! 66 to be exact. They're in His Word. You better RECOGNIZE! :o)

September 7
LISTEN TO YOUR CHILDREN!!!!
Psalm 8:2 ~ "Out of the mouth of babes and sucklings
hast thou ordained strength because of thine enemies,
that thou mightest still the enemy and the avenger."

I know that our ancestors taught us that children should be SEEN & NOT HEARD! Now think about how YOU felt as a child when you were treated like that. Now I'm NOT saying that children should NOT have MANNERS. Grown folks' business always remains GROWN FOLKS' BUSINESS! :o) I AM saying, DON'T treat children like "gum on your shoe" when they ask you questions or want to talk. A preacher who lived across the street from our church, loved to work on old cars. While underneath his car one day, the neighborhood kids called him repeatedly. He was too busy to respond, and hoped they'd go away. They kept calling. He came out from under the car to tell them to LEAVE HIM ALONE while he was working. The car came CRASHING DOWN off of the crates he had it propped up on! ~ LISTENING TO YOUR CHILDREN just might save your life, or you might LEARN SOMETHING!

September 8
Happy Birthday, KJV
Matthew 19:14 ~ "But Jesus said, Suffer little children,
and forbid them not, to come unto me:
for of such is the kingdom of heaven."

I've heard people who believe that you DON'T have a real Bible if you don't have the King James Version. I have many other versions that I use, especially in study. Remember that the Word of God was not inspired IN ENGLISH! Many words don't mean the same, even in English, as they did 404 years ago. In the verse before us, SUFFER meant to "allow" or "permit" in 1611 English. Some people even today act like it's a PAINFUL thing for children to come to Christ. So if you have a version that says, "Permit little children to come unto me...", you have an accurate translation of the verse! Christopher Wren was the great English architect who built over 50 of

England's greatest cathedrals. He began building his most famous work, St. Paul's Cathedral (Profile picture) in London around 1675. He finished in 1710. When Queen Anne went into the beautiful structure for the first time, she said to Wren, "This is AWFUL!!!" How could she INSULT such a world renown architect? SHE DIDN'T! In 1710 AWFUL meant "FILLED WITH AWE", or "AWE INSPIRING!" She simply said, "This FILLS ME WITH AWE!!!" Now, you have God's permission to get a faithful and readable version of the Word of God. :o)

September 9
Chandelier – More Light
Habakkuk 2:2 ~ "And the Lord answered me, and said,
Write the vision, and make it plain upon tables,
that he may run that readeth it."

A new pastor noticed that the sanctuary in the church had only ONE light in the ceiling. He asked a deacon to order a CHANDELIER for the church. The deacon agreed. Weeks passed & NO chandelier. The pastor asked the deacon what happened. He said, "Pastor, we tried to order it but no one could SPELL it. Then we realized that no one knew how to PLAY ONE. Then the board decided that what this church needed more than a chandelier, is MORE LIGHT!" Whatever your vision is, write it down and make it PLAIN!

September 10
Father Was in the Crib
Daniel 3:24-25 ~ "Then Nebuchadnezzar the king was astonished, and rose
up in haste, and spake, and said unto his counsellors,
'Did not we cast three men bound into the midst of the fire?'
They answered and said unto the king, 'True, O king.'
He answered and said, Lo, I see four men loose,
walking in the midst of the fire, and they have no hurt;
and the form of the fourth is like the Son of God.' "

I read about a grandfather who LOVED comforting his infant grandson. Whenever the boy would cry, his grandfather would get him out of the crib and hold him until he calmed down. The man's daughter (the child's mother), asked her father not to do that. She said, "He needs to learn to calm down on his own. He needs to know that we CAN'T BE THERE ALL THE TIME!" The father agreed he would NOT take the child of his crib again. Hours later the baby started crying. After a few minutes the crying stopped. The mother got angry because she knew her father had broken his word. When she went in the child's room, she broke down CRYING! Her FATHER was IN THE CRIB with the baby! If GOD doesn't get you out of a situation, He'll get IN IT WITH YOU, like He did with those THREE HEBREWS in the fiery furnace!

September 11
My Prayer for 9/11
Psalm 91:1 ~ "He that dwelleth in the secret place of the Most High
shall abide under the shadow of the Almighty."

My prayer for 9/11 is Psalm 91:1. I pray that we dwell undercover in the WITNESS PROTECTION PROGRAM of the ALMIGHTY GOD! If we're God's witnesses, we can claim this as part of the "Benefits Package"! If you're worried about terrorists, read verses 5-11! Those of you who still believe the verses are for Israel, God says "WE ARE" the Israel of God (Galatians 6:16). Paul also says that Christ has REDEEMED us from the CURSE of the Law, NOT THE PROMISES (Galatians 3:13)!

September 12
Make Her Happy for ONE YEAR!
Deuteronomy 24:5 ~ "When a man hath taken a new wife,
he shall not go out to war,
neither shall he be charged with any business:
but he shall be free at home one year,
and shall cheer up his wife which he hath taken."

The Bible says that ALL SCRIPTURE is "God-Breathed" and is beneficial and valuable…(2 Timothy 3:16). Deuteronomy 24:5 is a verse that can change your marriage, IF YOU DO WHAT IT SAYS! If you are not yet married, PREPARE to do this. If you have been married for a while, it's NOT TOO LATE to start …MEN! The onus (burden, responsibility) of this verse falls squarely on the HUSBAND or HUSBAND-TO-BE. Whenever I teach this verse in a marriage class, the MEN will inevitably ask me, "…but what do WE get out of it?" Sincere, but selfish question IF we intend to be LEADERS in our home. Leadership requires sacrifice, but the reward will be immeasurable! Remember, if you are already married, start yesterday!

Here's what the verse says. The verse says that when a man takes a wife, DO NOT ENLIST (or in those days he couldn't be drafted) in military service for ONE YEAR! The verse also says that the man is NOT TO TAKE any business interest, activities or investments (outside of the job needed to take care of his family). Now here's the shouting point for you ladies, (and men if you have the foresight to see where this can lead). The verse teaches that while you men are at home, spend 365 days (or 366) making your lady HAPPY or bringing her JOY! MEN, can you imagine what type of wife you will have in one year if you spend EVERY waking moment for the next 365 days figuring out ways to make her happy? At the end of one year you'll have a very happy wife, (unless you have a FOOL for a wife), and you will NOT have to ask the question "What do I get out of it?" Remember for ONE YEAR it's NOT about you, it's about HER! You also will have developed a HABIT of making & keeping her happy. Trust me, if SHE'S HAPPY ...YOU'LL BE HAPPY! :o)

September 13
Two BADLY BURNED Hands

John 20:24-29 ~ "But Thomas, one of the twelve,
called Didymus, was not with them when Jesus came.
The other disciples therefore said unto him,
'We have seen the Lord.' But he said unto them,
'Except I shall see in his hands the print of the nails,
and put my finger into the print of the nails,
and thrust my hand into his side, I will not believe.'
And after eight days again his disciples were within,
and Thomas with them: then came Jesus, the doors being shut,
and stood in the midst, and said, Peace be unto you.
Then saith he to Thomas, Reach hither thy finger,
and behold my hands; and reach hither thy hand,
and thrust it into my side: and be not faithless, but believing.
And Thomas answered and said unto him, My Lord and my God.
Jesus saith unto him, Thomas, because thou hast seen me,
thou hast believed: blessed are they that have not seen,
and yet have believed."

Thomas was the disciple who was NOT PRESENT when Jesus appeared to the other disciples after HIS (Jesus') resurrection. That's why Thomas needed PHYSICAL PROOF when he saw the resurrected Christ! ~ A man was walking by a burning house one day when he noticed a little boy and a little girl screaming from a second floor window in the burning building. As bystanders watched in horror, the man rushed into the house and came out a few minutes later with the children safe and sound in his arms. His hands had been BADLY BURNED. Unfortunately the parents of the children perished in the fire by the time firefighters arrived. When television station personnel at the scene began to ask how the children made it out safely, bystanders told of the mysterious man. "Where is he so we can interview him?" they asked. The man was nowhere to be found. They asked the children if the man was a relative? The children said they had NEVER seen him before. The children became wards of the state until relatives, who would care for them, could be found. No one came forward. The case and the fire were ran on television and in the local newspapers for weeks.

A court date was set for the claiming of the children. At the hearing, the judge ask a CROWDED courthouse if there were any relatives who would be willing to take the children and raise them. NO ONE STOOD! He asked several more times and told the court he did NOT want to send these children to foster care. If that happened, he said, there was a possibility they could be split up. He asked one last time. Someone stood up in the back of the courtroom. The judge asked, "Are you a relative?" He said, "No your honor." "Do you KNOW these children personally?", the judge asked. "No, your honor," the man said. "Then what gives you the RIGHT to claim these children?" The man, who had the attention of the entire courtroom at this time, simply lifted high in the air ...TWO BADLY BURNED HANDS!!! Everyone who had heard the story KNEW, he was the SAVIOR of those kids!

If you EVER wonder what gives JESUS the right to claim you as HIS OWN (1 Corinthians 6:19-20), I give you exhibits A & B ...HIS LEFT and RIGHT HAND! Oh, while you're at it ...check out His side, His forehead and His FEET! :o)

September 14
God KNOWS How You Feel

Hebrews 4:14-16 ~ "Seeing then that we have a great high priest,
that is passed into the heavens, Jesus the Son of God,
let us hold fast our profession.
For we have not an high priest which cannot be touched
with the feeling of our infirmities;
but was in all points tempted like as we are, yet without sin.
Let us therefore come boldly unto the throne of grace,
that we may obtain mercy, and find grace to help in time of need."

Have you ever felt like you were PRAYING to a God who was so MIGHTY & POWERFUL that He could NOT RELATE to what you were going through? You can be HONEST because GOD already knows! Now read the verses very carefully. They teach that our High Priest JESUS (Who IS GOD, 2nd Person in the Godhead - John 1:1;14; 10:30; Acts 20:28; Colossians 2:9), became flesh and was tempted (and/or tested) in EVERY WAY that we have been!!! JESUS has been through what we have been through and done many of the things we do as humans. He ate, slept, cried, got tired, was lied on, felt pain, felt betrayal, experienced jealousy and backbiting, yet HE NEVER SINNED. HE PASSED every test (verse 15)!

Now the next time you are burdened by something that's NOT your fault or tempted by something that IS, approach God freely in prayer and say, "Lord, you KNOW how I feel because you've BEEN THERE, DONE THAT, got the T-Shirt and the HAT! Now I NEED your mercy, your grace, and your help with what I'm going through (verse 16)!" After that, continue to DWELL in the ONLY PERFECT ONE. That's what and who, makes US PERFECT! :o)

September 15
As Far as the East Is from the West
Psalm 103:12 ~ "As far as the EAST is from the WEST, so far hath he removed our transgressions from us."

When Jesus took away your sins, did you ever stop to wonder if He just dumped them around the corner, and that you might come across them again somewhere in the future? Look at the verse. If I was David, I would have covered ALL of my bases and said, "As far as the EAST is from the WEST and the NORTH is from the SOUTH, so far hath he removed our transgressions from us." I'm so glad David DID NOT say that God has removed our transgressions as far as the NORTH is from the SOUTH. If you run your fingers NORTH on a globe, you can only go so far until you reach the apex we call the NORTH POLE. Then you change directions and start moving South, until you reach the SOUTH POLE. If you keep moving, you'll automatically change directions and start traveling NORTH AGAIN! There is a defined distance between NORTH and SOUTH. You can only go so far before NORTH meets up with SOUTH! But start moving EAST around the globe. You will NEVER run into WEST. If you do an about face and turn around, you will be traveling WEST and NEVER run into EAST! EAST and WEST NEVER MEET!!! When GOD removes our sins as far as the EAST is from the WEST, He's saying that we will NEVER ...run into them again! Now excuse me while I PRAISE HIM! :o)

September 16
Old Lady's House on the Hill
Proverbs 13:22~ "A good man leaveth an inheritance
to his children's children:
and the wealth of the sinner is laid up for the just."

An old lady worked about 35 years for a wealthy family. She lived in their home, and worked as a house cleaner and a cook. She had been a loyal employee until one day she was told by her boss that her services were no longer needed. She was UNCEREMONIOUSLY handed her dismissal papers with NO EXPLANATION, and told she would have to find somewhere else to live. She called a cab. The taxi driver knew her because he had regularly taken her to the market for her former employer. He noticed she didn't have her personal shopping cart, and asked why. She told the driver that she had been fired, and was told that she would have to leave the home. The driver knew her to be a great lady and asked her where she was going to live. She told him, "Just drive, and I'll tell you where to let me off. I have enough to pay you." The taxi driver started to drive.

After a few miles, the elderly lady said, "Turn right here." The driver made a right turn and went several more miles. They lady said, "At the next stop sign, make a left and go up the hill. When he got to top of the hill, she told him to stop. He looked out of his driver-side window and his heart sank. There was an OLD BARN that was barely standing! As the lady reached in her purse to pay the fare he said, "I can't take your money, and I'm not going to leave you here to live in a broken down barn!" She said, "You're looking out of the wrong window. I'm going to the OTHER SIDE of the street!" When he looked to his right, his jaw dropped! Sitting back about a hundred yards from the street was one of the most MAGNIFICENT HOUSES he had ever seen. He said, "WOW! You've got a NEW JOB already?" She started laughing and said to the driver, "I knew this day would come sooner or later. My former boss was not a nice man to work for. But he paid well. You've been driving on MY PROPERTY for the last 2 miles. I paid down on it 35 years ago when I started my last job. I had contractors start the house not long after that. Since I was living and eating rent free, my entire check went to paying off the house. Now I have something to leave my children and grandchildren who live in another state. Everything you see, I OWN free and clear …courtesy of my last employer!"

Once again - GOD CAN use your enemies to BLESS YOU, and the wealth of the sinner is INDEED stored up for the RIGHTEOUS! If you are God's child …that would be YOU!

September 17
In Deep Water
Psalm 107:23-24 ~ ""'They that go down to the sea in ships,
that do business in great waters;☐
☐These see the works of the LORD, and his wonders in the deep."

Years – no – DECADES ago I went as a young adult with some friends to the Russian River. I bragged all the way there about how well I could swim. In reality, I took swimming lessons in high school because it was a requirement to graduate. I swam just well enough to pass. When we got to the river, one of my male friends put me to the test. He stripped down to his swim suit and swam ACROSS the Russian River. When he got to the bank on the OTHER SIDE, he MOTIONED for me to swim across! Yeah, RIGHT!!! I don't remember what LIES I told that day to the mixed group that was on the shore with me. Needless to say, I didn't step foot in that water. He started swimming back toward us, but disappeared somewhere in the middle of the river. I thought to myself, "I can't sit here and do nothing!" I also had on my swimming trunks under my clothes. I looked up and said, "Lord, PLEASE don't make me go out into this water today and PROVE what a weak swimmer I am!" About that time, my friend's head popped up above the water and he returned safely to our side. (Please be patient, GOD is not through with me yet)!

We decided to rent a canoe and paddle down the river. There were three of us young men in the canoe. This was back in the day, before life-jackets were a requirement. We chose not to rent them. After all, my friends were strong swimmers and I didn't want to look bad in front of my boys. Once in the canoe and on the water, one of the guys decided to horse around and jump into the river. When he tried to get back into the canoe, he TIPPED IT OVER, and there I was IN DEEP WATER! Immediately, what I had learned in high school began to kick in automatically. I started my swimming stroke. There WAS a problem. Panic had set in and I had my eyes closed. I didn't know if I was swimming across or lengthwise the river! After a few minutes I opened my eyes, and I was STILL in the middle of the river! I felt that THIS WAS IT! The END of my life. With one last stroke, my hand hit something just below the surface of the water. It felt like a ROCK. I held on for dear life, then calmed down and got my bearings. I then proceeded to swim safely back across the river to the shore.

Now those of you familiar with the Russian River in California, know that there are NO ROCKS in the middle of it near the surface. At least not where I was! So what was it? I KNOW what I felt. It was a rock. I believe that ROCK ...was JESUS! When God drops you in DEEP WATER (any overwhelming situation), everything you have learned about FAITH will began to kick in automatically. You will see The WONDERS of God in the deep as He provides a ROCK for you to get your bearings, and then reminds you of the ABILITY he has placed in you for such a time! Or He just might take over all together. Just be VERY SURE while you're in DEEP WATER, that your ANCHOR HOLDS ...and grips the SOLID ROCK!!!

P.S. My friends had made it back to the boat and flipped it right-side-up. They were sitting in the canoe, LAUGHING AT ME! :o)

September 18
LET HIM IN!
Revelation 3:20 ~ "Behold, I stand at the door, and knock:
if any man hear my voice, and open the door,
I will come in to him, and will sup with him, and he with me."

1 Corinthians 6:19-20~ "What? know ye not that your body
is the temple of the Holy Ghost which is in you,
which ye have of God, and ye are not your own?
For ye are bought with a price: therefore glorify God in your body,
and in your spirit, which are God's."

There is an apocryphal story of a little boy who tried to get into a large suburban church one Sunday. Because of how he dressed and smelled, an usher met him at the door and asked him what he wanted. "I want to come to YOUR church today. I've heard that this church has great preaching and a wonderful choir." The usher said to the little boy, "Well perhaps you would feel more COMFORTABLE and AT HOME at one of the INNER-CITY churches. They have a lot of little boys just like you." The usher then REFUSED to let the little boy into the church. He started walking away with tears in his eyes.

The story goes that while walking, JESUS THE CHRIST HIMSELF appeared to the little boy and asked him what was the matter. The child said, "I went to that church down the street and they told me to go to ANOTHER church." JESUS SAID to the little boy, "Don't feel ashamed. I was at that church earlier myself ...and they WOULDN'T LET ME IN EITHER!!!"

It's a SAD day when JESUS CAN'T get into His OWN HOUSE. Does that sound like any churches YOU KNOW? Let HIM into your heart today. He doesn't need a wooden and concrete structure. YOUR BODY is the SANCTUARY of the Holy Spirit!

September 19
A Man, a Dog, and a Baby

2 Corinthians 5:7 ~ "Purge out therefore the old leaven,
that ye may be a new lump, as ye are unleavened.
For even Christ our passover is sacrificed for us."

Hebrews 11:1~ "Now faith is the evidence of things hoped for,
the evidence of things not seen."

A man who lived on a country farm was home ALONE taking care of his infant baby who was in her crib sleeping. He got an emergency telephone call that he figured would take him no longer than an hour to deal with. He didn't want to wake the baby. Just then his hunting dog came through the "doggie door" in the back of the house. He decided that the baby would be OK if she slept in her crib for another hour. He left his dog on the porch to scare anyone off who might come while he was gone. He left and RETURNED in about an hour.

To his HORROR, the dog was on the porch with BLOOD all over it's face. The man quickly rushed into the house and straight to his bedroom where the baby's crib was. The crib had been tipped over, there was NO SIGN of his daughter and there was a trail of BLOOD leading through the "doggie door" and into the WOODS in the back of the house. The man went CRAZY. He put 2 + 2 together and concluded that the dog had KILLED the child and dragged her little body into the woods like she was a bone. He ran to his closet, got his shotgun and fired several shots into what had been up to that time, a LOYAL DOG! The man picked up the telephone to call the sheriff and tell him that he had killed his dog, who had killed his daughter. As he picked up the phone, he heard A BABY CRY! It was coming from HIS BEDROOM. He dropped then phone and ran to his bedroom. His baby daughter was crawling out from under the man's bed, CRYING but UNHARMED! That's when he pick his baby girl up in his arms and sat down on the edge of the bed. He took a little more time to figure out what had happened. With his child in his arms, he followed the BLOOD trail out of the back door and a few yards into the woods. There, to his surprise, was a DEAD WOLF with a mortal wound to its throat! Now he knows what happened. The wolf had gotten into the house the same way the dog did. The dog followed the wolf into the man's room where the child was sleeping. The wolf tried to attack the child, tipping over the crib. The dog attacked the wolf and bit it in the neck. The WOUNDED WOLF made it out the "doggie door" and into the woods in the back of the house, WHERE IT DIED! The man had KILLED the one who had PROTECTED his daughter!

How many of us have jumped to conclusions, and our actions have caused harm to innocent people? THINK before you act! Then PRAY and TRUST GOD with EVERY situation. Things aren't always as they seem. That's why we walk by FAITH ...NOT BY SIGHT!!!

September 20
Forgiveness, and Divorce

Luke 23:34~ "Then said Jesus, Father, forgive them;
for they know not what they do.
And they parted his raiment, and cast lots."

1 Corinthians 7:11-13 ~ "But and if she depart,
let her remain unmarried or be reconciled to her husband:
and let not the husband put away his wife.
But to the rest speak I, not the Lord:
If any brother hath a wife that believeth not,
and she be pleased to dwell with him, let him not put her away.
And the woman which hath an husband that believeth not,
and if he be pleased to dwell with her, let her not leave him."

I'm going to try to set at least TWO people free with an expanded version of something I have shared before. If you take the time to read this entire post, you will either be made free or without excuse. One of the hardest things for people (including Christians) to do is FORGIVE! Whenever I tell someone that they need to forgive a person, I hear "...But Pastor, they DON"T DESERVE IT!" Guess what? It wouldn't be "forgiveness" if they deserved it! Neither we, nor the people who nailed Jesus to the cross deserve forgiveness. Yet there JESUS IS hanging on Calvary's cross in Luke 23:34 and the first words out of His mouth are "Father, FORGIVE THEM...!" One day I was reading about marriage & divorce when a QUESTION walk up UNINVITED and sat down next to me. It asked me: What do the words "FORGIVE" & "DIVORCE" have in common? In the New Testament they are the SAME WORD, the Greek word "af-ee'-ay-mee."

If you have a King James Bible, 1 Corinthians 7 uses the EXACT same word for "put away", "put away", and "leave" in verses 11, 12, & 13 when describing DIVORCE. The connection? BOTH words (forgive and divorce) mean to "SEND AWAY" or "GET RID OF". Here comes your freedom. In DIVORCE, you get rid of the PERSON & hold on to the GRUDGE. In FORGIVENESS, you get rid of the GRUDGE & hold on to the PERSON! THANK YOU LORD for getting rid of my SIN, and holding on to ME! ~ There is a wall photo by Johnny Hughes on my friend Rodrick Bates' page with these words: "Holding a grudge is letting someone live RENT-FREE in your head!" Don't give ANYONE that kind of power in your life! :o)

September 21
Follow, Chase, Pursue, Hunt Down
Psalm 23:6 ~ "Surely goodness and mercy shall follow me,
all the days of my life,
and I will dwell in the house of the Lord forever."

Every now and then I have to repost something I have posted previously because it weighs on my spirit. Not only that, I feel that SOMEONE needs to hear this today. The verse says "Surely goodness and mercy shall FOLLOW me ALL the days of my life..." The Hebrew word for "FOLLOW" means to pursue, chase, hunt. It's the SAME word used in 1 Samuel 26:20 of a man hunting a game bird in the mountains. Now read Psalm 23:6 again. "Surely goodness and mercy shall HUNT ME DOWN, all the days of my life..." Anyone ever had God's Goodness CHASE after you? Did Mercy HUNT YOU DOWN in the crack house, the gambling shack, the corner, the alley, despair, hopelessness? Because of what JESUS CHRIST did on Calvary, Goodness & Mercy will FIND YOU in places where mother, father, friends, family and even some CHRISTIANS WON'T GO! "ALL THE DAYS OF ..." aah, you can shout HERE!

September 22
Cockroach Churches
Jeremiah 3:15~ "And I will give you pastors according to mine heart,
which shall feed you with knowledge and understanding."

I have a message for all COCKROACH CHURCHES! A cockroach can live for sometime after its HEAD has been CUT OFF! It eventually dies from STARVATION. NO HEAD, CAN'T EAT! If your church has been without a PASTOR for some time, pray for one before you STARVE TO DEATH! (P.S. A lobster and a cockroach are in the same family. Think of a lobster as a cockroach on STEROIDS! ENJOY your dinner.)

September 23
Step Away from the Patient
Galatians 6:1~ "Brethren, if a man be overtaken in a fault,
ye which are spiritual, restore such an one in the spirit of meekness;

considering thyself, lest thou also be tempted."

I have a response to the recent FB criticism & gossip about saints who SEEM to have fallen in sin. When there's a horrific accident & someone is lying hurt on the ground, the first thing we do is to move the crowd back! Why? To allow room for those who know what they're doing to attend to the hurt! Now read Galatians 6:1. You who are spiritual, RESTORE THEM. The rest of you...STEP AWAY FROM THE PATIENT!!!

September 24
Street Lights and Tiffany Lamps
Matthew 5:16 ~ "Let your light so shine before men,
that they may see your good works,
and glorify your Father which is in heaven."

Dr. Gregory pointed out to a group of us in England an important difference between TIFFANY lamps & street lights. Tiffany lamps are made of pieces of stained cut glass. They were purchased by the wealthy to put in the middle of a table & draw attention to THEMSELVES! No one ever talks about how beautiful the street lights are, but they continue to light the way for travelers everywhere. What type of LIGHT ARE YOU? One that draws attention to itself, or points the way to Jesus?

September 25
How to Read Psalm 121:1-2
Psalm 121:1-2 ~ "I will lift up mine eyes unto the hills,
from whence cometh my help.
My help cometh from the Lord, which made heaven and earth.

Nina & I saw a good movie some years ago entitled "The Help." Am I the only one who noticed that most of the love, compassion, parenting, encouragement, wisdom, patience, etc. in that movie CAME from THE HELP? Now may I quote Psalm 121:1-2 as God intended? "I will lift up mine eyes unto the hills (Period). WHERE does MY HELP come from (Question mark)? MY HELP cometh from the LORD, which made heaven and earth!" When NO ONE ELSE WILL HELP YOU, He's a very PRESENT HELP! ~ Psalm 46:1

September 26
The Blood of Jesus KEEPS ON CLEANSING
1 John 1:7 ~ "But if we walk in the light, as he is in the light,
we have fellowship one with another,
and the blood of Jesus Christ his Son cleanseth us from all sin."

How many sins had YOU committed when Jesus died? ZERO! YOU WEREN'T HERE YET! If you're God's child, ALL of your SINS were FUTURE, yet STILL covered by the Blood of Jesus. That is the meaning of the PRESENT (Continuous) TENSE of the verb in 1 John 1:7, "...the blood of Jesus KEEPS ON CLEANSING...!" You are ALREADY forgiven if & when you cuss Pookie out NEXT MONTH (and I pray you don't)! Just apologize to GOD ...& POOKIE! Oh, & don't make sin A HABIT. :o)

September 27
Get the Right Stuff for Your Salad
1 Corinthians 2:1-5 ~ "And I, brethren, when I came to you, came not with excellency of speech or of wisdom, declaring unto you the testimony of
God.
For I determined not to know any thing among you,
save Jesus Christ, and him crucified.
And I was with you in weakness,
and in fear, and in much trembling.
And my speech and my preaching
was not with enticing words of man's wisdom,
but in demonstration of the Spirit and of power:
That your faith should not stand in the wisdom of men,
but in the power of God."

Paul was a VERY educated man, yet he chose to keep things plain & simple. Have you ever sat under teachers and/or preachers who knew their stuff, but left you more confused than when you sat down? Dr. Gregory put it like this, "If I invite you to my house for a summer salad from my personal garden; you want to see the tomatoes, lettuce & cucumbers ...NOT the SHOVEL, the GLOVES & the BUG SPRAY!!!" I WON'T apologize for trying to keep things simple! :o)

September 28
NO CONDEMNATION
Romans 8:33-39 ~ "Who shall lay any thing

to the charge of God's elect? It is God that justifieth.
Who is he that condemneth? It is Christ that died, yea rather,
that is risen again, who is even at the right hand of God,
who also maketh intercession for us.
Who shall separate us from the love of Christ?
shall tribulation, or distress, or persecution, or famine,
or nakedness, or peril, or sword?
As it is written, For thy sake we are killed all the day long;
we are accounted as sheep for the slaughter.
Nay, in all these things we are more than conquerors
through him that loved us.
For I am persuaded, that neither death, nor life, nor angels,
nor principalities, nor powers, nor things present,
nor things to come,
Nor height, nor depth, nor any other creature,
shall be able to separate us from the love of God,
which is in Christ Jesus our Lord."

I'm going to make this quick & painless for ALL CHRISTIANS. The verses teach that the ONLY ONE who can CONDEMN US (JESUS), is SITTING at the right hand of the Father ON BEHALF OF US, so that NOTHING can come between or SEPARATE US from the LOVE OF CHRIST! Now read that long list in those verses and you too will come to the conclusion that NOTHING, not even YOU, can separate YOU from God's LOVE! We LOVE Him because HE FIRST loved US! ~ 1 John 4:19. Excuse me a moment …HALLELUJAH!

September 29 (originally posted in 2011)
Facebook Payment Hoax
Matthew 7:15 ~ "Beware of false prophets,
which come to you in sheep's clothing,
but inwardly they are ravening wolves."

LISTEN, LISTEN, LISTEN!!! I'd like to think that those who visit this page THINK! I feel the need for a PUBLIC SERVICE ANNOUNCEMENT. I have tried to teach you all how to recognize a PHONY CHRIST when you see one. I pray that you would do the same with a PHONY MESSAGE! FACEBOOK IS NOT going to start charging for services!!!!!!!! Think about it!!! Why didn't they tell ALL OF US DIRECTLY? They have the POWER TO DO SO. I have been in contact with their page and there is a CHAIN LETTER circulating that is a HOAX. When I first saw it, I KNEW it was

NOT TRUE even before I checked! Learn to recognize PHONY when you see it! Do you KNOW how many accounts Facebook would lose if they did that overnight? They DON'T WORK LIKE THAT, PEOPLE! And if you could get the account for free just by COPYING something, what good would charging do them? Someone is out there LAUGHING at some of you right now. Be thankful they didn't ask for and receive VITAL INFORMATION from you to "keep your account free"! NOW CALM DOWN and STOP copying that craziness to your pages. I LOVE YOU!!! :o)

September 30
Ministers of the Mystery
Ephesians 3:1-8 ~ "For this cause I Paul,
the prisoner of Jesus Christ for you Gentiles,
If ye have heard of the dispensation of the grace of God
which is given me to you-ward:
How that by revelation he made known unto me the mystery;
(as I wrote afore in few words,Whereby, when ye read,
ye may understand my knowledge in the mystery of Christ)
Which in other ages was not made known unto the sons of men,
as it is now revealed unto his holy apostles and prophets by the Spirit;
That the Gentiles should be fellowheirs, and of the same body,
and partakers of his promise in Christ by the gospel:
Whereof I was made a minister, according to the gift of the grace of God
given unto me by the effectual working of his power.
Unto me, who am less than the least of all saints, is this grace given,
that I should preach among the Gentiles the unsearchable riches of Christ."

Pastor Van Lucas, who is a Son of Olivet, preached for us yesterday afternoon. He blessed us with a marvelous message! He told us that we are MINISTERS OF THE MYSTERY, then proceeded to share how another preacher explained that MYSTERY to a group of children. He had us visualize an illustration. Picture this: a glove laying down on the pulpit next to his Bible. Pastor Lucas SPEAKS to the glove. "Glove, pick up that Bible!" Nothing happens. He talks to the glove again, "GLOVE, I said PICK UP THE BIBLE!" Again nothing happens. Then he puts his HAND INSIDE THE GLOVE and says, "GLOVE, pick up the Bible!" Now the GLOVE has no problem picking it up because of the HAND inside of it. The kids say to the preacher, "Aw, there's NOTHING SPECIAL about that. The preacher says, "But THAT'S the MYSTERY, CHRIST INSIDE of us!!!" Only THEN can we become MINISTERS of the UNSEARCHABLE riches of Christ! CHRIST INSIDE of us, empowers us to do the work of the Kingdom of

God. Are YOU a minister of the MYSTERY? :o)

October

October 1
Dora the Explorer
John 14:6 - "Jesus said to him (Thomas),
'I am the way, and the truth, and the life.
No one comes to the Father except through me.'"

Our seven-year-old girl has taught us to be unselfish! She has invited an Hispanic girl into our home who has been a part of the family for almost seven years! Up until a little while ago, this girl laid on our daughter's bed, she sat on the floor in her bedroom, she stood in the corner of the room all day long and stays in the bathroom 24/7. Her name is "Dora The Explorer!" She's on the bed spreads, the garbage cans, the rug, the tooth brush & the tooth paste! DORA is a cartoon character (Profile picture) with a SINGING MAP in her back pack? Whenever Dora gets ready for an adventure, she consults her map. She pulls it out of her back pack and the map begins to sing:"If there's a place you gotta go, I'm the one you need to know, I'm the map... If there's a place you got to get, I can get you there I bet, I'm the map, I'm the map, I'm the map, I'm the map, I'm the map!"

Well, JESUS said the same thing in JOHN 14:6! If you need help with your problems He said, I'm the map. Trouble in school, I'm the map. Are your finances funny? I'm the map! Boss acting crazy? Jesus is the map! Problems with your children, church, health, marriage, relationships etc.? JESUS says, "I'm THE MAP, I'm THE MAP, I'm THE MAP, I'm THE MAP, I'm THE MAP!!!"

October 2
Can't Give What You Don't Have
2 Timothy 1:5 ~ "I am reminded of your sincere faith,
a faith that dwelt FIRST in your grandmother Lois and your mother Eunice
and now, I am sure, dwells in you as well." (ESV)

I was privileged to preach some years ago at the 90th Birthday Celebration of Mother Floydzell Banks. This sainted mother of nine (9) helped raise me! One of the sons told me that her children, grand-children, great grand-children and great great grand-child total 150+ !

I spoke from the verse up above. Paul tells Timothy, his son in the

150

ministry, that he sees an "non-hypocritical" faith in Timothy that he FIRST saw in Timothy's grandmother Lois and his mother Eunice! In other words, they instilled in young Timothy what was ALREADY in themselves! Mothers teach us what THEY KNOW about life and faith. Whenever I take an airplane flight, we are told at the beginning of every flight that in the event of decompression, or loss of cabin pressure, OXYGEN MASKS will drop down from the ceiling of the plane. WHAT do they tell you to do next? You GOT IT! PUT YOURS ON FIRST... before you try to help someone else with their mask!   The Late Pastor L.S. Rubin use to tell us, "You CAN'T TEACH what you DON'T KNOW, and you CAN'T LEAD where YOU don't go!" You can't TEACH someone what you yourself don't know or practice! You can't HELP someone if you haven't helped yourself! You can't LOVE someone if you don't LOVE YOU!!! Now tell somebody, "Excuse me while I do ME FIRST! I'm going to hook my oxygen up first, then I can help YOU!" :o)

October 3
Exceedingly, Abundantly
Ephesians 3:20 ~ "Now unto him that is able to do
EXCEEDINGLY ABUNDANTLY ABOVE ALL that we ASK or THINK,
according to the power that works in us..."

This is for those of you who may question one of the several birthday greetings I have left for many of you by way of Bible verse. The verse in question is the one before us, Ephesians 3:20. Some wonder how GOD can DO, bigger than I can THINK!!! At the risk of sounding presumptuous (arrogant, lifted up in pride), let me share the following. Remember that this, according to the verse, only works for those who have the same power that raised Jesus from the dead, God's Holy Spirit, dwelling in them! In other words, those who are saved by the Blood of Jesus Christ (Ephesians 1:19-20)!

Many of you have testimonies as well, so you can confirm that I'm not fantasizing! I am a preacher who has had virtually the same salary for over 20 years. Whenever I say that, it sounds like I'm complaining. It's actually just the opposite! I need you to know that I am NOT a wealthy preacher, so I can only credit GOD with what I am about to say. Just in the FEWWEEKS around the original writing of this post: 1) I found out that my childhood dentist, whom I feared because he was African American, was also a TUSKEGEE AIRMAN. That means he KNEW HIS STUFF! My son now cares for Dr. Richard Caesar's grave-site at the National Cemetery. 2) My daughter and son-in-law went to Rome, Greece and Turkey.3) Nina and I got back from Paris, France and London, England.4) Our 7 year old girl was in a program where she was playing golf ... AT PEBBLE BEACH!!! At the risk of upsetting the haters and non-believers, I'll stop here and say... "Now unto Him who is ABLE TO DO...!!!" :o)

October 4
No Hope, No Cash, & No Jobs?
Genesis 15:1~ "After these things the word of the Lord
came unto Abram in a vision, saying, 'Fear not, Abram:
I am thy shield, and thy exceeding great reward.' "

There is a POST out there that's good for a laugh and is very true, if you are NOT A CHRISTIAN! I must admit, I laughed when I first read it. Then I did what I normally do. I looked at it from a Christian perspective. What? Oh, I'm sorry! The post reads: "30 years ago we had Bob Hope, Johnny Cash and Steve Jobs. Today we have NO HOPE, NO CASH and NO JOBS!!!" I'll wait for some of you to finish laughing. Now I need the Christians to think about the CONTRADICTION that some of us are re-posting. 1) Titus 2:13 says that JESUS CHRIST IS our Blessed Hope, so the first one can't be true. 2) Genesis 15:1 says that GOD is our very great SALARY/WAGES, so the second one can't be true. 3) 1 Corinthians 15:58 teaches that we who are In The Lord ALWAYS HAVE A JOB! STRIKE THREE and this post is out of here as a declaration of what we believe as Christians! I've got hope, a lifetime job, and I'm EATIN'! That means I'm PAID!!! (I could strike out the side SEVERAL more times on each one of those, but YOU get the picture. Study it for yourselves as the church at Berea did (Acts 17:10-11), and see if what we're saying isn't the truth! It's a very CLEVER post, just not true for me. How about you? :o)

October 5
The Impala... and God's Comfort
2 Corinthians 1:3-5 ~ "Blessed be God, even the Father
of our Lord Jesus Christ, the Father of mercies, and the God of all comfort;
Who comforteth us in all our tribulation,
that we may be able to comfort them which are in any trouble,
by the comfort wherewith we ourselves are comforted of God.
For as the sufferings of Christ abound in us,
so our consolation also aboundeth by Christ."

Paul says that God COMFORTS US in our afflictions so that we might be able to COMFORT OTHERS going through the SAME TYPE OF STORM (verse 4)! Paul also said that if we trust GOD and NOT OURSELVES, God can handle our past, present, and future (verse 10)! An IMPALA is an African antelope (profile picture) that can jump up to 30 feet horizontally and 10 feet vertically, but you can contain it in a zoo with a 3 FOOT WALL! Why? I'm glad you asked! An Impala WON'T JUMP, if it CAN'T SEE where its feet will land! Common sense should tell the Impala that those of us who are staring at it from the other side of the wall are standing on SOMETHING SOLID. I'm Standing On HIS PROMISES! The SAME GOD that holds me up, can hold YOU up and deliver you yesterday, today and tomorrow as well. We walk by FAITH, not by Sight! ~ 2 Corinthians 5:7

October 6
Just Moved Upstairs
1 Thessalonians 4:13-18 ~ "But I would not have you to be ignorant,
brethren, concerning them which are asleep,
that ye sorrow not, even as others which have no hope.
14 For if we believe that Jesus died and rose again,
even so them also which sleep in Jesus will God bring with him.
For this we say unto you by the word of the Lord,
that we which are alive and remain unto the coming of the Lord
shall not prevent them which are asleep.
For the Lord himself shall descend from heaven with a shout,
with the voice of the archangel, and with the trump of God:
and the dead in Christ shall rise first:
Then we which are alive and remain shall be caught up
together with them in the clouds, to meet the Lord in the air:
and so shall we ever be with the Lord.
Wherefore comfort one another with these words."

There's been quite a bit of DEATH in the past couple of weeks. I'm on my way to a funeral service as I write this. It's the HOMEGOING of a lady who KNEW the Lord. That's ALWAYS much easier for me than those who didn't.

Paul says in verse 13 that Christian grief (sorrow) is DIFFERENT from the way those who don't know the Lord grieve. CHRISTIAN GRIEF contains HOPE! We know that we will see AGAIN loved ones who have died IN THE LORD JESUS CHRIST (14)!

A beautician lived in an apartment just above her beauty shop. Every morning she would get up early, get dressed, have breakfast, then go downstairs to her shop and open up. As she got older, her SKILLS were still INTACT, but her legs would not allow her to make it down the stairs like she use to. Her daughter, who lived with her said, "Momma, why don't you start working up here in the house, since you have a hard time making it down the stairs. The mother agreed, but over the next several weeks her business dwindled down to almost NOTHING!

The daughter was hurt that people would feel her mother was too OLD to do their hair as she had in the past. The mother didn't take it personally. She asked her daughter for a large sign-board and a permanent marker. The mother wrote on the board and asked her daughter to put it in the window of the shop downstairs. To the daughters surprise, within a few weeks, ALL of the mother's customers were BACK! The sign in the shop read ...NOT OUT OF BUSINESS, JUST MOVED UPSTAIRS!!!

Our loved ones who DIE IN THE LORD, are NOT out of business. They've just ...MOVED UPSTAIRS! :o)

October 7
Our LIFE and LIPS
Matthew 15:8~"This people draweth nigh unto me
with their mouth, and honoureth me with their lips;
but their heart is far from me."

Isaiah 29:13 ~ "Wherefore the Lord said,
'Forasmuch as this people draw near me with their mouth,
and with their lips do honour me,
but have removed their heart far from me,
and their fear toward me is taught by the precept of men...' "

The scribes and the Pharisees came about 75 miles from Jerusalem to Gennesaret to complain to Jesus about His disciples not adhering to CEREMONIAL hand washing (Matthew 15:1-2 ~ see Mark 7:1-4). Jesus uncovered their hypocrisy when he told them how they had broken God's laws by their oral law TRADITIONS which the rabbis said Moses passed down to the elders! Jesus gave an illustration of their hypocrisy. He remind them of how they had avoided responsibility by declaring their possessions to be "Corban" (Mark 7:11 = a gift in Hebrew). In other words, if they wanted to get out of a financial obligation such as taking care of aged parents (Honoring father and mother), just declare your money to be "Corban" (a gift) TO GOD! This not only dishonored parents, IT DISHONORED GOD who told us to HONOR them! Before you come down too hard on the scribes and the Pharisees, remember that they are

KINFOLK to some of us. How many of us have placed our loved ones in nursing or convalescent homes when we were WELL ABLE to take care of them, and then NOT EVEN VISIT THEM? Jesus then quoted Isaiah 29:13 by telling them in Matthew 15:8 that their words (a gift to God) didn't line up with their actions (dodging responsibility to their parents - Matthew 15:3-7)! How many people do you know who TALK like Christians but their ACTIONS don't line up with their talk? Sis. Rosia Robison put it like this in a message to or Mission Ministry, "Our LIFE and LIPS ought to AGREE!!!"

October 8
Meekness
Colossians 3:12 ~ "Put on therefore, as the elect of God,
holy and beloved, bowels of mercies, kindness,
humbleness of mind, meekness, longsuffering;"

MEEKNESS IS NOT WEAKNESS! One of my mentors, Dr. Warren Wiersbe, pointed out that meekness is POWER UNDER CONTROL! This word for meekness was used to describe a soothing wind, healing medicine, and a tamed horse. Winds can become storms. Too much medicine can kill you. Horses can run wild and hurt you. Meekness is when their POWER is under control.

A MEEK person has power to do HARM, but keeps it UNDER CONTROL. In 1 Samuel 24:3-12, David was hiding in a cave from King Saul. Saul was determined to kill David. GUESS which DARK cave Saul decided to take a TOILET BREAK in (verse 3)? Saul dropped his robe over his feet. David made his way in the dark cave toward Saul and secretly cut a piece from Saul's ROBE (verse 4). Then he waited until Saul was at a distance, stood outside the cave & waved the piece of cloth at SAUL (verse 11).

Saul KNEW how close he had come to death. David COULD HAVE cut off MORE than Saul's robe! He could have cut off his lineage and/or his life! That's MEEKNESS. I could hurt you, BUT I WON'T! :o)

October 9
Birds and Beef
Matthew 6:26 ~ "Behold the fowls of the air:
for they sow not, neither do they reap, nor gather into barns;
yet your heavenly Father feedeth them. Are ye not much better than they?"

Take heart from this verse in the midst of a bad economy. GODS

ECONOMY IS NOT TIED TO WALL STREET!!! Heaven is not BANKRUPT! The gold that we're fighting for here is use for walking on up there! By the way, the streets of heaven are NOT PAVED with gold. They are MADE OF GOLD – SOLID GOLD (Revelation 21:21)! A few years ago I ate at the indoor/outdoor cafe (GLASS ENCLOSED) across from UC Hospital in San Francisco. A man bought food for himself and his wife. He tripped on the way to the table and dropped his food! He cursed like a sailor, but the BIRDS didn't! That day the BIRDS had SHRIMP & TERIYAKI BEEF!!! Now if God can provide a FEAST for birds, don't you think He can take care of you? You're worth more to Him according to the verse, and according to His TRACK RECORD. God LOVES US, really – HE DOES! :o)

October 10
God's FAVOR
Ephesians 2:8-9~ "For by GRACE you have been saved □□through faith, and that not of yourselves; □it is the gift of God, not of □works, lest anyone should □boast." (NKJV)

You CANNOT WORK for God's FAVOR (Grace)! The "manna" God sent to feed his people in the wilderness fell AT NIGHT, when they were ASLEEP (Numbers 11:9)! YOU can't work when you're SLEEP! If you trust GOD, he'll rain down favor on you! Notice how the MANNA (which literally means "What is it?") only stayed fresh for that particular day (Exodus 16:19-21). That way they would have to TRUST GOD DAILY (Matthew 6:11)! When you get up each morning, take a spiritual look around. You will notice that GOD gives you BREAD (provisions/needs) from heaven (Exodus 16:4,15), DAILY (Lamentations 3:22-23), as MUCH as you can handle (Exodus 16:8) for any given day! Then the process starts all over again the next morning! That's why THIS DAY should be a BRAND NEW START for ALL OF US. GOD IS JUST THAT GOOD! :o)

October 11
Happy Birthday, Nina
Genesis 2:18 ~ "And the Lord God said, It is not good that the man should be alone; I will make him an help meet for him."

Today is the birthday of my "help meet" Nina Bailey. Just as in English, those words "HELP MEET" are TWO words in Hebrew. They mean "help suitable."

Did you notice that up until Genesis 2:18, EVERYTHING God made was GOOD (Genesis 1:4, 1:10, 1:12, 1:18, 1:21, 1:25)? Then after creating man, God looked back over all He had created and said it was VERY GOOD (Genesis 1:31)! Here in Genesis 2:18 is the FIRST time GOD says something is NOT GOOD! He said, "ALONENESS is NOT GOOD for man" (literal translation)! God also said in that SAME VERSE that He would make a SUITABLE HELP for the man. I looked up that word "SUITABLE." It means "in front, before your face, opposite to, parallel to, in the sight or presence of"! That should change your view of your OTHER HALF, men!

For those of you who don't know, that word "HELP" in the verse is MORE THAN just an assistant. It's the Hebrew word "ezer" which means, help, strength, power to accomplish a task! This word God used to describe the WOMAN, He uses to describe HIMSELF in several places in the Bible: Psalm 33:20 ~ ...He (God) is our HELP and shield. Psalm 70:5 ~ ...You (God) are my HELP and my deliverer. Psalm 121:1-2 ~ From where does my HELP come? My HELP comes from the Lord! Psalm 124:8 ~ Our HELP is in the name of the Lord. In each case it is the SAME word as in HELP meet!

To all my MEN out there, "Do you get the picture?" If GOD is important to you, then that lady in your life ought to be important, no, a necessity. That's because God uses the SAME LANGUAGE to describe HER, that He uses to describe HIMSELF! And because ALONENESS is NOT GOOD! :o)

HAPPY BIRTHDAY SWEETHEART! To you who stands in my presence opposite me to see what I can't see and strengthen me when I need it, I LOVE YOU DEARLY!!! ♥♥♥♥♥♥♥

October 12
Gossip
Proverbs 11:13 ~ "A talebearer revealeth secrets:
but he that is of a faithful spirit concealeth the matter."

1 Peter 4:8~ "And above all things have fervent charity
among yourselves: for charity shall cover the multitude of sins."

The story is told of a young girl who went to a priest and confessed that she had gossiped about her neighbor. "What shall I do?" she asked the priest. The priest said, "Take a FEATHER and put it on the step of every house in the neighborhood." The girl put out SEVERAL HUNDRED feathers! Then she went back to the priest and said, "OK. Now what?" The priest said, "Now go and pick them all up." The girl went back to the houses to pick them up, but MOST of them had been BLOWN AWAY by the wind. When she told the priest, he said, "Once you gossip, it's just like feathers in the wind ...ALMOST IMPOSSIBLE TO STOP!" Be CAREFUL how you talk about others. Check the facts! SOMETIMES, you might even need to cover a fault ...WITH LOVE!!! :o) ♥

October 13
Stupid Servant
Luke 12:40 ~ "Be ye therefore ready also:
for the Son of man cometh at an hour when ye think not."

Dr. Haddon Robinson shared with us in Dallas, Texas an Italian legend about a wealthy owner of a villa who had a servant that the owner considered to be stupid. One day the owner said, "Servant, I don't think there is ANYBODY more STUPID than you are. Take this staff (stick/cane), and if you ever meet someone more STUPID than you are ...you give him the staff." To show you how stupid the servant was, he AGREED! As the servant went day by day through the market place, he met a lot of stupid men. But he was never quite sure if they were worse than he was.

One day the servant returned to the villa and was ushered into his master's bedroom. The master said to the servant, "I wanted to talk to you. I'm going on a long journey." The servant said, "When will you be back?" His master said, "Well, I won't be coming back from this trip." The servant said, "Have you made preparations for this journey? Do you need me to do it?" His master said, "No, I've been too busy with other things." "Could you have made preparations?" the servant asked. The master said, "Yes, I just neglected it." The servant said, "Sir, you're going on a journey from which you will never return, and you could have made preparations for the journey and you failed to do so?" The servant took the staff, handed it to his master and said, "HERE SIR! At last I have met a man more STUPID than myself!"

Be careful how you judge others. Judging has a tendency to have a BOOMERANG effect (Matthew 7:1). Now answer this question. Will YOU be ready to take that journey when JESUS CALLS? Or will you be caught building "BIGGER BARNS" for stuff that won't last? See Luke 12:16-21!

October 14
Lotus Riverside Project (Start with the Foundation, AGAIN)

Matthew 7:24-27~ "Therefore whosoever heareth these sayings of mine,
and doeth them, I will liken him unto a wise man,
which built his house upon a rock:
And the rain descended, and the floods came,
and the winds blew, and beat upon that house; and it fell not:
for it was founded upon a rock.
And every one that heareth these sayings of mine,
and doeth them not, shall be likened unto a foolish man,
which built his house upon the sand:
And the rain descended, and the floods came, and the winds blew,
and beat upon that house; and it fell: and great was the fall of it."

1 Corinthians 3:11 ~ "For other foundation can no man lay
than that is laid, which is Jesus Christ."

The Lotus Riverside Complex is an 11 building project in Shanghai, China. Each of the 11 buildings has 13 stories (They are evidently NOT superstitious about the number 13 :o)! At approximately 6:00am on June 27, 2009, ONE of those buildings TOPPLED OVER virtually intact! The problem was the FOUNDATION ...or LACK THEREOF!!! Hollow pilings sunk into the ground were virtually all that was causing this (these) building(s) to stand upright! The pilings snapped like twigs!

"Improper planning and failure to stabilize structural foundation" during the construction of the property led to the residential building collapse, a preliminary investigation found. The under-construction building in the Lotus Riverside residential complex fell on its side, almost intact, killing a construction worker. A member of the team investigating the collapse, which angered some 500 homeowners of the still unoccupied complex, said: "No builder with basic construction knowledge should have made that error." The developers had sold 489 of the 629 flats in the 13-story building, and owners of the flats are demanding refunds or compensation. The event has sparked worries about construction safety in China. The building, one of 11 in a wider project, fell over when pillars that were supposed to be buried deep under the earth were uprooted.

That's what Matthew 7:26 teaches about OUR LIVES when we DON"T adhere to the teachings of Jesus. You may APPEAR to be intact. Truth be told, without Christ, an individual is like a building that was anchored in SAND! They are already fallen and don't know it!1 Corinthians 3:11 literally says that there is NO OTHER FOUNDATION that can be laid ALONGSIDE (para) the irreplaceable foundation that is already there! That would be JESUS CHRIST! Ironically in EARTHQUAKE prone areas such as where I live, something called a J-Bolt is required to anchor the building to a solid foundation. I call it a JESUS BOLT! That's the J-shaped bolt just below this post. The J-shaped end is anchored in concrete and the threaded end is bolted to the structure. They SHOULD BE all throughout the building foundation! If your life is on SHAKEN GROUND, try a J (JESUS) - BOLT ...that is anchored to the ROCK HIMSELF! :o)

October 15
Be Thankful Always
Philippians 4:6 ~ "Be careful for nothing; but in every thing
by prayer and supplication with thanksgiving
let your requests be made known unto God."

A man was looking forward to wearing a BRAND NEW pair of PANTS he had just bought. He asked his wife to iron them. While she was ironing them, she BURNED THEM! The man started to get mad because he was getting excited about wearing those NEW pants. He did something ALL OF US should do before we react. He stopped to think, then prayed, "Lord, I thank you that I wasn't IN THOSE PANTS when she burned them!" You can complain about your cup being half empty, or you can THANK GOD it's HALF FULL! There is ALWAYS a reason to be thankful! ~ Psalm 34:1 :o)

October 16 (originally posted in 2011)
Goshen and Goshen
Exodus 8:22-23 ~ "And I will sever in that day
the land of Goshen, in which my people dwell,
that no swarms of flies shall be there;
to the end thou mayest know that I am the Lord in the midst of the earth.
And I will put a division between my people and thy people:
tomorrow shall this sign be."

Dixie Lee Moss Climp Mayberry was born on a farm 6 miles west of Princeton, Missouri, and one mile from Goshen. She went home to be with the Lord on October 3, 2011. She was the mother of my good friend, Charlie Climp. I mention her because of where she was born.

Before there was a Goshen in Missouri, there was a GOSHEN in Egypt! While they were slaves, Israel dwelt in a part of Egypt called Goshen. It was the BEST of the land (Genesis 47:6, 11). God sent 10 plagues to force Pharaoh to let Israel go. Everyone in the land experienced the first 3 plagues, including Israel! On plague #4, God separated Goshen and made them distinct from the rest of Egypt! No swarm of flies in Goshen! Goshen became a place of PROTECTION for God's people, right there in the MIDDLE of all the trouble.

God can allow ALL HELL (the word is in the Bible, look it up!) to break out all around you, and NOT touch you! Dixie Lee was protected by the GRACE of God, and is now in the very PRESENCE OF GOD! I'm in Goshen, are YOU?

October 17
Mephibosheth: A Story of Grace
2 Samuel 9:1 ~ "And David said,
'Is there yet any that is left of the house of Saul,
that I may shew him kindness for Jonathan's sake?' "

GRACE is unmerited, undeserved favor! I know of NO OTHER picture of the Grace of God as BEAUTIFUL as the one in this chapter. "CHESED" (the word "kindness" in the verse) is another word for GRACE! David's arch enemy, king Saul, is dead. So is David's best friend Jonathan, who happened to be Saul's son! Saul had been trying to KILL DAVID when he found out that God had anointed David to take his (Saul's) place. Now David's worst enemy and best friend are both dead. This is what blows my mind whenever I read it. In 2 Samuel 9:1, David (who is now king) asks, "Is there anyone in my dead enemy's household that I can show GRACE to, because of my friendship with my enemy's son!

Notice that David DID NOT ask if there was ANYONE QUALIFIED for the blessing! If GRACE needed qualifications, we ALL would be without it! (Romans 5:8).The person that David ended up blessing, was Saul's grandson, Jonathan's son ...Mephibosheth! Mephibosheth felt absolutely UNDESERVING of David's Grace (2 Samuel 9:6-8). He was CRIPPLED, but ended up eating for the rest of his life at king David's table (9:13). By the way, those crippled legs were UNDER THE TABLE, COVERED by the King's GRACE! You can praise God right now, because He extended HIS GRACE to those of us who once were His ENEMIES (Ephesians 2:13-18). Not because we deserved it, but because of His SON ...JESUS!

October 18
Snakes!
Revelation 12:9 ~ "And the great dragon was cast out,
that old serpent, called the Devil, and Satan,

which deceiveth the whole world: he was cast out into the earth,
and his angels were cast out with him."

Why are we so shocked when people who DON'T have a relationship with JESUS, ACT like who they are?

The BIBLE verse makes it clear that the devil is a snake (serpent). I Matthew 12:34, JESUS called those who tried to trap and destroy Him ...children of SNAKES! If their mothers and fathers were snakes, that would make THEM snakes! Let me be clear that the Bible DID NOT SAY that every lost sinner is a "snake" or a "child of the devil," although lost sinners are called the "children of disobedience and wrath" (Eph. 2:1–3). But THERE ARE PEOPLE who mean you NO GOOD whatsoever! Their intent is to HURT YOU. These are the people the Word is speaking of when it talks about SNAKES.

Did you know that there are people who don't get much SLEEP because they stay awake devising ways to HURT YOU (Proverbs 4:16)?! By the way, SNAKES ...have no eyelids!!! Now the analogy makes sense. Snakes always appear to be looking at you, as if they never sleep. I'm just saying.

When you get ready to go to sleep, turn those SNAKES in your life over to YOUR HEAVENLY FATHER, who NEVER slumbers or sleeps (Psalm 121:4). Since God is ALREADY UP, let Him handle them. SOMEBODY needs to get some REST! Now go rest in PEACE ...before you R.I.P. :o)

October 19
Can an African Change His Skin Color?
Jeremiah 13:23 ~ "Can the Ethiopian change his skin,
or the leopard his spots? then may ye also do good,
that are accustomed to do evil."

Jeremiah is prophesying to Judah (the southern kingdom of Israel). They are facing Babylonian captivity. Jeremiah does a preemptive strike in verse 22 of chapter 13 when he tells them, "Before you go asking why this is going to happen to you, it's YOUR own fault!" Their sins were so deeply embedded in them, that they COULD NOT CHANGE! Then he asks them the following question in verse 23 to which they already know the answer!:"Can an African change his skin color, or can a leopard change its spots?" The answer to that question is a resounding NO! The reason they can't change who they are (not even with bleaching) is because WHO THEY ARE goes DEEPER than the surface. It's in their deoxyribonucleic acid (DNA)! Jeremiah goes on to ask, "Then how can you do good, who are so use to doing evil?"Why is it that WE think we can change people? We enter into marriages, friendships, business deals etc. thinking that we can mold this person or that person into what we desire them to be. They become a PROJECT! Then we are shocked, disappointed, devastated, hurt etc. when it DOESN'T HAPPEN!Since I try to make this page about GOOD NEWS ...HERE IT IS! Excuse me while I head to LEFT FIELD for a moment. I can bleach my skin until I am as WHITE as my friend Paul Shotwell, but that won't change the fact that African American is in my DNA! I may change my APPEARANCE, but it won't change WHO I AM! Changing who I AM took a SUPERNATURAL BLOOD TRANSFUSION! I have found only ONE person who could perform such a procedure ...JESUS, on Calvary!The PRAISE POINT comes right here! "...man looks on the outward appearance, but the LORD looks on the heart (1 Samuel 16:7). When discussing the RICH getting into heaven being as DIFFICULT as a CAMEL going through the eye of a SEWING NEEDLE, Jesus said, "...With men this is impossible; but with God (and JESUS IS GOD) ALL THINGS are possible. (Matthew 19:26). The BLOOD OF JESUS can, and WILL ...change you!

October 20
Big Ben
2 Timothy 3:16 ~ "All scripture is given by inspiration of God, and is profitable for doctrine, for reproof, for correction, for instruction in righteousness:"

Big Ben is actually the name of the largest of FIVE (5) bells in the clock tower of the Palace of Westminster in London. The name "Big Ben" has been extended to the entire four-faced clock tower.

When Nina and I were in England, we found out that BIG BEN is the most POPULAR tourist attraction in London. We also learned something about the PEOPLE who visit that famous 152 year old clock tower. Many of them SET THEIR WATCHES by Big Ben! It is the unofficial STANDARD for time in London! It is so accurate that when it gets off by maybe 1 SECOND per year, PENNIES are placed on or removed from the swinging pendulum, depending on whether it is 1 second fast or slow.

Did you know that GOD has an even MORE ACCURATE STANDARD for everyday living? It's called The Bible, His Word, Holy Scripture. The verse above says that scripture is literally GOD-BREATHED (inspiration). One of my Dallas instructors, Dr. Warren Wiersbe says THIS, about the rest of the verse. He says the scriptures are profitable for DOCTRINE (what is right), for REPROOF (what is not right), for

CORRECTION (how to get right), and for INSTRUCTION IN RIGHTEOUSNESS (how to stay right). You can SET YOUR LIFE BY IT! :o)

October 21
Mind the Gap!
Ezekiel 22:30 ~ "And I sought for a man among them,
that should build up the (moral) wall,
and stand in the (spiritual) gap before me for the land,
that I should not destroy it; but I found none."

This is a REVIEW of a message for the people of Olivet Baptist Church entitled, "MIND THE GAP!"

Nina and I were FREQUENT RIDERS of the Underground subway system in London, England. At virtually EVERY STOP, a voice could be heard inside the train, and outside in the station saying, "MIND THE GAP... between the train and the platform!" That was just a simple way of saying, "Pay attention to the distance between the train and the platform when the doors of the train are opened!"

If you have NOT claimed Jesus Christ as Lord and Savior of your life, PAY ATTENTION to the spiritual GAP between you and God every time the doors of the church are opened. The problem with gaps is DISTANCE. If the DISTANCE between the train and the platform is not dealt with, the consequences will be disastrous. In the above passage from Ezekiel, God's leaders (secular and religious), and the "common" people were acting in such a way as to put DISTANCE between themselves and God (verses 25-29)! Ezekiel records God as saying, "I looked for A MAN to rebuild the (moral) walls and bridge that (spiritual) gap, and couldn't find one (verse 30)!"

In Jeremiah 5:1, God tells Jeremiah to "act out his sermon" by running through the streets of a wicked Jerusalem and see if he could find ONE MAN that was righteous enough to cause God to CALL OFF the impending invasion of the city. We know that Jeremiah found none, and the city was invaded! So WHERE is that MAN that would "MIND THE GAP" between God and us? Paul identified Him in Ephesians 2:13 as JESUS CHRIST. Pilate also pointed Him out in John 19:5 when he said, "Behold...THE MAN!" Paul also told Timothy about the MAN that bridges gaps in 1 Timothy 2:5. If there is distance between you and God, MIND THE GAP by trusting His Son... The MAN, Jesus Christ! In the words of the secular group Salt 'N Pepa & En Vogue... "What a man, what a man, what a man, what a MIGHTY GOOD MAN!!!" :o)

October 22
Village Street Sweeper
"Romans 11:29 ~ "For the gifts and calling of God are without repentance."

The story is told of an elderly man who had a job sweeping leaves from the streets of a European village. A meeting was held by the people of the village about the inability to pay their debts. It was decided that the old man's services were no longer needed. They would let him go to save money.

Months later, a mysterious disease began to sweep through the village. Many of the people in the village got sick, and several died. Experts came in and traced the source of the disease to CLOGGED DRAINS full of ROTTEN LEAVES that had not been cleared since the old man was terminated!

Romans 11:29 simply says that what God called YOU to do is irrevocable! God DID NOT make a mistake. He DID NOT give you too little or too much to do. He DID NOT give you the wrong gift, or someone else's gift. What He gave YOU was NEEDED where He PLACED YOU!

Have you ever noticed that the smallest gift (letter wise - 1 Corinthians 12:28) in the list of spiritual gifts is the gift of "HELPS"!? Everybody can HELP somebody, even if it's something as simple as LISTENING to them! Never take lightly or for granted that which God has given YOU to do. Know that if you were to stop doing what God has gifted you to do, SOMEONE would miss you. For example, if those of you who encourage me on this page were to stop, I WOULD MISS YOU!

God has already BLESSED ME beyond, beyond (huper, huper) my wildest expectations on Facebook! Some of you who think your contributions to mankind are small and insignificant don't realize how you may have turned someone's day around just because you smiled, said THANK YOU, or held an elevator door for them! It doesn't take much. Ever had somebody say something kind to you, and it changed the way you felt for the rest of the day? There are those of you who do that for people, even when you don't realize it!

October 23
Jesus, Angry?
John 2:15-16 ~ "And when he had made a scourge of small cords, he drove them all out of the temple, and the sheep, and the oxen;
and poured out the changers' money, and overthrew the tables;

And said unto them that sold doves, 'Take these things hence;
make not my Father's house an house of merchandise.' "

Why was Jesus so ANGRY? Yes, these are the verses where Jesus made a whip and ran the money changers out of the temple. The exchange of Roman currency into Jewish currency was NECESSARY to pay temple dues. Now READ the verses carefully. Jesus' anger was focused on those who "SOLD DOVES!"

According to the law (Leviticus 5:7), doves (or common pigeons) were the sacrifice of the POOR. These men were TAKING ADVANTAGE OF THE POOR by selling to them what WE can go to a park & get for FREE! Did you notice in the verses that Jesus drove the sheep and oxen out of the temple as well, but He DID NOT TURN THE DOVES LOOSE?

God makes provisions for the poor. The money changers had turned God's house into a den of robbers. Remember that, next time YOUR CHURCH tries to SELL a $10 chicken dinner to a HOMELESS PERSON! I'm not telling you to STOP your fundraisers. My earthly father told me that many southern churches were built by chicken dinner sales and fish fries. (I prefer tithes and offerings! :o) Jesus' disciples SOLD PERFUME to raise money for the poor (Matthew 26:7-9)! But when a HUNGRY person stops by your church during that next dinner sale and can't afford to buy it, GIVE him or her a dinner!

And stop CHARGING PEOPLE to get into your church! There are sinners out there who don't understand why they couldn't get into the church because some CELEBRITY Christian was there and you were CHARGING at the door! That's what HOTEL BALLROOMS and ARENAS are for. Oops, I just lost about 10 friends!!!

October 24
"The Best Part of Waking Up..."
John 18:11~ "Then said Jesus unto Peter,
'Put up thy sword into the sheath:
the cup which my Father hath given me, shall I not drink it?' "

Some time ago, there was an episode of the "Bernie Mac" TV Show entitled "SIN CUP"! In that episode, Jordan convinces his baby sister Bryana that she has a SIN CUP that fills up whenever she does something wrong. He then tries to tell her how she can keep herself and the family "free from sin."

The BAD NEWS is that we ALL have a SIN CUP that we ourselves could do absolutely NOTHING about (Romans 3:23; 6:23). The GOOD

NEWS is that the verses at the beginning of this post teach that JESUS has partaken of that cup FOR US! There are actually several more verses, I just didn't want to burden you. :o)

For some of you today, the best part of WAKING UP will be Folgers (Starbucks, Kona, Earl Grey, or whatever you drink) IN YOUR CUP. For me, the best part of waking up is KNOWING that JESUS HAS DRAINED MY CUP! I don't have to drink the dregs of my sins today because of what JESUS did on Calvary. Isn't it great to know that JESUS drank that BITTER CUP that you and I couldn't? Enjoy your coffee, …or whatever! :o)

October 25
Should Preachers Be Called Reverend?
Psalm 111:9 ~ "He sent redemption unto his people:
he hath commanded his covenant for ever:
holy and reverend is his name."

I was in a bank one day when the teller wouldn't cash my check. I had all of the proper I.D., but the check was from another bank. I even had an ACCOUNT with the bank where I was trying to cash the check! (Notice I said "HAD")!

The teller told me she would have to call the other bank. I said, "Whatever," as in ...whatever you need to do to get this taken care of. I didn't know that in the language of the day, "WHATEVER" was not a nice thing to say! She (the teller) saw "Rev." on my check and said, "You are a REVEREND with an ATTITUDE like that?!" I wondered what in the hel...lo she was talking about. I also realized that it is the reason I keep the title on my checks and I sign my name, "REV. S.A. Bailey." It keeps me ACCOUNTABLE!

Now you won't find the title on this page, and I don't introduce myself as Reverend. But the reason I can't go into a store and purchase any kind of movie or item is because… 1) I LOVE the Lord. 2) The title REVEREND is on all of my checks and it's the way I sign my name!!! I'm just crazy enough to care what people think about me, because I now am a reflection of GOD!

That brings up a sensitive issue. Should preachers be called REVEREND? I'm not hung up on titles because there are TOO MANY of them. Nothing personal or biblical. THAT LONELY verse up there has been used AGAINST those who are called Reverend. Psalm 111:9 says, "…holy & reverend is HIS name"! SOME people say that you can't be REVEREND, because HE IS. If THAT is what this verse says, then I CAN'T BE HOLY EITHER!

Now listen carefully! I know that as preachers we need issues to argue and debate, but THIS isn't one of them! The Hebrew word in Psalm 111:9 for "reverend" is YARE (pronounced yaw-ray). It means to honor, revere, respect, inspire godly fear, etc. In Leviticus 19:3 we are told to YARE our mothers and fathers. In Joshua 4:14 we are told that the people had YARE for Joshua (their new leader) just as they had YARE for Moses (their old leader). In Genesis 32:11 Jacob said, "I YARE my brother Esau"!

There are MANY other verses, not just Psalm 111:9, which happens to be the only place where the exact same word is translated as reverend. Now, go ahead and call yourself Reverend. Just don't get lost in the title. :o)

October 26
One More Night With The Frogs

Exodus 8:8-10a ~ "Then Pharaoh called for Moses and Aaron, and said,
'Intreat the Lord, that he may take away the frogs from me,
and from my people;
and I will let the people go,
that they may do sacrifice unto the Lord.'
And Moses said unto Pharaoh, 'Glory over me:
when shall I intreat for thee, and for thy servants, and for thy people,
to destroy the frogs from thee and thy houses,
that they may remain in the river only?'
And he said, 'Tomorrow.' And he said,
'Be it according to thy word: that thou mayest know
that there is none like unto the Lord our God.' "

Then Pharaoh called Moses and Aaron and said, "Plead with the LORD to take away the frogs from me and from my people, and I will let the people go to sacrifice to the LORD." Moses said to Pharaoh, "Be pleased to command me when I am to plead for you and for your servants and for your people, that the frogs be cut off from you and your houses and be left only in the Nile." And he (Pharaoh) said, "Tomorrow..." (ESV)

In Exodus 8, The children of Israel are slaves to the Egyptians. Pharaoh was the leader of Egypt. God sends a plague of FROGS on Egypt. Frogs in the houses, frogs in the bedrooms, frogs in the beds and frogs in the ovens and mixing bowls (verse 3)!

In the verses up above, Pharaoh asked Moses, the leader of Israel, to beg God to take away the frogs (verse 8). Moses asked Pharaoh when he wanted him (Moses) to ask God (verse 9). Pharaoh said... TOMORROW (verse 10)!

Now, correct me if I'm wrong. If you had frogs EVERYWHERE in your house (especially in your bed!), and someone who knew someone who had the power to get rid of them asked you, "When do you want them gone?", how many of you would have said... YESTERDAY?!!! Yet Pharaoh said, TOMORROW! He chose to spend ONE MORE NIGHT WITH THE FROGS! Before you come down too hard on Pharaoh, how many of us could have had IMMEDIATE relief from some sin, storm or situation? Yet we chose to take... ONE MORE hit on the crack pipe. ONE MORE illegal job for the money. ONE MORE sleepover with someone else's husband or wife. ONE MORE sip of gin and juice. ONE MORE lie to cover our tracks. ONE MORE hit on The Chronic!

When you could have IMMEDIATE Grace, Mercy, Peace and Relief, why spend ONE MORE NIGHT WITH THE FROGS? (I just don't understand it! ~ That's just me talking to myself). :)

October 27
Don't Let Them Take You There
Ephesians 4:26 ~ "Be angry and do not sin;
do not let the sun go down on your anger..." (ESV)

Remember that song by the Staple Singers, "I'll Take You There?" Now they were talking about heaven, but SOME people want to take you to a place where you don't want to go... to a sinfully angry place! They may "take you there" but YOU DO NOT have to get out of the car! This post is for anyone who has had someone... TAKE YOU THERE!

Have you ever had someone tap dance on your LAST NERVE? You know that nerve you had locked away in a safe, and somehow they got the combination, removed it from the safe, threw it down on the floor and stomped all over it? The verse up top pretty much teaches us NOT to let folk push those buttons that move us PAST anger, and into sin. Someone is going to try "take you there" today at your job, in your home, at your school, at your church, on the freeway, on the bus, at the parade etc. :)

Righteous (justifiable) indignation (anger) has its place. It's OK to be angry over LEGITIMATE wrong and evil, but don't let that anger push that button that causes you to sin. Rev. Judy-Ann Young said at her 1st cousin's memorial service at our church, "I may have pushed your button, but I DIDN'T INSTALL IT!!!" Get rid of those buttons... before the sun goes down. Now excuse me while I go do some "BUTTON" demolition and removal from my own life! I REFUSE to give anyone that kind of power over me! :) :) :) ♥

October 28

The Truth Shall FREE YOU!!!!
John 8:32 ~ "And ye shall know the truth,
and the TRUTH shall FREE YOU!"

That word "free" means to make free, deliver, liberate, exempt from liability!

Have you ever been to jail? OK, have you ever gone just to VISIT? OK, remember when Pookie and Ray Ray went to jail and YOU had to BAIL them out, only to have them end up right BACK IN JAIL? That's because they were SET FREE, and not MADE FREE! Some people that the law set free on Friday will be back in jail on MONDAY!

When JESUS is Lord of your life, HE'S the TRUTH that MAKES YOU FREE. That's what the verse says. The TRUTH is PERMANENT, and can keep you from going into bondage ...CONTINUOUSLY. Can you HANDLE THE TRUTH, or are you CONTENT with TEMPORARY PAROLE?

P.S. I am about to write about Halloween for the next three days – and the TRUTH shall make you free! But it WILL make some of you MAD FIRST! :o)

October 29
Halloween, Part 1
John 8:32 ~ "And ye shall know the truth,
and the TRUTH shall FREE YOU!"

Truth: Halloween has in it the word HALLOW which means Holy and is considered a HOLIDAY which means a Holy Day! This is despite the fact that it is the biggest day of the year to worship ...SATAN!

Truth: Halloween started as a Druid (Celtic priest) festival which fell on November 1. These Celtic priests practiced sorcery and witchcraft! The earliest Halloween celebrations were held by the Druids in honor of "Samhain" who was the so called "lord of the DEAD"!

Truth: In ancient Britain and Ireland, the Celtic festival of Samhain was observed on October 31. It was the end of summer and the eve of the new year. It was the occasion of one of the ancient fire festivals when huge bonfires were set on hilltops to frighten away evil spirits. The festival acquired sinister significance, with ghosts, witches, hobgoblins, black cats, fairies and demons of all kinds said to be roaming about.

Truth: Halloween was thought to be the most favorable time for divinations concerning marriage, luck, health, and death. It was the only day on which the help of the devil was invoked for such purposes. The pagan observances influenced the Christian festival we know today as All Hallows' Eve or HALLOWEEN!

Truth: Traditionally at Halloween, Roman Catholic families purchased an envelope from the priest. Inside they wrote the name of a DEAD relative, and it was put on the altar so that the relative would not be forgotten in November's prayers for the DEAD. Thus the papist All Hallows' Eve was mixed with the pagan festival of the DEAD.

TRUTH ~ In Mark 12:26-27, JESUS told the Sadducees who didn't believe in the resurrection, that they needed to re-read what God the Father said to Moses at the burning bush in Exodus 3:6. God said, "I am the God of Abraham, Isaac and Jacob!" Now the Sadducees knew that these 3 men had been DEAD (as WE understand death) for some time. That's when Jesus hit them with Mark 12:27, "He is NOT the God of the DEAD ... but the GOD OF THE LIVING!

NEXT UP: How those practices like Jack-O-Lantern carving, black cats, bonfires and Trick or Treat started! More information at http://www.inhisstepsministries.org/:o)

October 30
Halloween, Part 2
John 8:32 ~ "And ye shall know the truth,
and the TRUTH shall FREE YOU!"

Truth: JACK-O-LANTERNS ~ Hundreds of years before Christ, on Halloween night each Druid dressed in hooded robes and slung over his shoulder on a cord, a large, hollowed-out turnip with an oil lamp burning inside. Carved into the side of the hollow turnip was a face, in an attempt to ward off evil spirits. When the Celts immigrated to the New World they found pumpkins, much easier to hollow out and carve than turnips. Among the English-speaking Celts the hollowed turnip or pumpkin was known as "Jock (or Jack) of the Lantern," referring to the spirit guide (Jock or Jack) who lived in them. Lore has it that Jack was too bad to get into heaven but wasn't permitted into hell because of a deal he had made with the devil, supposedly wanders the earth holding a carved turnip with a glowing coal from hell as his guide. This is "Jack's lantern."

Truth: TRICK or TREAT ~ The Druids (Celtic priests) had a strange diet. On the night of the Festival of Death they would go from home to home demanding these peculiar foods. If the people complied, they passed on in silence; if their demands were not met, the people and their home were cursed with trouble, sickness and death.

Truth: COSTUMES ~ The Celts and Druids believed that by wearing masks and costumes, they would confuse the spirits into thinking they were one of them. Therefore the evil spirits would leave them alone. They would usually wear these while dancing around the big Samhain "bonfires." During this night of rituals they sacrificed animals (and sometimes humans). Often they wore the skins of these animals. Dressed in this way, they would engage in fortune telling. Villagers also dressed in hideous masks and costumes in an effort to disguise themselves from the spirits. (Did they REALLY think that devil doesn't know who we are?)

Truth: BLACK CATS ~ From the 1500s through the 1700s, during the witch hunts in Europe, it was thought witches and warlocks flew threw the air to a meeting with the devil (who had by then replaced Samhain, lord of the dead) on Halloween. Some thought elves, fairies, and witches turned into black cats. Black cats hold a high significance to witches and Satanists. The black cat, they believe has special powers. To them they believe the black cat represents incarnated humans, malevolent spirits, or the "familiars" of witches. This is why many black cats are in danger around Halloween. Local ASPCAs won't even let anyone adopt a black cat around Halloween time, in fear that the cat might be harmed.

Truth: BONFIRES ~ Bonfires originally came from the nights of human and animal sacrifices where they would throw the remains of the bodies into the fire. The next morning all that was left were the ASHES and BONES. Thus the name of these fires were called "BONE FIRES." The ORANGE flames lit up the BLACK night, hence the COLORS of Halloween! Now READ Ephesians 5:11-12 :o)

http://www.inhisstepsministries.org/

October 31
Halloween, Part 3
John 8:32 ~ "And ye shall know the truth,
and the TRUTH shall FREE YOU!"

There are now THREE (3) separate posts here on Halloween in the book you are now reading. Below are some ALTERNATIVES to the traditional Halloween. Remember not to be legalistic or judgmental. Romans 8:1 says, "There is therefore now no condemnation for those who are in Christ Jesus." In the original text there is NOTHING after "...IN CHRIST JESUS" in the verse. NO CONDEMNATION – PERIOD!

God does not call Christians to be legalistic or self-righteous. Listed below are some alternatives to the common way of celebrating Halloween. The most effective means of counteracting the darkness of Halloween is to share the LIGHT of the GOSPEL. You can find the details for these alternatives at http://www.inhisstepsministries.org/, where the majority of this information comes from. There are also several other websites listed at the end of this post on Halloween and alternatives.

1) Harvest Festivals
2) Family Night
3) Glory Gatherings
4) Decorate yard and hand out candy and tracts
5) Judgment House or Christian Haunted House (I know, I know! Go to the site and find out HOW to do it!!! :o)
6) Celebration of Light

If you have been convicted by the Holy Spirit that Halloween is something that your family should not participate in, do not be burdened with guilt or condemnation. Just ask Jesus to show you HIS WILL for your family. Remember that pumpkins, black cats, apples, the colors orange and black, bonfires, etc. are not evil in themselves. It is what we do with them.

There are Christians who not only send their kids out for trick or treating, but actually let them dress as ghosts, witches, or other evil characters. And some send their children off to horrifying haunted houses which plant fear into their children and can even open them up to the demonic. Many people have been exposed to Ouija boards, seances, and other forbidden practices during Halloween.

Some of you may say, "We only do this for fun. We don't practice witchcraft." That which represents Satan and his domain cannot be handled or imitated "for fun." Such participation places you in enemy and forbidden territory and that is dangerous ground. Why would you want your children exposed to such practices?

Some may think that we are over-emphasizing the influence of the demonic during Halloween. Too much emphasis on witchcraft and the satanic. It is not as bad as we think. What about the presentation of violence, murder, blood, atmosphere of fear, and death during Halloween? Many more homes have ghoulish decorations. The violent and grotesque movies come out during Halloween are the number-one videos rented during Halloween. Halloween is preoccupied with death. More destructive acts are done during Halloween.

Once again. the Bible makes it very clear that we are to have nothing to do with the deeds of darkness. "And have no fellowship with the unfruitful works of darkness, but rather expose them. For it is shameful even to speak of those things which are done by them in secret." ~ Ephesians 5:11-12

November

November 1
Lyrics to "Angels Watching Over Me"
Psalm 91:11 ~ "For he shall give his angels charge over thee,
to keep thee in all thy ways."

I have a song on my heart. "Went to the bank, got no money. Went to my job, my boss acts funny. Gangs on the street, selling cocaine... bullets flying everywhere, got NO NAME. People drive DRUNK, the innocent killed. That could have been ME - Hallelujah STILL, HE'S WATCHING ...OVER ME!" (Lyrics to a song entitled "Angels Watching Over Me" by somebody named Steven Bailey). "LORD, ENLIST us in your Witness Protection Program so that the devil can do us no harm. In Jesus' Name...AMEN!!!" :o)

November 2
Bring Your Past to the ALTAR
Philippians 3:13-14 ~ "Brethren, I count not myself
to have apprehended: but this one thing I do,
forgetting those things which are behind,
and reaching forth unto those things which are before,
I press toward the mark for the prize
of the high calling of God in Christ Jesus."

Why do people allow their past to ruin their present? Satchel Paige said, "Don't look back, something might be GAINING on you!" Paul knew that anyone in a chariot or foot race couldn't afford to spend time LOOKING BACK!

When extending the invitation at our church one Sunday, Rev. Cordell Hawkins said, "You CAN'T ALTER your past, but you CAN bring your past TO THE ALTAR!"

From Warren Wiersbe: "Please keep in mind that in Bible terminology, 'to forget' does not mean 'to fail to remember.' Apart from senility, hypnosis and/or a brain malfunction, no mature person can forget what has happened in the past. We may wish that we could erase certain bad memories, but we cannot. 'To forget' in Bible language means 'no longer to be influenced by or affected by.' When God promises, '...their sins and iniquities will I remember no more' (Hebrews 10:17), He is not suggesting that He will conveniently have a bad memory! This is impossible with God. What God is saying instead is, 'I will no longer hold their sins against them. Their sins can no longer affect their standing with ME or influence MY attitude toward them.' "

November 3
Run Toward HIM!
Proverbs 18:10 ~ "The name of the Lord is a strong tower:
the righteous runneth into it, and is safe."

This verse reminded me of a friend of mine was walking toward a shed on a construction site where he was working, when the shed BLEW UP! The metal roof of the shed flew toward him, and he turned to run away. He said SOMETHING inside of him told him to TURN AROUND and run TOWARD the shed! As he turned and ran TOWARD the shed, the ROOF of the shed flew OVER his head and landed where he WOULD HAVE BEEN IF he had kept running away. My friend Beverly Chambers said some time ago, "When STORMS come, don't run FROM God ...run TOWARD HIM!" :o)

November 4
Hank Aaron in the 1958 World Series
Hebrews 12:2~ "Looking unto Jesus the author and finisher of our faith;
who for the joy that was set before him endured the cross,
despising the shame,
and is set down at the right hand of the throne of God."

Henry Louis "Hank" Aaron was major league baseball's HOME-RUN KING before Barry Bonds broke his record in 2007. Aaron retired in 1976 as the first, and ONLY other man to break George Herman "Babe" Ruth's home-run record of 714. Aaron had 755 home-runs, and was inducted into baseball's Hall of Fame in 1982.

During his career, which started with the "Indianapolis Clowns" of the Negro Leagues, Hank Aaron faced many obstacles that could have kept him from breaking the record of such a revered player as BABE RUTH! Aaron faced racism, taunting and death threats just to name a few. He didn't let those things cause him to lose focus to become one of the BEST baseball players of ALL TIME!

Hank Aaron was batting in the 1958 World Series when Hall of Fame New York Yankee catcher Yogi Berra decided to have some fun and taunt Aaron. While Aaron was at the plate, Berra told Hank, "You're holding the bat the wrong way. Turn the LABEL toward you, so you can read it!" (That's the way you were actually taught to hold the bat to cut down on the chance breaking it). Aaron IGNORED Berra and hit HOME-RUN in that at bat! As Aaron rounded the bases, touched home plate and was on his way back to the dugout, he looked back at Berra and said, "Hey Yogi, I came here to HIT ...NOT TO READ!"

Don't let your enemies get your FOCUS off of JESUS TODAY! They will certainly TRY! :o)

November 5
Stand Still and See the YESHUA

Exodus 14:13 ~ "And Moses said unto the people, 'Fear ye not, stand still, and see the salvation of the Lord, which he will shew to you today: for the Egyptians whom ye have seen today, ye shall see them again no more for ever.' "

It's interesting how YOU ALL can say things that cause scripture in my brain to be freed from the cobwebs in the corner of my cranium! :o)

My friend Terry Padilla said something in her comment on the last post that led me to this scripture! Speaking of the enemy who is always after us, and knowing where our help comes from, Terry said, "Bring it on!" The enemy WILL bring it (heartache, strife, backbiting, jealousy, etc.) you know, even WITHOUT an invitation or a forwarding address!

So what do you do when the enemy BRINGS IT ON? Do the SAME thing I told you to do in the last post! Exodus 14:13 is the Old Testament illustration of the revelation in Hebrews 12:2 from the previous post! It says, "Stand still and see the YESHUAH (the Hebrew word which means salvation, victory, deliverance) of God!" The word YESHUAH is also the Hebrew word for JESUS, which means "SALVATION" or "JEHOVAH SAVES" (John 1:21). Great name for a SAVIOUR! So, "Stand still and FOCUS ON the YESHUAH (JESUS) of the LORD"

Yes, JESUS WAS, before HE WAS! And He WILL save you from the attacks of the enemy. GOD said it here, LONG BEFORE legendary R&B singer James Brown did. God says, "Sit back, RELAX, and WATCH ME WORK ...through my Son JESUS!" :o)

November 6
Shamira and Her Duck

1 Peter 2:25 ~ "...Return to the Shepherd and Bishop of your souls!"

When she was a baby and before she could walk, our six-year-old girl used to take a bath with a YELLOW RUBBER DUCK. One day she taught me something about the BILLOWS (large waves or swells of water/trouble) that come in our lives from time to time.

My wife Nina had her at one end of the tub as her "yellow duckie" began to drift away to the opposite end of the tub. I thought my baby would get upset because she couldn't reach her duck. She did something that blew my mind. She lifted up both hands high in the air and came down on the water with her open palms, WHAM!!! She REPEATED that action over and over. I thought she was having a tantrum because the WAVES she was creating were causing the RUBBER DUCK to move farther away. She kept hitting the water until the duck hit the opposite wall of the tub.

Guess what happened? When the RUBBER DUCK had NOWHERE to go, it started floating BACK TOWARD SHAMIRA!!! Shamira then did ONE LAST THING that let me know that babies have more sense than we give them credit for! She would hit the water, forcing the waves form the opposite wall to push the duck back to her. Then she turned her palms upward and made a motion opening and closing all of her fingers as if to tell the duck, "COME BACK TO ME!" Eventually she had the duck SAFE and SECURE ...BACK IN HER POSSESSION!

GOD often ALLOWS WAVES of trial and sorrow in our lives to push us up against a wall, so that our only option ...is to come BACK TO HIM. He LOVES US that much! :o)

November 7
Jesus
Matthew 16:13~ "When Jesus came into the coasts of Caesarea Philippi,
he asked his disciples, saying,
'Whom do men say that I the Son of man am?' "

Jesus? The One who was, is & forever shall be? The One who is Living Water but can use water for a sidewalk or look at it & make it blush until it turns to wine, that Jesus? Jesus Christ, the One older than his mother & the same age as his Father? The Son of the Living God? The One Whose earthly father was told by an angel that his wife was pregnant by a ghost? That Jesus? Yeah, I know Him!

November 8
Our Daily Bread
Matthew 6:11 ~ "Give us this day our DAILY bread."

Why did Jesus teach His disciples to pray, "Give us THIS DAY our DAILY BREAD?" Why not teach them to ask for MONTHLY or YEARLY BREAD? Because God wants our DAILY TRUST! He would love to hear from us… DAILY!

If God gave us TOO MUCH at one time, SOME of us would forget and NOT talk to God again until we needed more bread (Proverbs 30:8-9)! FAITH is a DAILY walk. We need DAILY strength, DAILY encouragement, DAILY instruction, DAILY provision, DAILY protection etc. Sort of the reason some of you stop by this page, DAILY! :o)

November 9 (written in 2012)
Peace, Be Still
Mark 4:39 ~ "And He (Jesus) arose, and rebuked the wind,
and said unto the sea, 'Peace, be still.'
And the wind ceased, and there was a great calm."

My heart goes out to all who have lost family members and property on the East coast during HURRICANE SANDY. I commend our leaders for doing everything they can as fast as they can, but I do have one problem. I know it's not "politically correct", but when are we as a "God-fearing" nation going to at least ACKNOWLEDGE the one who can handle Sandy?!

I've heard politicians mention why the basketball game was canceled and why the marathon was not canceled. I even heard some leaders assure those affected by the storm that our prayers, (all religions pray in one way or another), are with them. Why isn't anyone publicly saying, WE KNOW SOMEBODY who can tell Sandy to BE STILL! The reason God "appears" to be asleep in these matters is because we call on the firefighters, police, FEMA, crisis responders, as well we should. But remember that they are set up to deal with the RESULTS of the problem and the devastation. Only God alone can short circuit THE PROBLEM ITSELF!

Jesus' disciples found that out when they went down into the ship during a devastating storm and found Him ASLEEP (verse 38)! See, right there?!!! Knowing what I now know about God, if I had been on that boat and saw the Master asleep, I would have laid down right next to Him!

The disciples already had The Lord's assurance that the would make it to the other side (verse 35)! But they woke Jesus up and asked Him if He cared that they were about to perish (38). Jesus got up and simply admonished SANDY and told the water, "Hush… Put a MUZZLE on it!" which is the LITERAL translation of "Peace, be still!"

November 10
King ME!

1 Samuel 8:5 ~ " 'Look,' the leaders of Israel told Samuel.
'You are now old, and your sons are not like you.
Give us a king like all the other nations have.'"

I pray that every eligible person exercised his or her right to vote, and yes... I DID! But remember, no matter WHO you voted for, 1 Samuel Chapter 8 tells us the true reason WHY things are the way they are. Before the events in 1 Samuel 8, Israel had NO HUMAN KING (leader, president)! GOD Himself was their "de facto" King. God's people decided they wanted a "king" like all the other nations had (8:5).

The prophet Samuel was not happy with that decision. So he prayed to the Lord (verse 6). God told Samuel, to give them what they asked for. "They haven't rejected YOU, but they don't want ME to reign over them!"said God (verse 7). God told Samuel in chapter 8, verse 9, to make sure that he (Samuel) let the people know what kind of king (human) would be over them. God gave Samuel a list for the people, of the things they could expect from a "flesh and blood" king. Tell me if these things sound familiar. God told Samuel to inform the people that this was the type of leader they would have, and how he would treat them (verse 11):

1. He will draft your sons for his army (11)
2. Some of your men will lead his armies, and others will plow his fields and harvest his crops (12).
3. Others will build weapons of war for your leader (12)
4. Your women will have to work (13)
5. He will take your property for his own purposes (14). (We call that "eminent domain")!
6. He will TAX you (15,17). God said, "You're going to cry out to me because of this "king" YOU have chosen for yourselves, and I WON'T HEAR YOU!"

WOW! No matter who our next HUMAN king is, we as Christians need to recognize who our REAL leader is. He's calling everyone of us. Listen.......! He's saying the same thing we said, when we crossed into enemy territory while playing that board game with the black and red checkers... KING ME!!!

November 11
Happy Veteran's Day
(official, not the changing observed date)
John 8:36 ~ "So if the Son sets you FREE,
you will be free indeed." (ESV)"

"...Oh say does that star-spangled banner yet WAVE, o'er the land of the FREE, and the home of the brave?!" ~ HAPPY VETERAN'S DAY!!! If you see a man or a woman in uniform, or if you know a veteran personally, THANK THEM for their service to this country.

Dr. Richard C. Caesar was born in Lake Village, Arkansas on April 12, 1918. In 1940, he graduated from Morehouse College in Atlanta, Georgia. He was then drafted into the military, which is why he is on this page today. During World War II, he rose to the rank of Lt. Colonel. Dr. Caesar was one of several awarded the Congressional Gold Medal in the Capitol Rotunda in April of 2007, by then President George W. Bush. After retiring from military service, Caesar earned a Doctor of Dentistry Degree in 1951 from Meharry Medical College. He had a dental practice in San Francisco, California for over 40 years. I should know, because Dr. Richard Caesar is the reason I still have most of my original teeth in my mouth!!! Yes, he was our family dentist when I was a child, and through my teenage years!

If you Google Dr. Caesar, you'll find out that he passed away on December 20, 2011 at the age of 93. My son now cares for his grave, at the Golden Gate National Cemetery in San Bruno, California. Dr. Caesar is buried there because he was also... an original TUSKEGEE AIRMAN!

As I talked to my son earlier today about the preparation for different events on Veteran's Day Sunday, he told me something that shocked me. I was trying to ascertain whether or not Dr. Caesar was a Christian. My son told me that he didn't know. I then asked if there was a CROSS on Dr. Caesar's headstone. (The CROSS being the symbol of Christians who believe that Jesus Christ freed us from the penalty of sin when He died on Calvary's Cross). This is the answer that blew me away."Dad, there are more than 137,000 headstones in that cemetery. There are more than twice as many people buried there, because some of the graves have up to FOUR people in them! Since I've been here, I have seen maybe TWO headstones that DID NOT have a CROSS on it!"

Now you and I both know that that percentage of veterans and their families being Christian is very improbable. But have you ever walked into a church where those TWO flags were on a stand somewhere on the premises, and you wondered why they were there? You see, after talking to my son, I realized that the flag on the right (The Cross), has to TEACH the flag on the left... HOW TO WAVE!!!

November 12
Lift Up Your Eyes
Psalm 121:2 ~ "I lift up my eyes to the hills.
From where does my help come?
My help comes from the LORD, who made heaven and earth." (ESV)

I shared with you some time ago how to read Psalm 121:1-2. The English Standard Version up top is how the verse should read. I lift up my eyes to the hills (period). Where does my help come from (question mark)? My HELP comes from the Lord...(period). Looking toward the hills just gets your head pointed in the right direction... UP!

Remember this, next time you seek help from the wrong people: James Garfield was our 20th President. 200 days into office, he was "assassinated" according to history. Garfield was actually shot, but the BULLET didn't kill him. He died from INFECTION when several WELL-MEANING people, with NO MODERN TECHNOLOGY, poked around in his body looking for the bullet! SOME people MEAN WELL, but do MORE HARM THAN GOOD poking around in your life! Do you know where your HELP truly comes from? It's in verse 2. :)

November 13
Get Your Thinking Straight
Romans 12:3 ~ "For by the grace given to me
I say to everyone among you
not to think of himself more highly than he ought to think,
but to think with sober judgment,
each according to the measure of faith that God has assigned." (ESV)

I wish I could convey in English the emphatic use of the Greek verb in this verse for THINK, which is "phroneo." It is used in some form, FOUR (4) times in the verse. I'll give it a shot anyway.

"For by the grace given to me, I say to everyone of you not to THINK of himself more highly than he ought to THINK, but to THINK with sober THINKING, based on the amount of faith that God has given each of us."

Here it is in plain English. "God has gifted me with the grace to tell you that just because He has also gifted you, you're NOT all that, a bag of chips and a side salad!!!"

God deliver me from folk who think that their grace gift is more important than someone else's! Before you stick your chest out about the gift God has given you, consider the following story. An elderly mother of a church lay dying in her hospital bed. She called for her pastor and the chairman of the Board of Deacons to come to her bedside. Filled with pride by the request, the two men went to see her in the hospital. Before the went to the hospital, they let as many people as they could know that one of the most important members in the church was dying, and she had asked specifically for them!

When they got to her hospital room, she asked each of them to stand by her on opposite sides of the bed. Maybe she was going to include them in her will, they thought. The deacon pulled out a small pocket Bible to read a scripture, while the pastor prepared to pray. With a weakened voice, the elderly woman looked up at both of them and said, "Now I can die just like JESUS died... between a ROBBER AND A THIEF!!!"

November 14
All, not Y'all
Romans 3:23 ~ "For all have sinned,
and come short of the glory of God..."

Why do some people read that verse up top as though they have a Southern accent? "Y'ALL have sinned, and come short of the glory of God!" Let me share a story that I heard from Deacon James Threat, that may help illustrate the verse clearly!

There was an old priest who got sick of all the people in his parish who kept confessing to the sin of adultery. One Sunday from the pulpit he said, "If I hear one more person confess to adultery, I'll quit!"

Well, everybody liked him, so they came up with a "code" word. Someone who had committed adultery would say they had "fallen." This seemed to satisfy the old priest, and things went well. The priest died at a ripe old age. About a week after the new priest arrived, he visited the Mayor of the town and seemed very concerned. The new priest said, "You have to do something about the sidewalks in town. When people come to confession, they keep talking about having 'FALLEN'! The mayor started to laugh, realizing that NO ONE had told the new priest about the code word. Before the mayor could explain, the priest shook an accusing finger at the mayor and said, "I don't know what YOU'RE laughing about! YOUR WIFE fell three times this week!!!" :)

November 15
Controversial!
Romans 16:1 ~ "I (Paul) introduce to you Phoebe our sister,
who is a SERVANT of the church in ☐Cenchrea..."

182

Forgive me for waxing controversial this evening, but I was in-boxed a question that I get quite often. The question was, "CAN WOMEN BECOME DEACONS IN TODAY'S CHURCH?"

Based on the above verse, not only can they become deacons, but there is NO SUCH THING in the Bible as a "deaconess"! I know that some of you are ready to hit the delete button, but you might want to hang on. After all, this page IS about getting at the TRUTH!!!

The word in Greek from which we get our word "Deacon" is DIAKONOS. The word "diakonos" means a servant or minister, one who SERVES! It's the word "DEACONS" in Philippians 1:1; the word "DEACONS" in 1 Timothy 3:8, 12; and it's the word "SERVANT" up there in the verse! You would have to ask the translators why they didn't call her a deacon. From the word "diakonos" comes the words "administration" in Acts 6:1; "serve" in Acts 6:2; and "ministry" in Acts 6:4. Stephen and Philip (Acts 6:5) as well as Phoebe, were all DEACONS! There is NO "deaconess" form of the word!

Now, for those of you who still believe that Paul had a problem giving authority to a woman, which is what he is doing in the context of the verse (see verse 2), look at Romans 16:7. You see the name Junia listed among the "noteworthy" APOSTLES? That's a WOMAN!!!

Many commentators avoid Romans 16:7. Others say that God gave us the FEMININE FORM of a man's name! REALLY??? Does God need to CONFUSE US any more than we already are? I think not! The Bible IS what it is, and says what it says loved ones! Now go SERVE where God has called you, ladies and gentlemen!

November 16
Upside Down
Acts 17:6 ~ "And when they found them not,
they drew Jason and certain brethren unto the rulers of the city, crying,
'These that have turned the world upside down are come hither also!' "

Did you know that everything you see with your natural eye is actually UPSIDE DOWN?! There is something in the back part of your eye-ball called the RETINA that receives the signals of what you see ...UPSIDE DOWN. Once the image enters your retina, your BRAIN actually processes things RIGHT-SIDE-UP! Isn't God amazing?! The Bible is true, we are reverently (there's that word "YARE" again talking about US!) and wonderfully made (Psalm 139:14)! What you see right-side-up, actually comes to you UPSIDE DOWN! So according to the verse, Luke says that those who were preaching JESUS CHRIST (Acts 17:1-4) …were just SETTING THINGS RIGHT-SIDE-UP by turning them UPSIDE DOWN!!! Jesus can make things right in your life ...IF YOU LET HIM! He may have to turn some things in your life UPSIDE DOWN in order to make them RIGHT! He said in Revelation 3:20, "Behold I stand at the door (of your heart) and KNOCK!..." Now He COULD knock the door down...BUT HE WON'T. Think about it! :o)

November 17
God Flips the Script
Daniel 6:18-22 ~ "Then the king went to his palace,
and passed the night fasting: neither were instruments of musick brought
before him: and his sleep went from him.
Then the king arose very early in the morning,
and went in haste unto the den of lions.
And when he came to the den, he cried with a lamentable voice unto Daniel:
and the king spake and said to Daniel,
'O Daniel, servant of the living God, is thy God,
whom thou servest continually, able to deliver thee from the lions?'
Then said Daniel unto the king, 'O king, live for ever.
My God hath sent his angel, and hath shut the lions' mouths,
that they have not hurt me:
forasmuch as before him innocency was found in me;
and also before thee, O king, have I done no hurt.' "

Daniel was at PEACE IN THE LION'S DEN when most of us would have stayed up all night worrying about the lions. King Darius (who ordered Daniel to be thrown into the den ~ 6:16) had NO PEACE IN HIS PALACE worrying about Daniel, when he (Darius) should have been asleep. The devil is like a roaring lion, walking around seeking whom he may devour (2 Peter 5:8). Got LION problems? Daniel had peace with the lions AND with THE LORD. If you TRUST GOD, He can FLIP THE SCRIPT!

November 18
Sorry, Rocks!
Psalm 98:8 ~ "Let the floods clap their hands:
let the hills be joyful together."

Isaiah 55:12 ~ "For ye shall go out with joy,
and be led forth with peace:

the mountains and the hills
shall break forth before you into singing,
and all the trees of the field shall clap their hands."

Have you ever been praising God and felt like someone was watching you and saying, "It doesn't take all of that!"? The verses teach that GOD'S CREATION has more praise for the CREATOR than SOME PEOPLE! Floods, mountains and trees all clap, sing and rejoice! If WE hold OUR peace, Jesus said we're inviting ROCKS to join the celebration (Luke 19:40)! Insert Praise HERE! ~ SORRY, ROCKS, I will BLESS the Lord at ALL TIMES!

November 19
Who's Going To Bell the Cat?
Isaiah 29:13 ~ "Wherefore the Lord said,
'Forasmuch as this people draw near me with their mouth,
and with their lips do honour me,
but have removed their heart far from me,
and their fear toward me is taught by the precept of men...' "

Once I asked my wife why she was laughing so hard in the room down the hall. She said our then 6-year-old girl asked her if we could have a cat. She knows that I am allergic to cats, so she immediately told my wife that "daddy" won't have to take care of the cat. "I'll take care of it," our little girl said. My wife asked, "Who's going to CLEAN UP after the cat?" Baby girl said, "Asa [my adult son] will!"

She reminded me of an apocryphal cat story that Dr. E.W. Roland shared in revival at our church some years ago. It seems that a group of MICE had a meeting one day about what to do about the harsh treatment they were receiving from the CATS in the neighborhood. One cat in particular was quite vicious. You could see the wounds that he had inflicted on several of the mice at the meeting. The focus of the meeting was on this one cat in particular who was wreaking so much havoc on the mice. A mouse who was missing part of one leg as a result of an encounter with the cat spoke first."Fellow Rats and Gentle Mice, I suggest that a BELL be procured, and tied to the neck of the cat. That way we will hear the cat as it approaches." Applause went up all around the meeting. "What a BRILLIANT idea!" they all said with one voice.

Another mouse who was missing part of an ear, and older than most at the meeting spoke up. "I AGREE. It's a WONDERFUL IDEA. I just have ONE question. Who's going to BELL THE CAT?" A motion was made and seconded to dismiss the meeting, with still NO solution!

Do you know people who can ALWAYS recognize and can even tell you HOW to solve the problem, but NEVER want to be PART OF THE SOLUTION. They can tell YOU how to fix YOUR marriage or raise YOUR children, but don't want to be part of their own advice in solving their own problems. Many of them are people who go through the motions of FAITH for outward appearances. That's what the verse says. They SPEAK well ABOUT GOD and FOR GOD with their lips, but their hearts are far FROM GOD! I know the verse was NOT talking about you. The verse is for Pookie and Ray Ray down the street and around the corner. :o)

November 20
Don't be Crabby
Philippians 2:3-5 ~ "Let nothing be done
through strife or vainglory; but in lowliness of mind
let each esteem other better than themselves.
Look not every man on his own things,
but every man also on the things of others.
Let this mind be in you, which was also in Christ Jesus:"

Do you know anyone with a CRAB mentality? (This is a RHETORICAL QUESTION! That means it's to provoke thought. (Please don't put any names on my Facebook page. You MIGHT find YOUR NAME there! :o) Ever dealt with LIVE CRAB? If you put them in a bucket and walk away, there will be NO COVER required on the bucket. It's the reason there is no lid on the LOBSTER tank at the Red Lobster (at least not in our area)! When you come back, you'll have the SAME number of crab (or lobster), that were in the bucket when you left!Why don't you need a lid on a bucket of crab? Because when one crab tries to climb OUT of the bucket, ANOTHER CRAB will REACH UP and PULL it back DOWN!

Please don't let that be YOU doing the pulling. Let's LIFT ONE ANOTHER UP! As a matter of fact, the reason we go to church is to exhort, encourage, and/or lift each other up! (Hebrews 10:25). So stop using that excuse about how "...you can worship God at home!" That's TRUE, but you can't ENCOURAGE ME ...IF YOU'RE AT HOME! If we LIFT one another up, we can ALL get out of this CRAZY CRAB COFFIN ...TOGETHER! :o)

November 21
Dress Codes

1 Peter 3:3 ~ "Whose adorning let it not be that outward adorning of plaiting the hair, and of wearing of gold, or of putting on of apparel..."

Here is another one of those verses that has been taken out of context. Christian women have been told that they should not braid their hair or wear jewelry. This verse has also been connected with 2 Kings 9:30 about Jezebel, which says she painted her face (eyes) and tired (beautified or crowned) her head. Some people have said if a woman wears make-up, jewelry or has her hair braided, she is a Jezebel! Jezebel anticipated her death, and wanted to DIE LIKE A QUEEN! The verse has NOTHING to do with her being seductive, as has been suggested.

Can we straighten out ONE MORE THING today? 1 Peter 3:3 is NOT a prohibition to making yourself look better! If you can't wear jewelry or braided hair, then you CAN'T WEAR CLOTHES EITHER! The "wearing of apparel" is in the same verse. The verse simply says, don't let OUTWARD things determine WHO YOU ARE in the eyes of those watching you. A person should love you whether your hair is braided on your head, or on a Styrofoam head on the dresser. They should love your beautiful teeth, no matter if they are in your mouth, or in a glass on the bathroom counter!What draws people to you ought to be the GODLY person on the INSIDE according to verse 4, not what you do to the outside. Please don't get things twisted. You should do whatever you can do to make your OUTWARD APPEARANCE as beautiful as possible.

But remember, "You can PAINT THE PUMP, but it won't change the QUALITY of the WATER!"Almost 40 years ago, before I knew the Lord real well, I got a traffic ticket for driving TOO SLOW in the fast lane! When the ANGRY highway patrol officer pulled me over, he took one look at me and got ANGRIER. I was on my way to CHOIR REHEARSAL, dressed in a full length BLUE LEATHER coat, DOUBLE KNIT pants and top with silver studs from the cuff to the shoulder on the top. The same silver studs went from hip to ankle on the pants. Blue leather boots (you all stop laughing!) to match the coat! The officer said, "What are you doing driving this piece of junk in the fast lane. You're going to get somebody killed! LOOK AT YOU! You need to be on a HORSE, not in a car!" He just called it, AS HE SAW IT. Appearances ARE important, but they shouldn't determine someone's judgment of who you are. I DID NOT look like who I was representing. OK NOW, pants up, hemlines down ...FORWARD MARCH!!! :o

November 22
Where God Abides

Psalm 22:3 ~ "But thou art holy,
O thou that inhabitest the praises of Israel."

God "abides in" the praises of His people. Praise isn't always
PERFECT. Choirs and musicians should be trained (Psalm 33:3), but
personal praise is PERSONAL! If the person praising God next to you at any
given service is out of tune, off key, or unable to speak in the king's English,
know that GOD understands it! What do YOU do when your child messes
up that Easter or Christmas SPEECH or SONG? You say, "Go ahead baby
(sweetheart if you're of a different culture :o)! That's MY child (baby)!"God
inhabits GENUINE PRAISE, no matter how OFF-KEY it may be, or WHO
is offering it! A young pastor, after his first Sunday at his new church,
decided to let an Elderly Church Mother know that her prayer during the
devotion was FULL of INCORRECT ENGLISH. She quietly said, "With all
due respect Pastor, I WASN'T TALKING TO YOU"! God understands
IMPERFECT PRAISE & PRAYERS. Grandma said, "I may not be able to
sing like angels or preach like Paul..." Go on & praise HIM, with your
IMPERFECT SELF!!! ~ Romans 8:26

November 23
Just Obey
1 Samuel 15:22 ~ "Obedience is better than sacrifice."

Remember when some of us were taught that if you DID NOT OBEY
authority, you would pay (sacrifice) dearly! We were KEPT IN LINE by a
threat of DIVINE VENGEANCE. That's NOT what this verse says! When
you committed a sin under the Law, you said you were SORRY to God and
had your sins COVERED by sacrificing an INNOCENT animal. In the
verse, God says "JUST OBEY ME! That's BETTER than trying to make up
for it by KILLING (sacrificing) all of those poor animals! Now you
understand why MANY families had LARGE HERDS of Cattle & FLOCKS
of Sheep!!! :o)

November 24
We All Have Issues
Mark 5:25 ~ "And a certain woman,
which had an issue of blood twelve years..."

What do the words rheumatic fever, rheumatoid arthritis, and
rheumatism have in common? The ROOT word "rheuma". Rheuma comes

from the Greek word "rhusis", which means "to flow"! It's the word "ISSUE" in this verse. This woman's ISSUE was a constant menstrual flow. WE ALL have issues! What's YOURS? Faulty finances, fickle family, horrible health, jacked-up job, bi-polar believers or schizophrenic saints? Focus on what JESUS did for us on Calvary. Then the ISSUES flowing from your heart (as Pastor Hezekiah Walker would say) will become GRATEFULNESS!

November 25
When Money Tells of Its Travels
1 Timothy 6:17-18 ~ "Charge them that are rich in this world,
that they be not highminded, nor trust in uncertain riches,
but in the living God, who giveth us richly all things to enjoy;
That they do good, that they be rich in good works,
ready to distribute, willing to communicate."

In keeping with the Thanksgiving spirit, I heard an apocryphal story about a group of monetary BILLS having a discussion and BRAGGING about their travels.

The THOUSAND-DOLLAR BILL said, "I've been in the pockets of some of the RICHEST people in the world!"

The HUNDRED-DOLLAR BILL said, "I've traveled to foreign lands in all parts of the globe."

The FIFTY-DOLLAR BILL said, "I've been to some of the finest restaurants in the world."

The TWENTY-DOLLAR BILL said, "I've been in some of the most popular department stores anywhere."

The TEN-DOLLAR BILL chimed in, "I've been to grocery and corner stores everywhere!"

The FIVE-DOLLAR BILL told the group, "I've been an allowance in the pockets and purses of little kids everywhere for years."

The BILLS noticed that the ONE-DOLLAR BILL wasn't responding, so they asked him, "...and WHERE have you been?"

The ONE-DOLLAR BILL said, "I've been ...TO CHURCH!"

In the spirit of Thanksgiving, let's do better than that same old DOLLAR in our giving to the Kingdom of God ...especially those of us who INVEST in churches and organizations that HELP OTHERS! :o)

November 26
How to Have a Happier Thanksgiving

Proverbs 25:17 ~ "Withdraw thy foot from thy neighbour's house;
lest he be weary of thee, and so hate thee."

THANKSGIVING is an EMOTIONAL holiday. Family members travel THOUSANDS OF MILES to see people they only see ONCE A YEAR, and then they are rudely reminded of EXACTLY WHY! (This is a re-post of my friend Bartin Mrooks' status from last year at this time. The scripture and the following comment are mine). Here's how to BIBLICALLY avoid this problem. After you have eaten and exchanged pleasantries this wonderful Thanksgiving Day, the scripture says, "Withdraw thy foot from thy neighbor's house; lest he be weary of thee, and hate thee." Translation: GO HOME BEFORE THEY GET TIRED OF YOU, and not like you very much! (This works for more than just Thanksgiving!!! :o)

November 27
Freely Give
Matthew 10:8 ~ "Heal the sick, cleanse the lepers, raise the dead, cast out devils: freely ye have received, freely give."

This verse has been so often misquoted that it just seemed appropriate during this THANKSGIVING HOLIDAY Season to look at it again! The verse does NOT say "...freely you give, freely you shall receive"! The season IS NOT about receiving! Read Matthew 10:8 again S-L-O-W-L-Y. Jesus was trying to teach his disciples that just as YOU have RECEIVED so much from ME (context), GIVE to others in the same way! "...Freely you HAVE RECEIVED (from me), freely GIVE!" Stop GIVING in order to GET. Give because of what you HAVE RECEIVED...like salvation, grace, mercy, protection, healing, favor, etc. All from HIM! Again, HAPPY ThanksGIVING! :o)

November 28 (originally written in 2011)
How to REALLY Occupy Everything
Luke 19:13 ~ "And he called his ten servants,
and delivered them ten pounds, and said unto them,
'Occupy till I come.' "

This probably won't be popular, but then again God did NOT call me to be popular. I will however share the TRUTH of His Word. The King James Version of this verse says, "OCCUPY until I come!"
The way to defeat GREED is NOT to OCCUPY WALL STREET or

any other street. All THAT does is TICK OFF everyday people who are trying to get through those streets others are occupying!!!

Isn't it ironic that JESUS instructed His disciples, by way of this parable, to do the OPPOSITE of what the "OCCUPY" movement is trying to do? We can defeat greed on WALL STREET, by INVESTING in The Kingdom on STRAIGHT STREET (Acts 9:11)! That would be any BUSINESS that helps build the Kingdom of God!

The Greek word "OCCUPY" in Luke 19:13 means to "do business, invest, or carry on the business of a BANKER or TRADER!" OCCUPY (Invest …or NOT) with your MONEY, not your body!

If you have a problem with the price of things, STOP SUPPORTING those places. I guarantee you their prices will go down, or THEY will go out of business! The CIVIL RIGHTS MOVEMENT was WON because Dr. Martin Luther King Jr. and others convinced African Americans NOT to INVEST in a bus company that wouldn't let us sit in ANY available seat on the bus! They didn't have to BLOCK the buses. They just STOPPED spending their money to ride them! Eventually the buses were virtually EMPTY, therefore headed for bankruptcy.

Now OCCUPY – INVEST in the Kingdom, until JESUS COMES! :o)

November 29
What do Snakes and Sin Have in Common?
John 1:29 ~ "The next day John saw Jesus coming toward him, and said, 'Behold the Lamb of God, who takes away☐ the sin of the world.' "

Years ago I took my son Marcus to what was then Marine World. A SNAKE TRAINER by the name of Steve was out in the open, near the entrance of the park holding a 12 ft. SNAKE! As he held the head of the snake in his hands, the middle of the snake's body was draped over his shoulder and the rest of the snake was on the ground! Steve was answering questions. The question & answers went something like this:

Question: "How long will the snake GROW?"
Steve: "As long as I feed it!" (So does SIN!)
Question: "Do COLORS bother it?" (Asked by a lady wearing a BRIGHT RED outfit!)
Steve: "Snakes are virtually COLOR BLIND!" (So is SIN!)
Question by my son Marcus: "CAN I HOLD IT?"
Steve: "No son. What will happen is, he'll end up HOLDING YOU!" (So will Sin!)

By the way, something caught my attention about Steve as he HELD the snake! Steve only had 8 FINGERS! I'm just saying! Stay AWAY from snakes, and CLOSE to the ERASER. His name? JESUS!!! John 1:29 is still GOOD NEWS. :o)

November 30
Come Out, Come Out, Wherever You Are
Luke 13:34 ~ "O Jerusalem, Jerusalem, which killest the prophets, and
stonest them that are sent unto thee;
how often would I have gathered thy children together,
as a hen doth gather her brood under her wings,
and ye would not!"

I was better at the game of JACKS than most girls or boys, (stop laughing)! We threw jacks (see profile picture) on a level surface and a little red ball in the air. The ball bounced once while we picked up the jacks in a sweeping (gathering) motion, one at a time, then 2, 3 (1'sees, 2'sees, 3'sees etc....). Then we caught the ball. If a jack had rolled too far away, (like under a chair or a table), it was hard to GATHER! Jesus wants to GATHER (save) US TO HIMSELF. Will you LET Him? Then COME OUT FROM UNDER whatever you are hiding under, and let JESUS have your life! :o

December

December 1
The Story of the Candy Cane
Matthew 1:21~ "And she shall bring forth a son,
and thou shalt call his name Jesus:
for he shall save his people from their sins."

It started as a straight white stick. Christians used changes in the item to teach. A RED STRIPE represents the blood of OUR SAVIOR on a background of WHITE (purity). A German choirmaster is said to be responsible for the hook at the end that looks like a SHEPHERD'S CROOK (Psalm 23). Upside down it looks like a "J", for JESUS (Matthew 1:21)! When I give a child a CANDY CANE, that's my story & I'm sticking to it :o)

December 2
Total Commitment
Romans 12:1~ "I beseech you therefore, brethren,
by the mercies of God,
that ye present your bodies a living sacrifice,
holy, acceptable unto God, which is your reasonable service."

A pig & a chicken in the back of a truck saw a sign: "Ham & Eggs, $3.50."

Pig: "I'm getting out!"
Chicken: "Let's go a little farther."
They saw another sign, "Ham & Eggs, $2.50."
Pig: "I'm gone!"
Chicken: "Let's see what the end will be."
Pig: "I already know! When people eat ham & eggs, it only requires a little INVOLVEMENT from you. For ME, it's a TOTAL COMMITMENT!"

Are You TOTALLY COMMITTED?

December 3
Really BAD Tea Partying (and Not in Politics)

Luke 12:15 ~ "And he said unto them,
'Take heed, and beware of covetousness:
for a man's life consisteth not in the abundance
of the things which he possesseth.' "

Beware of COVETOUSNESS, & SHARE with others. Covetousness is wanting more & more of what you have enough of, ALREADY (Haddon Robinson)!

"I had a little tea party, this afternoon at three - it was very small, three guests in all - Just I, Myself & ME. Myself ate all the sandwiches, While I drank up the tea - It was also I, who ate the pie - And passed the cake TO ME!" Are you guilty of Tea Parties for ONE?

December 4
Open The Book!
Hebrews 1:1-2 ~ "God, who at sundry times and in divers manners spake
in time past unto the fathers by the prophets,
Hath in these last days spoken unto us by his Son,
whom he hath appointed heir of all things,
by whom also he made the worlds."

Why are we concerned when PEOPLE stop talking to us? We have been in the presence of famous people who haven't said a word to us. We have RELATIVES who don't speak to us! It doesn't matter because verse 2 says GOD speaks to us, IN HIS SON (by way of His Word). Dr. Warren Wiersbe told a group of us in Dallas, Texas in 2003 that when we open the Bible, GOD SPEAKS! Do you need someone to talk to you? OPEN THE BOOK! :o)

December 5
In Due Season
Galatians 6:9 ~ "And let us not grow weary of doing good,
for in due season we will reap, if we do not give up." (ESV)

In December 2012 I gave a heart-felt THANK YOU to Timothy Dupre, Sally Carter, and the Fellowship Bible Institute and College of Urban Studies for conferring upon me (and others) a degree that was earned almost 20 years ago. Transitions within the school itself put the conferring of the degrees on hold until yesterday. Back then, during the early through mid 90's, I simply did the work and left the rest in God's hands.

A better understanding of the verse up top is a result of the long wait. The word for "due season" in the verse, is KAIROS. It means an opportune or seasonable time! The degree means more now, than it would have back then. I can also encourage YOU ALL now! Encourage you to do what? To hang in there, no matter what. You WILL REAP (enjoy the fruit of your labor)... at the right time (due season).

December 6
Will Somebody Please, Please Tell Me Why?
Psalm 127:3-4 ~ "Behold, children are a HERITAGE from the LORD,
the fruit of the womb a reward. Like arrows in the hand of a warrior
are the children of one's youth." (ESV)

Please don't misunderstand what I am about to say. I love children and young people dearly. I would go to the mat for them. But they need to be taught that they belong to GOD (His heritage, possession, property), and WE (parents and elders) have been made stewards over them. That's what the verses up top say. According to verse 2, we are to guide young children in the right direction like a warrior guides an arrow to its target! So why are 10-year-olds on the streets at two in the morning with cigarettes in their mouths?

December 7
Mountain High
Matthew 17:9~ "And as they came down from the mountain, Jesus charged
them, saying, 'Tell the vision to no man,
until the Son of man be risen again from the dead.'"

Mark 9:9~ "And as they came down from the mountain,
he charged them that they should tell no man
what things they had seen,
till the Son of man were risen from the dead."

Luke 9:37 ~ "And it came to pass, that on the next day,
when they were come down from the hill, much people met him."

Peter, James and John have just witnessed the TRANSFIGURATION of Jesus (a glimpse of the GLORIFIED Christ)!
I remember a great Sunday evening in years past. The wife and I, (as special guests of Maestro Curtis and his lovely wife Nola Curtis), got a

chance to have an ADULT NIGHT (kid free) out at the Wyndham Parc 55 Hotel in San Francisco! Thank you to my daughter Sheree Scott for watching our little girl that day.

Nina and I felt like proud parents as our sons Aaron Bailey (bass) and Adam Bailey (keyboards), and our God-son Roland Wiley II (drums), played for the legendary Dorothy Morrison. She is the writer and singer of the ORIGINAL "Oh Happy Day" with the Edwin Hawkins singers. They also played behind Dalon Collins, the lead singer for Kirk Franklin and the Family. That night was INDEED a MOUNTAIN HIGH! Many of us were on a MOUNTAIN HIGH ...yesterday.

Now from the mountaintop experience (lets say, SUNDAY), back down the hill and often into the valley (lets say, MONDAY). Ever feel that way the DAY AFTER Sunday Service, let's say oh...TODAY? Peter wanted to pitch three tents (Mark 9:5) and STAY THERE (on the mountain).

NEWS FLASH! Ministry was waiting for them at the foot of the mountain. There's MORE WORK to be done ...DOWN HERE! Enjoy your Monday...in the VALLEY! :o)

December 8
Made for God's Glory
Isaiah 43:7 ~ "Even every one that is called by my name:
for I have created him for my glory,
I have formed him; yea, I have made him."

I don't expect much response to this, but I believe most of you come to this page for the TRUTH! This verse says that we were made for GOD'S GLORY! We can better understand why Paul told the church at Corinth that our BODIES are the Holy of Holies (naos) of the Holy Spirit (1 Corinthians 6:19-20). The "naos" was MORE than just the Temple. It was the MOST HOLY PLACE in the Temple! He also said that we DO NOT belong to ourselves. We have been BOUGHT with a price. That price was the DEATH of His Son JESUS on Calvary! Is what you are doing with your body glorifying God? Be careful WHAT you PUT IN your body, and WHO you give ACCESS to your body! And for God's Glory, Jesus said ...PLEASE "REST YOUR BODY" (Mark 6:31)! The disciples had worked so hard, they hadn't even taken time TO EAT! Some of us wouldn't be so MEAN if we just took a VACATION every now and then. It doesn't have to be expensive, and it doesn't always have to be long. Just TURN ASIDE ...and REST A WHILE! You'll feel so much better when you come back, and so will the people AROUND YOU! :o)

December 9
Bless My Bones
2 Kings 13:21 ~ "And it came to pass,
as they were burying a man,
that, behold, they spied a band of men;
and they cast the man into the sepulchre of Elisha:
and when the man was let down, and touched the bones of Elisha,
he revived, and stood up on his feet."

Elisha had BEEN dead long enough for there to be nothing left in his tomb, except HIS BONES! Some Israelites were burying a man, when a band of Moabites attacked. They HASTILY threw the man into Elisha's tomb. When the dead man's BODY touched Elisha's BONES, the dead man's body REVIVED and STOOD UP! Are you living so that the LEGACY you LEAVE ON EARTH, will bring LIFE TO A DEAD SITUATION ...LONG AFTER YOU'RE GONE? Now I understand what those old preachers meant when they said, "BLESS MY BONES!!!" :o)

December 10
We STILL Win!
Revelation 12:7-11 ~ "And there was war in heaven:
Michael and his angels fought against the dragon;
and the dragon fought and his angels,
and prevailed not;
neither was their place found any more in heaven.
And the great dragon was cast out, that old serpent,
called the Devil, and Satan, which deceiveth the whole world:
he was cast out into the earth,
and his angels were cast out with him.
And I heard a loud voice saying in heaven,
'Now is come salvation, and strength, and the kingdom of our God, and the power of his Christ: for the accuser of our brethren is cast down, which accused them before our God day and night.
And they overcame him by the blood of the Lamb,
and by the word of their testimony;
and they loved not their lives unto the death.' "

This is how I watch a ballgame on my DVR. I fast forward to the end of the game and check the score. If the team I wanted to win LOST, I erase the game. If they WON, I go back to the beginning and watch the game. I

know that no matter how my team messes up, WE STILL WIN! No matter
how many dropped balls, fumbles, strikeouts, errors, missed shots, etc., WE
STILL WIN! No matter how far down the team is at any point in the game, I
ALREADY know the outcome! That's how I taught myself to read the Bible.
I was reading Revelation 12:7-11 one day and saw that the devil lost …and I
WON. Then I started reading from the book of Genesis knowing that no
matter what happens, in CHRIST I WIN! Now about that last BATTLE you
were in that didn't come out so well, Click DELETE!!! Now remember that
the devil is ALREADY DEFEATED. You can rewind to the beginning, you
know, over there in Genesis where GOD created everything? As you read,
you can watch the entire story of humankind unfold KNOWING that GOD
has a plan (Jeremiah 29:11)! Because of what the Lord JESUS did on
Calvary, here's why we can watch with confidence this drama of life unfold.
No matter how MANKIND sins, messes up, fumbles and falls, misses the
mark, etc., the devil is already defeated. Those of us in CHRIST …HAVE
ALREADY WON! Now ENJOY your life, and your day, and THANK GOD
for the VICTORY we have …IN CHRIST. :o)

December 11
Amen Friends
Proverbs 27:6 ~ "Faithful are the wounds of a friend;
but the kisses of an enemy are deceitful."

Some people won't listen to the "CONSTRUCTIVE CRITICISM" of
friends. If you're a FRIEND receiving or giving advice, that would be
"loving correction" based on verses 5. We ought to have friends that are
NOT AFRAID to correct us "IN LOVE" when we are wrong. That's better
than them keeping it to themselves according to verse 5. Not letting me
know my short-comings can be destructive for me down the road! Verse 6
also teaches that everybody in your face, is NOT YOUR FRIEND! As the
O'Jays (an R&B group from Canton, Ohio) have told us, "They smile in you
face, but all the time they want to TAKE YOUR PLACE!" Those are what
they called "BACK-STABBERS!" REAL friends may from time to time
BRUISE (wound) you with honesty, but it will NEVER be BEHIND your
back.A BRUISE is not deadly, as is a STAB in the back! The "BRUISES" of
a real friend are both edifying and instructive. The Hebrew word for
"FAITHFUL" in verse 6 is "AMAN" (reliable, trustworthy, confirming). It's
where we get our English word AMEN! If a REAL FRIEND "wounds or
bruises" you with advice, you can TRUST that it's for your GOOD. Do you
have any "AMEN FRIENDS"?

December 12
What's In a Name?
Matthew 1:21~ "And she shall bring forth a son,
and thou shalt call his name Jesus:
for he shall save his people from their sins."

Be careful what you allow people to call you. It may stick! Do some research BEFORE you name your baby. Jesus means "SAVIOR". What an appropriate NAME for the one who died for our sins! Ladies ARE NOT "bitches" and "whores"! Check their birth certificates people if you're NOT SURE! (Both words are in some version of the Bible, so get over it). Hey Kobe, I'm sure you know that a Black Mamba is a DEADLY AFRICAN SNAKE that LOVES hanging IN and AROUND TREES!

December 13
Enjoy Your Tree
Jeremiah 10:3-5 ~ "□For the customs of the people are vain:
for one cuts a tree out of the forest,
the work of the hands of the workman, with an axe. □
They deck it with silver and with gold;
they fasten it with nails and with hammers so it can't move..."

Now about those CHRISTMAS TREES you have bought or are about to buy. I know what SOME people are going to teach you this Christmas season. Many will use these verses to support there claim that CHRISTIANS should NOT have decorated (decked) trees in their homes. Jeremiah had NO IDEA how we would celebrate Christmas in 2011.These verses have ABSOLUTELY NOTHING to do with your purchase of a TREE for CHRISTMAS! That is, unless you plan to put REAL GOLD and SILVER on the tree and bow down to it! Israel had picked up the dangerous habits of the heathen nations, such as worshiping TREES! ANYTHING you put in GOD'S place becomes an IDOL. God reminded them through the prophet Jeremiah that He (GOD) alone was the one and only TRUE GOD! He said, "Those trees stand upright, but CAN'T TALK" (verse 5). "You have to carry the trees because they CAN'T WALK", He told Israel in that same verse. Now when you trim that tree, teach your kids about the Tree of Life and the Light of the World. His name is JESUS! Jeremiah 10:7 reminded Israel (and us) that there is NO ONE like the TRUE GOD! Enjoy your TREE. :o)

December 14

(written in 2012, in reference to the Sandy Hook tragedy)
Matthew 18:6 ~ "But if anyone causes one of these little ones
who trusts in me to lose faith, it would be better for that person
to be drowned in the DEEP PART of the sea...
with a heavy millstone tied around their neck."

The words of the Lord Jesus Christ HIMSELF! WOW! The mass murder of CHILDREN! Is there anyone out there that still thinks that we as a people, don't need God MORE THAN EVER?! Psalm 127:3 says that children are God's Property!!! How could ANYONE abuse God's property that way? The answer is simple, anyone who would do this CANNOT KNOW CHRIST as Lord of their lives!

I'm going to pray for those responsible for this heinous crime, as well as for the victims. Yes, I SAID IT! Do you know why we should pray for those who did this? Because of what Jesus HIMSELF said about those who would do something like this, that may cause some of those children to NOT BELIEVE in Him. It's in the verse up there!

Four weapons and a bullet-proof vest... in an ELEMENTARY SCHOOL?!!! For real??? Parents, PRAY for the families of the children involved... then go find your children, and HUG them tightly! Oh, tell them how much you LOVE THEM!!!

December 15
(written in 2012, in reference to the Sandy Hook tragedy)
Luke 13:34 ~ "O Jerusalem, Jerusalem,
the city that kills the prophets and stones those who are sent to it! How often
would I have gathered your children together
as a hen gathers her brood under her wings,
and you would not (allow me, or choose me)!"

The sentiments voice how I'm feeling after yesterday's tragedy. I saw this poster on several of your pages. I saw at least one negative reaction to the poster. Someone told a good friend of mine that the poster was "baloney" because God is everywhere. That individual evidently has a problem with the word "allow" on the poster. They also evidently HAVE NOT read the verse up top.

First, let me say that being a red-blooded American, I LOVE baloney, especially fried! Second, Most Christians that I know have common sense! We know that God is omnipotent and can do whatever He desires. We also know that He is omnipresent, and therefore everywhere at the same time. But we ALSO know that from the beginning of mankind (in the garden of

Eden), God has given humans "free will"! That's why Jesus, who has ALL POWER (Matthew 28:18), said in the verse up there that He was "not allowed" to love and protect Jerusalem as he desired! When it comes to things concerning Himself, God says CHOOSE! (Check out how many times in the Bible the word "choose" is used!).

Yes, He could FORCE us to do whatever He wanted us to do, but He ALLOWS us to choose NOT to "ALLOW" or "ACCEPT" Him in certain areas of our lives. We have DISALLOWED prayer, Bible, and certain parts of the "Pledge of Allegiance" (Under God!), in many of our public schools. Therefore in a very REAL sense, we have DISALLOWED GOD in our schools. Now, I didn't suggest that... JESUS DID! Read it, it's up there! Now excuse me while I pass the BALONEY (or Bologna for the sensitive folk!)!!!

December 16
Mama, Mamie, and Job
Job 13:15 ~ "Though He slay me, yet will I trust in Him..." (Authorized King James Version) "Even if he killed me, I'd keep on hoping..."
(Eugene H. Peterson ~ "The Message Bible").

This day in 2017 would have been my mother's 94th Birthday! Clemmie Lee Bailey went home to be with the Lord in 1989 at the age of 65.

I eulogized our CENTENARIAN (100-year-old member) six years ago. Mamie Ruth George, who made 100 years old on September 3, 2011, went home to be with the Lord on December 9, 2011. I thought about her long life and the goodness of God as I meditated on this verse from the Book of Job this evening.

WHY would Job say he had HOPE, even if God TOOK HIS LIFE?! Do you think Job had inside information, and already KNEW what Mama and Mamie now KNOW? Jesus is REAL, and HE IS the Resurrection and the Life (John 11:25)!

Mama and Mamie's TRANSITION CELEBRATIONS, ("funerals," for those who have NO hope), were EASY to do because of the Blessed Hope I have ...IN CHRIST JESUS (Titus 2:13)! My question to you would be, who is YOUR HOPE IN? Mama, Mamie, and Job ...have already spoken! :o)

December 17
Order My Steps
Psalm 119:133 ~ "Direct (order) my steps by Your Word,
and don't □let iniquity have dominion over me." (NKJV)

While driving to a Homegoing service one day, I saw something that caught my attention. It was a group of children around the ages of 4-6 years old walking on the sidewalk, evidently on a field trip. I assumed that because these children were wearing the same T-shirts, and were accompanied by ADULTS in the FRONT and ADULTS in the BACK of the group!What really caught my eye was that the ADULTS in the front and back of the group, were holding a ROPE around the perimeter of the children! Then it hit me that the rope was to keep the children together, and to keep them from wondering into the street! I also had a question. Couldn't those small kids just duck UNDER the rope and dash into the street?Then I realized that the rope was just there to WARN the children that there was DANGER... OUTSIDE OF THE ROPE! It was the WATCHFUL EYES of the ADULTS that actually kept the children safe! When I saw these children, the verse at the beginning of this post came to me. God's WORD is like that rope. It serves to WARN us of the dangers, or even death if we go OUTSIDE of its parameters. If you "duck" underneath the Word and escape its protection by running into the evils of the STREETS (this world), INIQUITY WILL get control over you as the verse says! I lost about half of you right then, didn't I? Just do as the verse says and let God's Word (the rope) direct where you will walk. It's much safer inside of the PARAMETERS of His Word! I DO have good news for those of us who are tempted to STRAY, and wander underneath and outside of the rope from time to time. We are ALWAYS under the WATCHFUL EYE of God the Father! Now STAY inside the rope. GOD IS WATCHING, but some folk in the STREETS... ARE NOT!!!

December 18
Relax about the "X"
Matthew 1:16 ~ "And Jacob begat Joseph the husband of Mary,
of whom was born Jesus, who is called Christ."

I'm on my way to Stockton, CA. to teach a college class on basic Biblical Greek. Before I go, I want to help at least TWO PEOPLE with something I have shared with the class. I keep hearing people tell us not to let THEM (whoever THEY are) take the "CHRIST" out of "CHRISTMAS". They have gone as far as to say, DO NOT write "XMAS" or buy anything that has "XMAS" on it. The claims are that this is just another attempt to take CHRIST out of Christmas. NOT TRUE! "Xmas" has been used as an abbreviation for "Christmas" for CENTURIES! The same with Xian (Christian) and Xianity (Christianity). XMAS was REGULARLY USED in

England by CHRISTIANS in the mid-1500's. That's DECADES BEFORE there was ever a King James Bible! We use abbreviations all the time and no one complains. Do you STILL know what Rev., Dr., M.D., R.N., Mr., Mrs., Sis., and Bro., mean? Here's what I shared with the Greek class some weeks ago. In Koine (common, biblical as in the verse) Greek, the word CHRIST is spelled chi-rho-iota-sigma-tau-omicron-sigma. I wish Facebook would allow me to use the GREEK FONT on my computer so you could see it. I CAN give it to you in English, since the FIRST letter in Greek and English look EXACTLY the same! It's XRISTOS! "X" is the FIRST letter in CHRIST throughout the New Testament. You CAN'T SPELL CHRIST in the bible without the first letter "X" (Chi). You frat brothers and sorority sisters ought to recognize that letter. :o)Those of our ANCESTORS who could neither READ or WRITE, use to sign their names with an "X." I WONDER why they chose THAT particular letter? You think our ancestors knew something that their EDUCATED CHILDREN didn't know? My profile picture is a blown up portion of the word for CHRIST from Matthew 1:16, in it's original Bible language. It came from my Greek Bible. Click on the Profile Picture at the top left of this PAGE, and see if you can find the word "CHRIST." It's spelled the same throughout the New Testament. Then take a CHILL PILL and relax. Merry Xmas, or CHRISTMAS for those of you who are still offended. :o)

December 19
(A post from the wife of my Son in the Ministry, Maya Scott)
Philippians 3:13-14 ~ "Brethren, I count not myself
to have apprehended: but this one thing I do,
forgetting those things which are behind,
and reaching forth unto those things which are before,
I press toward the mark for the prize
of the high calling of God in Christ Jesus."

THERE IS A REASON why the windshield in your car is LARGER than the rear view mirror! Simple yet true. You CANNOT drive while consistently looking in the rear view mirror, without CRASHING into something! The rear view mirror is for OCCASIONAL glances, not total focus. Life is the same way. We gain perspective from the past. We hope to learn from past mistakes, but we cannot live in the past and build a future. Now, let's have MORE looking through the windshield …and less looking in the rear view mirror! :o)

December 20
Ecclesiastes 3:4 " ... A Time to LAUGH!"

**************** BREAKING NEWS *****************
The SUPREME COURT has ruled that there cannot be a NATIVITY
SCENE in the United States' Capital this CHRISTMAS season! This ISN'T
for any RELIGIOUS reason. They simply have NOT been able to find Three
Wise Men in the Nation's Capital. A search for a VIRGIN continues. There
was NO problem, however, finding enough ASSES TO FILL THE
STABLE!!!

(This is a repost from my deacon, Al Carter's status over a year ago.
Enjoy your day. :)

December 21
Redeemed from the Pit
Psalm 103:4 ~ "Who redeemeth thy life from destruction;
who crowneth thee with lovingkindness and tender mercies..."

The verse tells us to BLESS GOD who redeems our lives from the
"PIT" (destruction in the KJV, or grave). Here is a simple message for those
who find yourself in an emotional, psychological or financial hole (pit) this
Christmas season, after spending so much time investing in others. I was
reminded by Rev. Aaron Casey of something Joel C. Gregory told us in one
of our City-Wide Revivals. Dr. Gregory said, "When you find yourself in a
hole, STOP DIGGING! You'll CATCH that by the time you return from
wherever you are going! :o)

December 22
Under the Sun, Under the Son
Psalm 139:14 ~ "I will praise thee;
for I am fearfully and wonderfully made..."

Ecclesiastes 1:3 ~ "What □does man gain
by all the toil at which he toils under the sun?"

Today's technology is amazing. My doctor said to me, "You don't get
OUTSIDE MUCH, do you?" I asked, "Why do you say that?" (I really
wanted to know how he KNEW THAT!). He said (based on blood test taken
earlier), "You have a Vitamin D deficiency, and we get most of our Vitamin
D ...from THE SUN!"

WOW! I have a physical deficiency because I don't spend enough time UNDER THE SUN! Sitting there in the doctor's office is where it hit me that those of you who are NOT spending time under the SON (The Lord Jesus Christ), have a Vitamin D deficiency. Spending time under the SON... brings Deliverance, Determination, Discipline and Destiny! Have you had your dose of Vitamin D from the SON today? I'm WORKING on that SUN thing! :)

December 23
You Do Have a Gift To Give
Luke 1:41-44 ~ "And it came to pass, that,
when Elisabeth heard the salutation of Mary,
the babe leaped in her womb;
and Elisabeth was filled with the Holy Ghost:
And she spake out with a loud voice, and said,
'Blessed art thou among women,
and blessed is the fruit of thy womb.'
And whence is this to me,
that the mother of my Lord should come to me?
For, lo, as soon as the voice of thy salutation sounded
in mine ears, the babe leaped in my womb for joy."

For those of you who believe you have NOTHING TO GIVE this Christmas, the Bible teaches that there's something in your VOICE that can GIVE JOY to others! John the Baptist was just a 6-MONTH-OLD FETUS in the womb of Elisabeth when he JUMPED for joy at the VOICE of Mary saying HELLO! Does the sound of YOUR voice GIVE joy to those IN your presence, or does it make them want to run FROM your presence?

December 24
Avoid the Stampede
Luke 12:15 ~ "And he said unto them,
Take heed, and beware of covetousness:
for a man's life consists not
in the abundance of the things which he possesses."

Are people SERIOUS???!!! This verse teaches that what makes a person is NOT their POSSESSIONS! Why would anyone even desire to be part of a STAMPEDE to get a $180 pair of ATHLETIC SHOES?
Some years ago, a couple of the male members of our church came to a

rehearsal with boxes and smiles. They had DISCOVERED a "new" athletic shoe for $50 in multiple colors! These "new" $50 shoes were called PF Flyers! The older people reading this are laughing right now! That's because PF Flyers are NOT NEW! PF stands for "Posture Foundation". (I LOVE IT)! The patented insole technology was developed in 1933, and set a new standard in athletic shoe comfort. The insole technology was first used in BF Goodrich shoes (YES, the TIRE company). They have a wedge-like insert (promoted as the "magic wedge") that moves weight to the outside of the foot, evenly distributing weight and thus reducing leg strain. As the success of the sneakers with the "Posture Foundation" insole technology grew in 1937, it became the basis for the brand name, "PF Flyers." Now go get THREE pair of comfortable shoes that will help you stand UPRIGHT! Then get your CHANGE, and let those OTHER people stand in LONG LINES and get trampled if they so desire! :o)

December 25
Merry Christmas
Micah 5:2 ~ "But thou, Bethlehem Ephratah,
though you are little among the thousands of Judah,
yet out of you shall HE (Jesus) come forth unto me
that is to be ruler in Israel;
whose goings forth have been from of old, from everlasting."

In this verse, Micah prophesied the birth of JESUS... almost 800 years BEFORE it was to happen in Matthew 2:3-6! It also says that GREATNESS (A ruler = Jesus) would come out of this SMALL town and clan. Did you know that GOD can bring GREATNESS out of your circumstances, no matter how insignificant YOU think they are?! Something good CAN come out of the HOOD!

The fact that Jesus would "go forth" (into time) out of the EAST (old) of ETERNITY is also in the verse. This caught my attention because my home office and also my bedroom face the EAST. GUESS what comes up in my face every morning? You GOT IT, the SUN! The Spirit spoke to me while reading this verse and reminded me that the Sun CONTINUES to exist, even when I can't see it. So does the SON. He's always there and ALWAYS has been!

One last thing I saw in this verse. The NAME Bethlehem means "House of Bread." The name Ephrata(t)h means "Fruitful, place of fruitfulness, vineyard." If you aren't shouting yet, then you missed it. The Bread (His body) and the fruit of the vine or the wine (His Blood)! YES! Jesus was BORN in a place whose very NAME speaks of His Broken Body and Shed Blood! HAPPY BIRTHDAY JESUS!!! Whenever I take the Lord's Supper, I'm going to remember WHERE you were born!

December 26
Donkeys and Destiny

1 Samuel 9:3 ~ "Now the donkeys of Kish, Saul's father, were lost. So Kish said to Saul his son, 'Take one of the young men with you, and arise,
go and look for the donkeys.' " (ESV)

Can I share a story that ought to bless you if you follow me? Some donkeys belonging to Saul's father Kish, got lost. Kish told his son Saul to take one of the servants and go look for them (1 Samuel 9:3).The two went through several places and could not find the donkeys (verse 4). When they got to a place call Zuph, Saul said to the servant, "Let's go home, or my father will stop worrying about the donkeys and start worrying about us (verse 5)!"

The servant told Saul that there was a man of God (Samuel) in Zuph that could help them out (vs.6). God had told Samuel ahead of time that He (God) would send Saul to him, and Samuel was to ANOINT Saul as the FIRST King of Israel (verses 15-16)! Are you praising God yet, or did you miss it? Saul went looking for DONKEYS, and found his DESTINY! Stop complaining about the "jack-asses" in your life. God may be using them... to get you to your DESTINY! Say what? Yeah, daddy's donkeys were recovered (10:2)! :)

December 27
God's Masterpiece

Job 1:21 ~ " ...the LORD gave, and the LORD hath taken away; blessed be the name of the LORD."

Job had just lost his property and his children (vs.14-19). Instead of being ANGRY with God, he bows down and WORSHIPS GOD (vs.20)!!! In verse 21 Job realizes that whether God is ADDING TO or SUBTRACTING FROM your life, HE IS STILL the BLESSED BLESSOR! That's the same conclusion that James came to about the story of JOB (James 5:11). We have HEARD about Job's patience (he really wasn't that patient after chapter 2). James encourages us to take a look and SEE how that story ended! What God had TAKEN AWAY from Job, He GAVE JOB DOUBLE in the end (Job 42:10) ...WHEN HE PRAYED FOR (act of

FORGIVENESS) his friends! The Lord GIVES, and He TAKES AWAY. Either way, We're BLESSED!If you still haven't gotten it, consider this. A painter and a sculptor are BOTH ARTISTS who have TWO DIFFERENT approaches to art. One GIVES, the other TAKES AWAY! A PAINTER GIVES paint to the canvas, while A SCULPTOR TAKES AWAY rock from the original slab of stone until in the end ...BOTH HAVE A MASTERPIECE!!! You are God's Masterpiece, whether He's giving or taking from you. :o)

December 28
More than Nikes!

Romans 8:35-39~ "Who shall separate us from the love of Christ?
shall tribulation, or distress, or persecution, or famine,
or nakedness, or peril, or sword?
As it is written, For thy sake we are killed all the day long;
we are accounted as sheep for the slaughter.
Nay, in all these things we are more than conquerors
through him that loved us.
For I am persuaded, that neither death, nor life, nor angels,
nor principalities, nor powers, nor things present,
nor things to come,
Nor height, nor depth, nor any other creature,
shall be able to separate us from the love of God,
which is in Christ Jesus our Lord."

1 Corinthians 15:54-58 ~ "So when this corruptible
shall have put on incorruption,
and this mortal shall have put on immortality,
then shall be brought to pass the saying that is written,
'Death is swallowed up in victory.'
O death, where is thy sting? O grave, where is thy victory?
The sting of death is sin; and the strength of sin is the law.
But thanks be to God, which giveth us the victory
through our Lord Jesus Christ.
Therefore, my beloved brethren, be ye stedfast, unmoveable,
always abounding in the work of the Lord,
forasmuch as ye know that your labour is not in vain in the Lord."

I just want to ENCOURAGE a few people with God's Word today! In Genesis 42:36 Jacob, (later named Israel), THOUGHT that everything going on in his life at the time was working AGAINST him. Paul teaches (Romans

8:28) that if you loved God and are called for His purpose, it's ALL WORKING for your GOOD! In the verses before us (Rom.8:35-39), we see a comprehensive list of things that COULD work against us if it wasn't for the fact that Christ died (context). Now we are "HYPERNIKAO" according to Paul in Romans 8:37. We are HYPER (MORE than, as in "hyper active"), NIKAO (from the root word NIKE) which means "victorious or conqueror." We are MORE THAN CONQUERORS, IN CHRIST JESUS! The word NIKE is the Greek New Testament word for VICTORY used 3 times in 1 Corinthians 15:54-57. If you bought (or help your child buy) $200 Nike shoes, at least TEACH THEM what the name means. Read I Corinthians 15:58, shout, and have a GREAT DAY! :o)

December 29
Please Kill the Spider!
Romans 6:14 ~ "For sin shall not have dominion over you:
for ye are not under the law, but under grace."

You will know you are under GRACE and not under the Law when sin no longer DOMINATES your life. If you are a Christian, you WILL sin! Just don't be CARNAL and make a HABIT out of it! Those verses in 1 John 3 (e.g. verses 4,6,8,9,...) have "participles" which put an "ing" on the words in English (committING, abidING, sinnING). Those verses also speak of PRESENT TENSE and CONTINUOUS ACTION! When you pray, ask and allow God to ACTIVATE the power of the Holy Spirit He has placed in you to deal with the ROOT CAUSE of sin in your life. A man who attended prayer meeting regularly would end his prayer every week, "Lord, take the cobwebs out of my heart, and Lord get rid of the cobwebs in my soul!" He routinely ended with those same words each week, "Lord, take the cobwebs out of my heart, and Lord get rid of the cobwebs in my soul!" A deacon who also attended the meetings got TIRED of hearing that same prayer one night. He got up behind the man's prayer and said, "Lord, While you're at it, PLEASE KILL THE SPIDER!"

December 30
Where Are You, Lord Jesus?
Revelation 22:20 ~ "Surely I come quickly..."

These are the words of Jesus Himself. If you have a "good" Bible, the words are probably in red letters. So then WHAT HAPPENED?! Where ARE YOU, JESUS?

There are critics of Christianity who use verses like this to buttress their claims that the Bible is a book full of false teaching. They point to a passage like this and say, "See, it's been over TWO THOUSAND years and He (Jesus) hasn't come yet!"

But QUICKLY is an ADVERB! Adverbs modify VERBS! That would be the ACT of His coming itself! "Quickly" in Greek is "tachu." We get the word "tachometer", which is an instrument you can find on the dashboard of a car. A "tachometer" can tell you HOW FAST the car goes from A to B, ONCE YOU GET STARTED! That's what Paul was saying about JESUS in 1 Corinthians 15:52 and 1 Thessalonians 4:16-17.

WHENEVER Jesus comes, the EVENT (His coming) will happen QUICKLY! The question is, "Will you be ready?" :o) or :o(

December 31
Stop Going In Circles!
Deuteronomy 2:3-4 ~
"…You have circled around this mountain long enough.
Turn northward and command the people,
'You are about to pass through the territory of your brothers, the people of
Esau, who live in Seir; and they will be afraid of you. So be very careful.' "

Do you have a PLAN for the coming year? Or are you like the songwriter who wrote, "I'm an ever-rolling wheel, without a destination real. I'm an ever-spinning top, whirling around 'till I drop. But what am I to do? My mind is in a whirlpool. Give me a little hope. One small thing to cling to. You got me GOING IN CIRCLES!!!"

Do those words sound familiar? Then you're probably a "Friends of Distinction" or Isaac Hayes fan! God says HE KNOWS the PLANS (thoughts) HE HAS for you (Jeremiah 29:11)! HE said in Deuteronomy 2:3 that the children of Israel had been circling the SAME MOUNTAIN LONG ENOUGH! We do that when we do the same thing with minimal results. It was time to head NORTH! If you look at a map, that would be …UPWARD!!! Deuteronomy 2:4 teaches us to be careful in 2016. Not everyone you will come in contact with, means you well! That includes some family members!

Scripture Index

August 12 – Ezra 3:1-3

Job
March 5 – Job 42:7
April 9 – Job 29:27-30
July 28 – Job 1:6
December 16 – Job 13:15
December 27 – Job 1:21

Psalms
January 13 – Psalm 145:4
January 16 – Psalm 107:23-24
January 20 – Psalm 7:15-16
January 31 – Psalm 56:8
February 8 – Psalm 24:1
February 12 – Psalm 23:6
February 19 – Psalm 119:18
February 20 – Psalm 95:7-8
March 11 – Psalm 33:3
March 13 – Psalm 14:1
March 22 – Psalm 73:1-3
April 1 – Psalm 51:10
April 14 – Psalm 124, complete
April 26 – Psalm 103:12
April 28 – Psalm 110:1-4
May 26 – Psalm 146:1
May 27 – Psalm 149:6
June 3 – Psalm 116:15
June 8 – Psalm 23:1
June 13 – Psalm 55:12-14
June 14-- Psalm 23:5
June 16 – Psalm 30:5
July 10 – Psalm 51:1
July 23 – Psalm 139:10
July 31 – Psalm 139:14
August 2 – Psalm 7:15-16
August 13-- Psalm 81:15
August 14 – Psalm 46:1
August 15 – Psalm 118:23-24
August 18 – Psalm 27:1
August 20 – Psalm 42:1
August 21-- Psalm 27:10
August 29-- Psalm 119:133

September 3 – Psalm 14:1 and 53:1
September 6 – Psalm 119:18
September 7 – Psalm 8:2
September 11 – Psalm 91:1
September 15 – Psalm 103:12
September 17 – Psalm 107:23-24
September 21 – Psalm 23:6
September 25 – Psalm 121:1-2
October 25 – Psalm 111:9
November 1 – Psalm 91:11
November 12 – Psalm 121:2
November 18 – Psalm 98:8
November 22 – Psalm 22:3
December 6 – Psalm 127:3-4
December 17 – Psalm 119:133
December 21 – Psalm 103:4
December 22 – Psalm 139-14

Proverbs
January 15 – Proverbs 20:30
January 26 – Proverbs 10:19
February 14 – Proverbs 18:22
May 3 – Proverbs 24:17-18
May 6 – Proverbs 22:28
June 12 – Proverbs 13:22
June 17 – Proverbs 3:5-6
August 17 – Proverbs 31:10-31
September 16 – Proverbs 13:22
October 12 – Proverbs 11:13
November 3 – Proverbs 18:10
November 26 – Proverbs 25:17
December 11 – Proverbs 27:6

Ecclesiastes
February 16 – Ecclesiastes 10:20
July 12 – Ecclesiastes 9:11
December 20 – Ecclesiastes 1:4
December 22 – Ecclesiastes 1:3

Isaiah
January 30 – Isaiah 64:6

February 5 – Isaiah 43:7
March 15 – Isaiah 65:24
March 28 – Isaiah 41:10
April 22 – Isaiah 55:8
April 30 – Isaiah 53:5
May 9 – Isaiah 40:31
August 9 – Isaiah 53:5
August 11 – Isaiah 53:3
August 16 – Isaiah 53:6
October 7 – Isaiah 29:13
November 18 – Isaiah 55:12
November 19 – Isaiah 29:13
December 8 – Isaiah 43:7

Jeremiah
January 17 – Jeremiah 29:11
March 21 – Jeremiah 18:1-6
July 8 – Jeremiah 2:1-2
September 22 – Jeremiah 3:15
October 19 – Jeremiah 13:23
December 13 – Jeremiah 10:3-5

Lamentations
April 13 – Lamentations 3:21-22

Ezekiel
January 24 – Ezekiel 16:49
October 21 – Ezekiel 22:30

Daniel
May 29 – Daniel 3:24-25
September 10 – Daniel 3:24-25
November 17 – Daniel 6:18-22

Amos
January 25 – Amos 5:24

Micah
December 25 – Micah 5:2

Nahum
January 9 – Nahum 1:7

Habakkuk
May 19 – Habakkuk 2:2
September 9 – Habakkuk 2:2

Malachi
July 14 – Malachi 3:6
July 22 – Malachi 3:3
August 5 – Malachi 3:17

Matthew
January 2 – Matthew 6:33
January 8 – Matthew 6:25
January 12 – Matthew 7:6
January 28 – Matthew 10:8
February 2 – Matthew 10:29-31
March 1 – Matthew 7:3-5
March 3 – Matthew 12:43-45
March 14 – Matthew 26:21-22
March 17 – Matthew 28:19
March 26 – Matthew 10:16
May 2 – Matthew 12:38
May 18 – Matthew 5:13
May 21 – Matthew 24:4, 36, 44
June 18 – Matthew 7:3
June 20 – Matthew 6:16-18
June 22 – Matthew 6:34
June 29 – Matthew 25:1-13
July 1 – Matthew 27:24
July 11 – Matthew 11:29
July 12 – Matthew 10:22
July 13 – Matthew 6:19-21
July 17 – Matthew 8:17
July 24 – Matthew 7:13-14
August 7 – Matthew 18:20
August 27 – Matthew 5:16
September 4 – Matthew 12:43-45
September 8 – Matthew 19:14
September 24 – Matthew 5:16
September 29-- Matthew 7:15
October 7 – Matthew 15:8
October 9 – Matthew 6:26
October 14 – Matthew 7:24-27
November 7 – Matthew 16:13
November 8 – Matthew 6:11

November 27 – Matthew 10:8
December 1 – Matthew 1:21
December 7 – Matthew 17:9
December 12 – Matthew 1:21
December 14 – Matthew 18:6
December 18 – Matthew 1:16

Mark
April 18 – Mark 15:6-15
November 9 – Mark 4:39
November 24 – Mark 5:25

Luke
January 23 – Luke 9:62
January 31 – Luke 12:7a
February 11 – Luke 12:17
February 15 – Luke 9:31
March 28 – Luke 11:23
April 5 – Luke 24:5-6
April 18 – Luke 9.58
May 11 – Luke 12:15
August 1 – Luke 5:12-14
August 8 – Luke 13:6-9
September 20 – Luke 23:34
October 13 – Luke 12:40
November 28 – Luke 19:13
November 30 – Luke 13:34
December 3 – Luke 12:15-21
December 7 – Luke 9:37
December 15 – Luke 13:34
December 23 – Luke 1:41-44
December 24 – Luke 12:15

John
January 4 – John 1:35
January 10 – John 4:24
February 10 – John 14:6
February 18 – John 17:21-23
March 4 – John 10:9
March 6 – John 8:32
March 10 – John 3:16
March 12 – John 6:38 and 10:15

March 18 – John 14:5-6
April 4 – John 20:7
April 18 – John 19:30
April 20 – John 20:4-7
May 2 – John 12:20-21
May 14 – John 8:44
June 6 – John 3:16
July 4 – John 19:11
July 5 – John 2:1-11
August 28 – John 1:3 and 15:5
September 13 – John 20:24-29
October 1 – John 14:6
October 23 – John 2:15-16
October 24 – John 18:11
October 28-31 – John 8:32
November 11 – John 8:36
November 29 – John 1:29

Acts
June 11 – Acts 1:8
June 23 – Acts 16:6-7
November 16 – Acts 17:6

Romans
January 1 – Romans 8:34
February 28 – Romans 8:28
March 9 – Romans 8:28
March 19 – Romans 14:16
April 20 – Romans 13:12 and 13:14
June 1 – Romans 14:16
June 5 – Romans 12:3-5
June 25 – Romans 8:3
July 2 – Romans 3:23
July 21 – Romans 8:3
July 27 – Romans 12:3
August 19-- Romans 5:20-21
August 23 – Romans 11:29
August 24 – Romans 8:28
September 28 Romans 8:33-39
October 22 – Romans 11:29
November 13 – Romans 12:3
November 14 – Romans 3:23
November 15 – Romans 16:1

December 2 – Romans 12:1
December 28 – Romans 8:35-39
December 29 – Romans 6:14

I Corinthians
January 18 – I Corinthians 13:1
January 27 – I Corinthians 2:1-5
February 26 – I Corinthians 13:5
March 12 – I Corinthians 15:24-25
April 12 – I Corinthians 2:9-10
April 15 – I Corinthians 13:5
April 21 – I Corinthians 15:58
May 2 – I Corinthians 1:22-24
May 31 – I Corinthians 1:2
June 10 – I Corinthians 6:19-20
July 9 – I Corinthians 15:55
July 27 – I Corinthians 15:10
August 12 – I Corinthians 3:11
September 18 – I Corinthians 6:19-20
September 20 – I Corinthians 7:11-13
September 27 – I Corinthians 2:1-5
October 14 – I Corinthians 3:11
December 28 – I Corinthians 15:54-58

II Corinthians
January 5 – II Corinthians 4:2
January 29 – II Corinthians 11:13-15
February 9 – II Corinthians 5:17
April 16 – II Corinthians 5:21
May 11 – II Corinthians 5:17
May 14 – II Corinthians 11:14-15
June 6 – II Corinthians 11:13-15
June 15 – II Corinthians 6:14
July 19 – II Corinthians 5:7
September 19 – II Corinthians 5:7
October 5 – II Corinthians 1:3-5

Galatians
February 7 – Galatians 6:10
February 27 – Galatians 5:15

July 7 – Galatians 6:7
September 23 – Galatians 6:1
December 5 – Galatians 6:9

Ephesians
January 7 – Ephesians 4:29
January 14 – Ephesians 5:16
January 22 – Ephesians 2:8-9
January 24 – Ephesians 2:18
March 7 – Ephesians 2:8
March 8 – Ephesians 5:25-26
April 6 – Ephesians 6:12
April 20 – Ephesians 6:11
March 25 – Ephesians 2:8-9
May 16 – Ephesians 5:15
May 21 – Ephesians 4:14
May 22 – Ephesians 1:15-23
June 2 – Ephesians 1:3-4
June 28 – Ephesians 6:16
June 29 – Ephesians 3:20
July 15 – Ephesians 5:2
July 25 – Ephesians 3:20
September 2 – Ephesians 4:15
September 30 – Ephesians 3:1-8
October 3 – Ephesians 3:20
October 10 – Ephesians 2:8-9
October 27 – Ephesians 4:26

Philippians
March 16 – Philippians 2:3-5
March 24 – Philippians 3:13-14
May 15 – Philippians 4:6
July 7– Philippians 4:19
July 18 – Philippians 4:19
October 15 – Philippians 4:6
November 2 – Philippians 3:13-14
November 20 – Philippians 2:3-5

Colossians
January 7 – Colossians 4:6
February 1 – Colossians 3:23

March 29 – Colossians 3:5
April 20 – Colossians 3:10 and 3:12
April 23 – Colossians 4:6
May 8 – Colossians 2:5-7
July 30-- Colossians 1:18 and 2:10
October 8 – Colossians 3:12

I Thessalonians
June 1 – I Thessalonians 5:22
June 4 – I Thessalonians 5:17
June 19 – I Thessalonians 4:11
July 26 – I Thessalonians 5:9

I Timothy
February 6 – I Timothy 4:8
February 17 – I Timothy 2:5
April 19 – I Timothy 6:17-19
November 25 – I Timothy 6:17-18

II Timothy
II Timothy 1:5 – May 10
II Timothy 1:5 – October 2

Titus
May 4 – Titus 1:10-11
August 5 – Titus 2:14

Hebrews
February 25 – Hebrews 10:17
March 12 – Hebrews 1:3
March 17 – Hebrews 9:14
May 1 – Hebrews 13:5
May 23 – Hebrews 11:1
May 24 – Hebrews 4:14
June 24 – Hebrews 12:2
June 26 – Hebrews 13:18
July 29 – Hebrews 12:2
August 4-- Hebrews 8:12 and 10:17
August 21-- Hebrews 13:5-6
September 19 – Hebrews 11:1
November 4 – Hebrews 12:2
December 4-- Hebrews 1:1-2

James
February 21 – James 1:22
February 22 – James 1:23
March 21 – James 1:2-4
May 7 – James 5:11
May 13 – James 1:19-22

I Peter
February 13 – I Peter 5:8
March 17 – I Peter 1:2
April 3 – I Peter 5:8
April 7 – I Peter 5:8
April 8 – I Peter 3:15
June 9 – I Peter 3:7
October 12 – I Peter 4:8
November 6 – I Peter 2:25
November 21 – I Peter 3:3

I John
January 6 – I John 4:4
April 15 – I John 1:5
May 30 – I John 4:4
August 10 – I John 1:7
August 22 – I John 1:9
September 1 – I John 3:17
September 14 – Hebrews 4:14-16
September 26 – I John 1:7

Revelation
April 10 – Revelation 12:10-11
April 24 – Revelation 13:8
April 30 – Revelation 21:21
June 24 – Revelation 22:13
August 26 – Revelation 3:20
October 18 – Revelation 12:9
December 10 – Revelation 12:7-11
December 30 – Revelation 22:20

216

www.ingramcontent.com/pod-product-compliance
Lightning Source LLC
Chambersburg PA
CBHW022126080426
42734CB00006B/246